France and the Great War, 1914–1918

KU-018-585

The latest addition to *New Approaches to European History*, Cambridge's successful textbook series, *France and the Great War* tells the story of how the French community embarked upon, sustained, and in some ways prevailed in the Great War. Synthesizing many years of scholarship, the book unfolds both chronologically and thematically, using different types of historiography to discuss the various phases of the war. The authors examine the origins of the war from a diplomatic and military viewpoint, before shifting their emphasis to socio-cultural and economic history when examining the civilian and military war culture. They look at the "total" mobilization of the French national community, as well as the military and civilian crises of 1917, and the ambiguous victory of 1918. The book concludes by revealing how traces of the Great War can still be found in the political and cultural life of the French national community.

LEONARD V. SMITH is Frederick B. Artz Professor of History at Oberlin College, Oberlin, Ohio, USA. He was awarded the Paul Birdsall Prize from the American Historical Association for his book: *Between Mutiny and Obedience: The Case of the French Fifth Infantry Division During World War I* (1994) and is the editor of *France at War: Vichy and the Historians* (with Sarah Fishman *et al.*, 2000).

STÉPHANE AUDOIN-ROUZEAU is Professor of Modern History at the Université de Picardie-Jules Verne, Amiens, France. His previous publications include *Cinq Deuils de Guerre, 1914–1918* (2001), *14–18 Retrouver la Guerre* (with Annette Becker, English edition forthcoming), and *Men at War: National Sentiment and Trench Journalism in France during the First World War* (1992).

ANNETTE BECKER is Professor of Modern History at the Université de Paris X–Nanterre, France. Her previous publications include *War and Faith: the Religious Imagination in France, 1914–1930* (1998), and *Humanitaire et Culture de Guerre, 1914–1918: Populations Occupées, Déportés Civils, Prisoniers de Guerre* (1998).

New Approaches to European History

Series editors
WILLIAM BEIK *Emory University*
T. C. W. BLANNING *Sidney Sussex College, Cambridge*

New Approaches to European History is an important textbook series, which provides concise but authoritative surveys of major themes and problems in European history since the Renaissance. Written at a level and length accessible to advanced school students and undergraduates, each book in the series addresses topics or themes that students of European history encounter daily: the series embraces both some of the more 'traditional' subjects of study, and those cultural and social issues to which increasing numbers of school and college courses are devoted. A particular effort is made to consider the wider international implications of the subject under scrutiny.

To aid the student reader scholarly apparatus and annotation is light, but each work has full supplementary bibliographies and notes for further reading: where appropriate chronologies, maps, diagrams, and other illustrative material are also provided.

For a list of titles published in the series, please see end of book.

France and the Great War, 1914–1918

Leonard V. Smith
Stéphane Audoin-Rouzeau
Annette Becker

French sections translated by
Helen McPhail

CAMBRIDGE
UNIVERSITY PRESS

PUBLISHED BY THE PRESS SYNDICATE OF THE UNIVERSITY OF CAMBRIDGE
The Pitt Building, Trumpington Street, Cambridge CB2 1RP, United Kingdom

CAMBRIDGE UNIVERSITY PRESS
The Edinburgh Building, Cambridge CB2 2RU, UK
40 West 20th Street, New York, NY 10011-4211, USA
477 Williamstown Road, Port Melbourne, VIC 3207, Australia
Ruiz de Alarcón 13, 28014 Madrid, Spain
Dock House, The Waterfront, Cape Town 8001, South Africa

http://www.cambridge.org

First published 2003

Printed in the United Kingdom at the University Press, Cambridge

Typeface Plantin 10/12 pt   *System* LaTeX 2$_\varepsilon$ [TB]

A catalogue record for this book is available from the British Library

ISBN 0 521 66176 5 hardback
ISBN 0 521 66631 7 paperback

À nos enfants,
Ian, Raphaël, Ambroise, Eloi, et Sarah-Laure

No historian has yet managed to measure the effects of the First World War, "the Great War," as Frenchmen still call it – on the French nation. It is easy to cite statistics of physical damage or loss of life or decline in industrial production; it is much harder to assess the moral and psychological impact of this vast calamity, its permanently debilitating results, its traumatic effect on large parts of the population. Nations, like the individual human beings that compose them, are remarkably resilient things; history furnishes many examples of their vigorous recovery from periods of disaster. Perhaps that very resilience tends to conceal some of the deeper effects that endure beneath the surface of the system and that surprise observers by their long-range consequences. Such lesions are more likely to be concealed when a nation seems to triumph over disaster – when the long strain of war ends in what men call victory. Nations that are beaten undergo long examination and self-examination; the effects of the war may even be exaggerated to the point of producing a national neurosis. Nations that triumph are generally assumed to be, and assume themselves to be, healthy organisms that have somehow been spared by the plague.

Gordon Wright, France in Modern Times (1960)

Contents

Plates

Maps

Preface

This book is a work of synthesis rather than original research, in which we tell the story of France and the French in the Great War in the context of a huge and mostly new historiographical literature. The elements of "conventional" history are all here – diplomacy, strategy, battles, and the "high politics" of the National Assembly and prime ministers. But we focus more on the society and culture of the French at war. What, throughout the book, we call "war culture" refers to a broad-based system of representations through which the French made sense of the war, and persuaded themselves to continue fighting it. Much of this book recounts the social and cultural history of a national community that mobilized, remobilized, suffered, mourned its sacrifices, and in the end "won," or at least failed to lose the most terrible war in its long history. We argue that traces of the Great War are still visible in France today. We note aspects of the war still not well understood by historians, and thus in a general way point to directions for future research.

In keeping with the practice of the *New Approaches to European History* series, we have kept footnotes to a minimum. We include a comprehensive bibliography of works in French and in English. Most of our footnotes are there to avoid disruption of the main body of the text. They provide additional necessary explanation of points made in the text or document points made from works less likely to be of general interest. Most of the time, we cite primary accounts in the main body of the text, by author, title, and date of publication. We footnote primary sources when providing this information in the text seems too cumbersome. While some accounts from French combatants have been translated, most of the best have not. We cite English versions when available in the Bibliography. However, many published English translations are quite old and inelegant. Consequently, we frequently retranslated short quotes. Certainly hundreds and probably thousands of images from the Great War have been published. We have concentrated here on images unlikely to be familiar to readers in the English-speaking world, and most especially on images that illustrate French war culture.

The authors would like to thank William Beik of Emory University for originally approaching us to write this volume, as well as the other series editor, T. C. W. Blanning, of Sidney Sussex College, Cambridge University, and also R. W. Scribner, of Harvard University. Elizabeth Howard provided welcome counsel throughout the writing of this volume, as did Sophie Read and Helen Barton while Elizabeth was on maternity leave. We particularly appreciate the patience of Cambridge University Press in giving us the latitude to work out a complex collaboration of three authors on two continents working in two languages over a period of nearly four years. Helen McPhail provided invaluable assistance in beginning the process of turning the French contributions into English. The project would have taken much longer to complete without her. The help provided by our superb copyeditor, Sara Adhikari, in smoothing out the translation and catching gaffes proved invaluable. Thanks also go to Caroline Fontaine and the Historial de la Grande Guerre in Péronne for their help with the illustrations. We happily acknowledge our great debt to Ralph Douglass for computer generating the maps.

The writing of this volume was greatly facilitated by electronic mail, which has done so much to transform the lives of us all. Chapters could be flung more or less instantaneously from Ohio, to Paris, to Lille, to Cambridge, England. But even today, nothing can quite replace personal contact. In the last stages of completing this volume, collaboration among the authors was made possible by a visiting appointment for Leonard Smith at the Université de Paris 7-Jussieu, UFR-Sciences des Textes et Documents. Particular thanks go to Carine Trevisan for making possible this opportunity.

Introduction

On November 6, 1915, Sarah Bernhardt performed a dramatic poem by Eugène Morand, *Les Cathédrales*, at the Théâtre Sarah Bernhardt in Paris. Even the "Divine Sarah," then seventy-one years old and still the greatest actress of the French stage after a career spanning more than fifty years, had seldom taken to the stage under more remarkable circumstances. It was her first performance in Paris after her return from the Bordeaux region, where she had fled as the Germans approached Paris in August 1914. Bernhardt herself was no stranger to war. She had opened a hospital for the wounded at the Odéon theatre in Paris during the Franco-Prussian war of 1870–1. According to legend, she left Paris in 1914 only after her friend and future wartime premier Georges Clemenceau told her she was on a list of hostages to be taken by the Germans if they captured the city. Moreover, the aging star was herself recuperating from major surgery – the amputation of her leg, which had finally become gangrenous after years of mistreatment of an old injury.

In itself, *Les Cathédrales* is a work remote in form and content from today's aesthetic sensibilities. It recounted the dream of a young and courageous French soldier who has grabbed a few moments of sleep near the front, in the department of the Nord, invaded by the Germans. Though his unit had been retreating, he could not take his eyes off his devastated native village, or the ruins of his own house, and he fell asleep out of sheer exhaustion. During his dream, a number of the great cathedrals of France appeared to him as allegorical figures. They praised the courage of all young soldiers, on whom they know the salvation of the country depends. They recounted the suffering of France since August 1914. Notre Dame de Paris lamented:

> The German eagle cast its immense shadow upon us
> From the first days, he reviled me.
> At the hour of prayer,
> My people were assembled at the foot of my towers,

The thunder that he held in his claws,
He made it fall on me, on me, Paris.[1]

In about the middle of the piece, Bernhardt appeared as the Alsatian cathedral of Strasbourg, which had been under German control since 1871. Seated on an ornate dais, she recounted the sorrow of her long separation from the rest of France. She lamented the trials of the cathedral in Rheims in the Champagne, bombarded by the Germans in 1914: "Queen of cathedrals,/ Seeking Heaven through the poked-out eyes of her windows,/ Is like a martyr in the hands of her torturers."

Yet she foretold allegorically that Strasbourg, still the hostage of the invader, would one day seal the doom of Germany. Her own spire would ascend heavenward and skewer the eagle symbolizing the ancient enemy. The eagle would die a grisly death. Plainly, her prediction was only symbolic up to a point. Real, flesh and blood Germans should expect no gentler treatment. During this protracted speech, Bernhardt managed as if miraculously to bring herself to a standing position on her one remaining leg, as her unforgettable voice rang forth:

> . . . Now part, my spire! And whistle! And rise!
> Pierce the sky with your lightning!
> Great arrow of iron!
> Arrow of God that nothing can chip,
> Strike him in the heart, pitiless arrow,
> Part, my arrow of five hundred feet!
> Ah! Ah, you have struck him, my arrow! He falls,
> The assassin of cities, he who slits the throats of doves!
> How long it takes him to fall. He falls! He falls!
>   Finally!
> Drained of all his blood, deprived of his feathers,
> Cast against the rocks, in the eddies of foam,
> The eagle, the German eagle, has fallen into the Rhine!
>   *Pleure, Pleure, Allemagne,*
>   *L'Aigle, l'aigle Allemand est tombé dans le Rhin!*
>   (Weep, Weep, Germany,
>   The Eagle, the German eagle, has fallen into the Rhine!)

Little seemed to justify faith in such an outcome in November 1915. An Anglo-French offensive in the Artois and the Champagne had come and gone that autumn, with no meaningful gains and heavy casualties. The allies of France fared no better. The Russians had been driven from the Habsburg province of Galicia, while the British, Australians, and the French were being massacred in the fruitless offensive against the

---

[1] Eugène Morand, *Les Cathédrales* (Paris: Librairie Théâtrale, Artistique & Littéraire, probably 1916). Unless otherwise noted, all translations are our own.

Ottoman Turks in the Dardanelles. People in the United States, while enraged over the German sinking of the *Lusitania* in May 1915, remained overwhelmingly isolationist. For France, ahead lay the carnage of Verdun, the Somme, and the Chemin des Dames, and the near collapse in 1918.

Sarah Bernhardt was not the consummate performer of her age for nothing. Clearly, she sought, in these unpromising circumstances, to symbolize embattled France itself – aged, mutilated, but almost miraculously still in the fight. She and the nation had plenty of battle scars, inflicted from within as well as from without. But both maintained a remarkable resilience still little understood outside France. Her performance spoke to a uniquely French war culture in the conflict of 1914–18 that lies at the heart of this book. By "war culture," we mean the many varieties of representation through which the French understood the war and their commitment to winning it. Bernhardt's particular performance of this war culture had its roots in nineteenth-century sentimentality, and can seem melodramatic and even silly to many people today. Yet even across the considerable expanse of time, we cannot deny the sincerity of *Les Cathédrales*, indeed its deadly seriousness. The national community that adored Sarah Bernhardt knew, at a certain level, what it wanted out of the war and accepted the perils, the sacrifices, the hatreds, and the cruelties of fighting it.

Barely a year and a half later, on May 18, 1917, and directly across the square from the Théâtre Sarah Bernhardt at the Théâtre du Châtelet, premiered the Ballet Russe production of *Parade*. The proceeds of the performance were go to a fund to help wounded soldiers and their families. The collaborators in *Parade* comprised a "who's who" of the artistic avant-garde of Paris. Impressario Serge Diaghilev staged the ballet, at the same theatre where his production of Igor Stravinsky's *Le Sacre du printemps* (The Rite of Spring) had caused a riot in 1913. Jean Cocteau wrote a one-page script, Erik Satie wrote the music, Léonide Massine did the choreography, and Pablo Picasso designed the sets and costumes. Guillaume Apollinaire wrote the program notes.

By May 1917, the fortunes of France in the conflict had never been lower. The Chemin des Dames offensive had failed, and a major mutiny was brewing within the French army. The tsarist regime had fallen in Russia, and that country's future participation in the war had become uncertain. To be sure, the United States had entered the war on the side of the Allies in April 1917. But militarily speaking, the American colossus was still a world away. It had plenty of money, but no army to speak of and no infrastructure for war production. The French could not expect serious material assistance from the United States any time soon.

The meanings of *Parade* are as diffuse as the message of *Les Cathédrales* is focused – and that, perhaps, is the point. Ostensibly, it is a work fixated on curiosities, on what in the grim spring of 1917 must have seemed like tasteless trivialities – a Chinese magician, acrobats, and the antics of an American girl. The work seemed directed toward anything *but* the war that at that very moment was tearing apart the France that so easily understood Sarah Bernhardt. Satie's music freely adopted both French and American popular music, and was full of kitschy and catchy tunes. As if this were not enough, he drew on sounds quite removed from the concert hall – sirens, whistles, a revolver, and even a typewriter. The French term "*parade*" means a sideshow, set up alongside a traveling theatre to draw in customers. As such, the *parade* in the ballet failed miserably. The audience in the piece became so fixated on the sideshow that no one ever bothered to go inside to the "actual" performances, despite the increasingly frantic efforts of three managers attired in Picasso's cubist costumes. They finally collapsed on each other as the magician, the acrobats, and the American girl tried to convince them and the audience, in Cocteau's words, "*que le spectacle se donne à l'intérieur* [that the spectacle takes place inside]."

Certainly, at least part of the audience was displeased, though the stories of the premier of *Parade* got better with the telling. Cocteau proclaimed, rather grandly, that "I have heard the cries of a bayonet charge in Flanders [probably not true, in fact], but it was nothing compared to what happened that night at the Châtelet Theatre."[2] Several critics were hostile. Satie in particular was accused of *bochisme*[3] ("Hunism" or "Krautism"), of writing music so disrespectful and inappropriate that it undermined the war effort and gave aid and comfort to the enemy. In a career-defining episode, Satie sent a series of obscene postcards to one critic, calling him "not only an asshole (*con*) but an unmusical asshole." The critic sued for libel, nearly bankrupting Satie but solidifying his position as the premier avant-garde French composer of the day.

On the surface, *Parade* seems like a very familiar avant-garde embrace of the radically new, of trying to shock an audience for its own sake. Wild costumes, irreverent music, and distinctly non-classical choreography pointed to a violent rupture with the sentimental and patriotic aesthetic of Sarah Bernhardt. But *Parade* was as much a cultural production

---

[2] Cocteau had served for a time as a nurse near but not actually in the front lines. Jean Cocteau, "Parade: Ballet Réaliste In Which Four Modernist Artists Had a Hand," *Vanity Fair*, September 1917, quoted in Frank W. D. Ries, *The Dance Theater of Jean Cocteau* (Ann Arbor, MI.: UMI Research Press, 1986), p. 188.

[3] *Boche* became the preferred racial epithet that the French applied to the Germans in World War I, the reference being to having a wooden head.

of the Great War in France as *Les Cathédrales*. The war haunted *Parade* far more than its frivolous exterior suggested. For who in France in 1917 could imagine that the real *spectacle*, wherever it "actually" took place, was anything but the war itself? Cocteau, after all, insisted on a subtitle of "*ballet réaliste*." The humor of the work aside, it raised abstract but troubling questions about what was internal and what external to the spectacle. Apollinaire, wounded in the head at the front in 1916 and later a casualty of the influenza epidemic at the end of the war in 1918, carried the "realism" of *Parade* one step further. In his program notes, he contended that the marriage of music, dance, painting, and costumes had created something more than real, something "*sur-réal*." Although Apollinaire did not mean the same thing by this term as later surrealists, he too believed that the new France that created the spectacle and was being created by it required new representational modes. *Parade*, he wrote, hailed a new artistic era. The ballet was "so pure and so simple that one recognizes within it the marvelously lucid spirit of France herself."[4] The charge of *bochisme* against Satie, in fact, was quite misplaced. The very outlandishness of his music was a nationalist reaction to what Satie considered the overblown and ponderous Germanic symphonic tradition. *Parade* was an idiosyncratic but fiercely patriotic work, in its way as much so as *Les Cathédrales*.

We propose in this book to tell the story of the national community and the war culture that produced two such apparently divergent artistic works, which actually said many of the same things. We examine the national community that embarked upon, sustained, and in some way prevailed in the conflict of 1914–18. We explore how the national agony of the war inaugurated what Jean-Jacques Becker called "the great mutation"[5] of France, and consider how the war shaped the history of that country in the rest of the twentieth century and beyond. One could reasonably question the rationale for writing this sort of national history, at the beginning of a century when the meanings of nationhood are in flux across the world, nowhere more so than in Europe. There is indeed a paradox underpinning this volume, in that the authors firmly believe that the future of the study of World War I and of European history in general lies in international and comparative scholarship.

The national community matters first and foremost here because it mattered first and foremost to people at the time. World War I proved, at least to date, the last general conflict among European nation-states.

[4] Guillaume Apollinaire, "Parade," in Pierre Caizergues and Michel Décaudin, eds., *Apollinaire: Oeuvres en prose complètes*, 3 vols. (Paris: Gallimard, 1991), vol. 2: p. 865.
[5] Jean-Jacques Becker, *La France en guerre, 1914–1918: la grande mutation* (Brussels: Éditions Complexe, 1988).

The nation-state remained the basic military, political, economic, social, and cultural unit for the duration, even though universal ideologies became more engaged as the war became "total." Certainly, European states dragged their empires into the war, and it ended to no small degree thanks to intervention from outside Europe, from the United States. But unlike World War II, World War I was primarily a European conflict that came to absorb other parts of the world. The "European" focus of the war mattered particularly to the French in reflecting on the twentieth century, given that the defeat by Germany in 1940 suddenly and dramatically removed most of France and most of the French from most of World War II. Consequently, the traditional French term *la Grande Guerre* (the Great War), probably more accurately describe the conflict of 1914–18 than "World War I."[6] Ultimately, we invoke the nation as the central category here, whatever its instabilities, because we believe the comparative study of World War I must rest on a thorough knowledge of just what is being compared. In this sense, we see this book as a companion to the volume by Roger Chickering in this series, *Imperial Germany and the Great War, 1914–1918* (1998).

In the Great War, the Western Front played the role played by the Eastern Front in World War II – the theatre where the outcome of the war was decided. And France was the country where virtually all of the Western Front was located. As we will show, the position of the Western Front and the character of the fighting that took place there made the Great War a life-or-death struggle for France. France, to be sure, had lost most of two large and prosperous provinces, Alsace and Lorraine, in its defeat by Prussia in 1871. But Bernhardt's protestations aside, the "lost territories" were borderlands, where people spoke German and Alsatian dialects at least as much as they spoke French. Few in France would admit it after 1914, but France had managed to remain France without them. Not so for the large swath of northeastern France conquered by the Germans in August 1914. Much of French coal and steel production came into German hands. And as a matter of principle, the French could not let stand another massive appropriation of national territory by Germany. To remain "France," the national community had to reconquer not just northeastern France, but the older "lost territories" as well – even if the experience of "total war" would in time invoke the destruction of the national community that embarked on it. On this basis,

---

[6] World War II, we would argue, began as two distinct continental wars in Europe and Asia. But by the end of 1941, following the German invasion of the Soviet Union, the Japanese attack on Pearl Harbor, and the German declaration of war on the United States, these wars became a single and genuinely global conflict of massive geopolitical, military, and ideological blocs.

the French came to justify practically an open-ended commitment to the war, and to a vindictive and unworkable peace once it concluded.

We will tell the story of the "great mutation" of France in the Great War through a double narrative structure. Our book unfolds both chronologically and thematically. At different phases of the war, different varieties of history take center stage. Chapter 1 begins with politics, diplomacy, and the military. We explore how the legacy of war in the nineteenth century had shaped France at the beginning of the twentieth century, then the outbreak of war in 1914. We focus on the origins and contours of the grim resolution that sustained the French throughout the conflict. The military stalemate that resulted from the battles of 1914, coupled with the loss of northeastern France to the Germans, made a compromise peace impossible. Chapter 2 explores the implications of this impasse, and emphasizes social, cultural, and economic history. Recovering the occupied territories both required and justified the "total" mobilization of the French national community. We argue that the very success of French national mobilization at least makes comprehensible a military strategy that otherwise seems not just cruel, but insane. For the irresistible force of national commitment ran into the immovable object of the war of the trenches. The massive grief that afflicted France after 1918 began during the war itself. Chapter 3 begins with military strategy, and the soldiers' war culture that resulted from it. The pre-war doctrine of the offensive persisted in the grim setting of the stalemated war. Bit by bit, French military strategy came apart in ways that made the survival of France *qua* France a more dire matter than ever. Of course, the war exacted the greatest price from the soldiers who fought it. Yet we argue that soldiers were not just victims of their experience in the trenches, but were active participants in negotiating it in their own war culture, distinct from but closely connected to that of the civilians.

France, like the other European protagonists in World War I, experienced a period of national crisis, when its continued participation in the war could by no means be taken for granted. *Parade* premiered during a phase of national vertigo lasting most of 1917, in which France could neither win the war nor relinquish it. Chapter 4 emphasizes social and political history, and examines the multiple crises of 1917 – mutiny at the front, strikes in the interior, and bitter divisions in the government resolved by a quasi-dictatorship under the government of Georges Clemenceau. Yet in the end, the national community proved remarkably adaptable, and a "second mobilization" (alongside critical support from the Allies) made it possible for France to emerge from the war as something of a victor. Chapter 5 examines how France tried but only partly succeeded in ending the war. We show how an incomplete military victory led to a bitter peace that ultimately failed to resolve the conflict. Commemoration sought to console individuals in deep mourning, and to construct a narrative of national triumph not actually there in the Versailles treaty of 1919. In our conclusion, we explore how a grieving France came to reject the Great War, and then to forget and repress much of its experience in the Great War after World War II, only to return to it, and to traces of its abiding grief, at the end of the twentieth century.

1   The national community goes to war

In *The Old Regime and the French Revolution* (1856), Alexis de Tocqueville described the French as a people "talented enough at anything, but who excel only at war. They adore chance, force, success, flash and noise, more than true glory. More capable of heroism than virtue, of genius more than good sense, they are suited more to conceiving immense plans than to completing great enterprises." Up to a point, Tocqueville knew his compatriots well. Over the course of the nineteenth century, France had gone to war many times and, in general, had fared poorly at it. The French had mainly themselves to blame. The century began in a blaze of Napoleonic glory, followed by complete national defeat in 1815. Not that this prevented the French from erecting to Napoleon their greatest military monument, the Arc du Triomphe, an unusual tribute to a defeated commander. Some victories came at mid-century, against the Russians in the Crimean War of 1853–6, and against the Habsburg Monarchy in Italy in 1859. Yet these were classic nineteenth-century "limited" wars, in which France ventured and gained relatively little. But the "immense plan" of Emperor Napoleon III (allegedly the illegitimate nephew of Napoleon Bonaparte) to install his protégé, Archduke Maximilian (the brother of Habsburg Emperor Francis Joseph), as emperor of Mexico in 1861 ended in utter failure. France had nothing to show for it but the famous 1867 painting by Édouard Manet of Maximilian's execution by Mexican patriots.

Worst of all, France provoked a war with Prussia in 1870, over what seemed the relatively minor matter of the succession to the Spanish throne. In fact, Napoleon III wanted to forestall the unification of Germany under Prussian leadership. He had reason for concern, but blundered without allies into a war that invoked the very thing he sought to prevent. The overconfident French army met defeat within two months, and on January 18, 1871, the victors proclaimed the creation of the German Empire. To maximize the humiliation of their foe, the Prussians chose to do so in France, in one of the most splendid spaces created by the old monarchy – the Hall of Mirrors at the palace at Versailles. According to the armistice with the new republican government of France signed a few days later, France had to pay a large indemnity and surrender Alsace-Moselle and most of Lorraine, two wealthy provinces now absorbed into the Reich. France could fume and swear one day to get its revenge, but not much else. Worse, a new Great Power had been created at its doorstep, far more dangerous to France than Prussia had ever been. The Third French Republic had to prepare for a new war with Germany virtually from the day of its inception. France would never again feel safe from Germany until the Allies divided Hitler's Third Reich after World War II.

Yet Tocqueville, who died in 1856, did not live long enough to see the whole picture. Perhaps he was too taken with his idealized version of the young republic in the United States to see his own country clearly anyway. The French economy boomed through most of the nineteenth century, and French literary and artistic life remained the envy of the West. By the end of a century of war, revolution, and social turmoil, the French, in part through a massive investment in institutions such as the education system and the army, had forged one of the most cohesive national communities in the world. France had also become the only republic among the Great Powers of Europe. The Third Republic proved more cautious about going to war than the regime of Napoleon III. The guardians of the republic made alliances, in order to contain a Germany much larger, wealthier, and militarily stronger than itself. Those among the French who sought Napoleon's sort of military glory did so mainly through the vast French global empire. The French military, as we will see, had many problems, in doctrine, funding, and leadership. But the army and navy of France continued to be feared throughout Europe and even the world. Moreover, despite decades of civil–military turmoil, democracy took hold in the French military. Unique among Europeans mobilized in 1914, the French soldier served neither kaiser nor tsar nor king, only himself and his compatriots. Even before the outbreak of the war, he was a citizen-soldier.

But success in the great enterprise of national rehabilitation came at a price. The alliances made by the Republic, in the end, provoked rather than deterred Germany and its ally Austria-Hungary, and thus helped render the diplomatic situation in Europe more perilous. In the crisis of August 1914, France had little room for maneuver, because of diplomatic and military choices made decades earlier. But this did not obscure the fact that Germany and not France chose war in 1914, because of the inflexibility of prewar German military planning. France had war forced upon it more than any other European country except Belgium and perhaps Serbia. German aggression in August 1914 responded to a long-term threat posed by the alliances made by France. But it was aggression all the same.

The French greeted the outbreak of what they saw as the most just of wars with grim resolution rather than patriotic fury. Yet from the beginning, the French were very determined to win the war, and to regain Alsace and Lorraine in the process. The return of the "lost provinces" proved the most consistent French war aim, from the first days of the Great War to the last – the symbol, in fact, of making France safe from the enemy across the Rhine. Yet their initial military effort seemed scripted by Tocqueville's assessment of the national character. The French offensive in Alsace and Lorraine failed miserably, while the Germans poured into northeastern France. The Battle of the Marne in September 1914 drove the Germans back, and partly reversed this initial disaster. But the first month of fighting proved the bloodiest in the entire war. Although the "miracle of the Marne" became understood as the greatest victory of French arms since Napoleon, it led to the descent into trench warfare, and to four years of fighting that was as bloody as it was indecisive.

Diplomacy: France as a Great Power, 1871–1914

The main preoccupation of French foreign and military policy between 1871 and 1914 was the threat of a new war with Germany. Heading off this threat required the reestablishment of France as a Great Power. The French sought to deter Germany, not through creating strategic parity, but through superiority. The leaders of the Third Republic concluded early on that France should never again fight Germany alone. But breaking out of diplomatic isolation proved difficult for about twenty years after the defeat. Otto von Bismarck, Prussian chancellor in 1870–1 and Imperial chancellor until 1890, effectively pursued his own policy of deterrence through superiority, by cultivating alliances with Russia and Austria-Hungary. Keeping France isolated removed the threat of a two-front war, and thus forcibly muted nationalist cries in France for *la revanche* (revenge). But Bismarck's policy began to break down, even before his forced retirement in 1890. Tensions grew between Russia and Austria-Hungary over the Balkans, particularly over who would pick up the pieces of the crumbling Ottoman Empire. Germany sided with Austria-Hungary in this evolving struggle, as its only reliable ally.

After Bismarck's departure, the French began to court Russia in earnest. Some peculiar political theatre resulted, as well as, over time, a dramatic reversal of French fortunes. In July 1891, the French navy paid an official visit to the Russian port of Kronstadt, where Tsar Alexander III, autocrat of the most reactionary regime among the Great

Powers, stood at respectful attention while a military band played "La Marseillaise," which sang the death of tyrants. The French side, for their part, transformed the tsarist regime, which had invoked the ruin of Napoleon in 1812, into a somewhat exotic but treasured counterweight to the enemy across the Rhine. A variety of cultural exchanges followed, the most famous of which proved Diaghilev's Ballets Russe, which electrified the Paris dance scene beginning in 1909. Of more diplomatic import was a massive flow of French capital into Russia, mostly to finance Russian industrialization. In 1888, Russia borrowed 500 million francs on the French market; by 1913, the French had invested 12 billion francs in Russia, more than in any other country. France stood to lose a great deal of money should its ally fall.

What came to be known as the Dual Alliance between France and Russia began in the winter of 1893–4, as a straightforward defensive response to the Triple Alliance of Germany, Austria-Hungary, and Italy. It committed Russia to war against Germany in the event that Germany attacked France, or if Italy attacked France supported by Germany. Likewise, France would be obligated to go to war with Germany should Germany (or Austria-Hungary supported by Germany) attack Russia. The alliance was upgraded in 1899, largely through the efforts of the secretive, hard-working, and durable French Foreign Minister Théophile Delcassé, who more or less personally ran foreign policy from 1898 to 1905. After 1899, the two countries committed themselves not just to mutual security, but to maintaining the balance of power in Europe. Just what this meant in practice, however, remained ambiguous until August 1914. In the meantime, Republican France kept the public about as ignorant of the great strategic choices being made as did autocratic Russia. The French public was not even told about the Alliance until 1897, and many of its secret clauses remained unknown even to senior officials until war broke out. Nor did France confine secret diplomacy to its relations with Russia. In 1902, Italy promised, in a secret agreement, to remain neutral should Germany or Austria-Hungary attack France. Britain also found itself drawn subtly and secretly into the anti-German alliance.

In addition to its alliances, France based its status as a Great Power on its overseas empire. France had been acquiring colonies since the seventeenth century. By 1914, France had a global empire second only to that of Britain, with territories ranging from North and West Africa, to Indochina, to a number of islands in the Indian, Pacific, and Atlantic Oceans, as well as in the Caribbean. Some of these colonies, such as St. Pierre and Miquelon, two fishing islands off the Canadian coast, and the Caribbean islands of Martinique and Guadeloupe, remain French today.

Like its rivals, France greatly extended its imperial conquests in the late-nineteenth century, for diverse reasons. In the mercantilist tradition of colonialism, France sought raw materials and markets for finished goods. The Third Republic also sought global expansion as an alternative to brooding about an unattainable *revanche* in Alsace and Lorraine. It could cloak imperialism in the rhetoric of a "*mission civilisatrice*," or "civilizing mission" to bring the blessings of Frenchness to distant parts of the world. Such an approach earned expansionists scorn, indelicately expressed, from the nationalist Right. "I had two sisters [Alsace and Lorraine]," proclaimed Right-wing deputy Paul Déroulède, "and you are offering me two domestic servants."[1]

More than was the case elsewhere, French imperial expansion was the creature of the colonial army. Often on their own initiative and not always rationally, colonial officers would launch expeditions that would net vast tracts of economically dubious land, such as most of the Sahara Desert. These acquisitions would then have to be administered and, as the expression of the day had it, "pacified." One colonial officer, Charles Mangin, who would hold several major commands during the Great War, argued in 1910 that France should raise a huge colonial army that could definitively solve the problem of France's demographic inferiority to Germany.[2] Mangin's scheme drew criticism from those appalled at the prospect of metropolitan France depending on non-white soldiers for its defense. But like Mangin, most French officers and politicians sought expansion as some form of long-term geopolitical investment. Countries acquired colonies before World War I much the same way they acquired battleships, and for much the same reasons. Imperialists, in France, and elsewhere, foresaw a twentieth century in which huge geopolitical blocs far larger than the nation-states of Europe would dominate the world. One such bloc had plainly formed in the United States; many saw the potential for another in Russia. Imperialists concluded that if Europe expected to dominate international politics in the twentieth century as thoroughly as it had in the nineteenth, empires would have to move from the margin to the center of strategic thinking.

Imperial politics both complicated and clarified the position of France in Europe by August 1914. The great rival of France in the quest for colonies at the end of the nineteenth century was not Germany, but Britain. The nadir of this rivalry came in 1898, during the "scramble for Africa," when much of the continent was divided up among competing European powers. An entrepreneurial French officer, Colonel

---

[1] According to one version, Déroulède said "and you are offering me twenty Negroes."
[2] Charles Mangin, *La Force noire* (Paris: Hachette, 1911).

Jean-Baptiste Marchand, led a mission of a few Frenchmen and some 150 Senegalese soldiers to claim southern Sudan. The French sought thereby to control the upper Nile River and thus the main water supply of the British protectorate of Egypt. In September 1898, Marchand's outpost at Fashoda encountered a much larger force led by H. H. Kitchener (later British minister of war during the Great War). After a tense military and diplomatic stand-off that nearly brought France and Britain to war, Marchand was ordered to withdraw, in the greatest international humiliation France had experienced since 1871.

Yet whatever ill will the French might bear the British over Africa, France very much needed Britain's support on the continent. Attaching Britain to the Franco-Russian alliance could help deter a general war in Europe. Moreover, the world's greatest naval and financial power would prove a critical ally if prewar plans for a short, decisive war went awry – as indeed proved the case. Britain and France resolved their colonial rivalry gradually in the ten years preceding the outbreak of the Great War. In 1904, France agreed to give Britain a free hand in Egypt, in exchange (again in a secret clause) for British support for what proved to be the last great French imperial conquest before 1914, its protectorate over Morocco. Germany, now clearly worried about the resurgence of its enemy across the Rhine, invoked two major diplomatic crises over Morocco, in 1905–6 and again in 1911–12. Both times, French primacy over Morocco was affirmed, thanks largely to British support. Even more important, Anglo-French naval cooperation closely linked the fortunes of the two countries. Britain, greatly concerned about the expanding German navy, needed allies at sea. A series of secret letters in the fall of 1912 between British Foreign Minister Sir Edward Gray and French Ambassador to Britain Paul Cambon affirmed that the British navy would assume primary responsibility for guarding the English Channel, while the French navy would do the same in the Mediterranean. The latter was of crucial interest to the British because of the Suez Canal, which guaranteed British access to India. These letters did not, to be sure, obligate Britain to join a general European war. But they did give Britain a strategic interest in heading off a French defeat on the continent that had not been there in 1870–1.

While the French position became more secure in the West, the Franco-Russian alliance, still the cornerstone of French security, came under pressure in the last years before 1914. The problem was the seething cauldron of the Balkans, where France had no strategic interests and where Russian interests could not have been stronger. Russia, Austria-Hungary, the ever-crumbling Ottoman Empire, and a proliferating array of (often mutually antagonistic) nationalist groups all vied for influence over the Balkans. The Congress of Berlin in 1878 had awarded administration of the former Ottoman province of Bosnia-Herzegovenia to Austria-Hungary. Germany's support of this move had helped create the Franco-Russian alliance in the first place. But when Austria-Hungary formally annexed Bosnia-Herzegovenia in 1908, a furious Russia invoked a major diplomatic crisis. France offered no support, and Russia had to climb down. But Russia returned the favor in 1911–12, when it declined to support France in the second Moroccan crisis. Diplomats throughout Europe came to wonder just what sort of crisis *would* bring the alliance into force.

But as the political meaning of the Franco-Russian alliance seemed increasingly ambiguous, its military provisions became increasingly precise. Among other things, this indicated a serious lack of communication between the Foreign Ministry and the Ministry of War in France. As early as August 1911, and at French urging, the Russian army committed itself to taking the offensive immediately against Germany in the event of war, the chronic logistical difficulties of the tsar's forces notwithstanding. The French supreme commander Joseph Joffre visited Russia in the summer of 1913 and further clarified mutual obligations. France would take the offensive within eleven days of the outbreak of war, Russia within fifteen. It was assumed (correctly) that Germany would direct the bulk of its forces toward France at the outset of a general conflict. It was also assumed (incorrectly) that the speediest possible Russian attack would help guarantee the success of the French Plan XVII, as will be explained further below.

All this being said, from a position of defeat and isolation in 1871, the politicians and diplomats of the Third Republic had reestablished France as a Great Power, in Europe and in the world. Yet new dangers replaced the old. Through the Russian alliance, the French had indirectly tied their fate to the perpetually volatile Balkans, where everyone agreed France had no particular interests. Doubts lingered over the stability of the tsarist regime itself, particularly after the near-revolution of 1905. Moreover, France had revived its fortunes at the risk of helping to create the conditions for the general European war its alliances had been constructed to deter. Germany, in effect, had become encircled. No one doubted that France, Russia, and Britain could bring to bear more men, materiel, and money than Germany and Austria-Hungary – in the long run. German military planners concluded, therefore, that they could not permit a two-front war to *have* a long run. German generals bet on fortune favoring the swift, as it had in 1870.

The army and the Republic

War shaped the entire history of the Third Republic, its predilection for diplomacy over military conflict notwithstanding. The regime was born at war against Germany in 1871 and died at war against Germany in 1940. Conflict with the Reich, actual or potential, haunted each of the 100 or so governments that presided over France in between. French military revival after 1871 took place against the backdrop of the contentious and at times tortured relationship between the French army and the French republic.

Throughout the history of the Third Republic, parties and factions at all points on the political spectrum fought over the soul of the army. Catholics and monarchists admired and advocated traditional military virtues of order and hierarchy. But militarism also had roots on the political Left. Revolutionaries since 1789 had echoed the cry of Jean-Jacques Rousseau: "Every soldier a citizen, every citizen a soldier." Universal male conscription, which ended completely in France only in June 2001, institutionalized the *levée en masse* of 1793, in which the Republic ordered its entire population of young men to organize in battalions bearing the banner "The French people risen against tyranny." French political culture profoundly shaped the French army, and vice versa. The French army of August 1914 reflected a variety of antagonisms and compromises at work in the preceding decades.

Their admiration for militarism during the Revolution notwithstanding, most Republicans looked on the army with suspicion or worse. Few dared raise a voice against Napoleon, the greatest guardian of French *gloire*. But had not a certain General Bonaparte swept aside the Republic after 1799 in favor of personal military rule? In the decades before 1914, distrust centered on professional officers, who Republicans saw, sometimes correctly, as enemies of the regime. General Georges Boulanger, a charismatic figure who could draw support from workers and Socialists as well as monarchists, led an unfocused and ultimately unsuccessful political movement against the Republic in 1887–8. Its primary result was to reinforce Republican suspicions of professional officers who went into politics.

Far more serious was the protracted Dreyfus Affair. In December 1894, Captain Alfred Dreyfus was convicted of having given secret French military documents to the Germans. Initially, little controversy surrounded the conviction. Even later defenders of Dreyfus, such as Radical politician Georges Clemenceau and Socialist Jean Jaurès lamented that he had been given a life sentence on Devil's Island rather than the death penalty. Only the Dreyfus family, wealthy Jewish industrialists from Alsace who had chosen French citizenship in 1871, continued to believe Dreyfus's protestations of innocence. They lobbied tirelessly for a review of the conviction, gradually gaining ground among intellectuals and a few influential politicians. The "Affair" proper began on January 13, 1898, when France's most famous man of letters, Émile Zola, published his famous open letter to the president of the Republic in Clemenceau's newspaper *L'Aurore*. Titled "J'accuse," Zola's letter accused the War Ministry of a willful miscarriage of justice.

From the beginning, the case against Dreyfus rested on evidence manufactured by his former colleagues in the counterespionage unit of the army general staff.[3] Yet as suspicions of the handling of the case mounted, the professional officer corps closed ranks. The counter-espionage unit continued to provide evidence of its own invention, and the senior command silenced voices of dissent within the army itself. This made the Affair a matter of professional autonomy versus the rule of law. The Nationalist Right, led by writer Maurice Barrès and a host of like-minded notables, came to the defense of the army. The archbishop of Paris and the Catholic press intervened in ways that highlighted the anti-Semitic overtones of the Affair. As Right and Left mobilized against each other, the Dreyfus Affair became one of the great domestic political crises of modern France. The army tried Dreyfus again in the summer of 1899, when a divided court martial arrived at the bizarre verdict of guilty of treason with attenuating circumstances. He was sentenced again, to ten years' detention. But by this time, the political landscape had changed in favor of the Dreyfusard forces. A Center-Left "government of republican defense" was formed that arranged for a presidential pardon. But the fallout from the Dreyfus Affair had barely begun.

The coalition that came to power in 1899 saw its first task as settling scores with what it perceived to be the institutional enemies of the Republic – the professional army and the Catholic Church. Military promotions became strictly centralized under the Ministry of War, now under the direction of only the most reliable Republican figures. Reformers meant to break what they saw as the Catholic and monarchist hold over the officer corps, even at the expense of professional competence. General Louis André, minister from 1900–4, wrote: "To attain my goal, my first preoccupation was to seek out among the anonymous and silent mass of officers, those whose republican sentiments could single them out for my attention . . . How did one recognize them? I resolved to fix my attention

---

[3] Documents were indeed being passed to the Germans, before and after the conviction of Dreyfus. It is now generally agreed that the guilty party was another officer in the counterespionage section, Major Ferdinand Esterhazy.

upon those recommended by no one." In 1904, the Affaire des Fiches broke when it became known that the ministry had gathered information on candidates' political and religious views from the Masonic Grand Orient. In 1905, the National Assembly renounced the 1805 Concordat between France and the Catholic Church, thus separating church and state. The state ceased to pay clerical salaries, and assumed title over all church property. The most strident anticlericals insisted on adding insult to injury by making the army participate in the mean-spirited enterprise of taking inventories of individual churches. The Republic thus ordered Catholic officers to choose between faith and country, the Pope having expressly commanded Catholics in France to resist the new legislation. Civil-military relations reached their lowest level since the Third Republic began.

Yet the army and the Republic could not remain enemies forever, if only because of the increasingly dangerous international situation. And while many officers bitterly resented "civilian interference" in the Dreyfus Affair and were appalled at efforts to "republicanize" the army, few saw any realistic alternative to the Republican regime. The army and the Republic gradually came to terms in the last years before the Great War. The French army of August 1914 is best viewed as a collection of compromises, representative of the *modus vivendi* at work in the national community as a whole.

One such compromise involved conscription. We have already seen that compulsory military service had deep roots in France before 1914 and in the Republican tradition. The obligation to take up arms for the Republic, in Richard Challener's words, constituted "both the badge and the moral consequence of citizenship."[4] Each young man had a "class" indicated by the year in which his cohort turned twenty. Elaborate rituals involving parades, bands, costumes, and much else evolved in localities throughout France to celebrate the induction of each class to military service. These comprised rites of manhood as much as citizenship. There is no question that conscription and the cultural baggage it carried continually reinscribed the essentially male nature of citizenship in France through most of the twentieth century.

This being said, there existed a wide range of views in France on conscription and the citizen-soldier it produced. While conservatives and reactionaries certainly advocated a large standing army, they believed that the recalcitrant masses drafted into the colors could be controlled only by a powerful and professional officer corps – the very corporate entity

---

[4] R. D. Challener, *The French Theory of the Nation in Arms, 1866–1939* (New York: Columbia University Press, 1955), p. 4.

that had worked so hard to frame Dreyfus. Centrist opinion remained suspicious of a professional military caste. Republicans writ large wanted conscription to be fair and to produce a large, efficient, and egalitarian army, and to do so cheaply. Republican objectives thus proved mutually inconsistent. Generally speaking, the Left detested conscription as the tool of militarists, imperialists, and industrialists, who saw the army as tool with which to break strikes. Yet the sentiment was far from universal. Socialist leader Jean Jaurès in *L'Armée nouvelle* (1911) advocated an armed citizen's militia on the Swiss model, led by a tiny officer corps of 4,000 professionals drawn from the working class.

Conscription law in France reflected a continuing compromise among these opinions. Before 1913, the trend involved reducing the term of active service and eliminating categories of exemption, so that the obligation of military service fell more equally over the whole male population. The 1872 law provided for five years of active service, though the number of men actually called up from a given class varied from year to year, depending on need, as determined by the war ministry. A lottery determined just who would be called upon to serve. An 1889 law reduced service to three years, and made some restrictions on exemptions. A 1905 law, passed at the height of the ascendance of the Dreyfusards and in the same year as the law separating church and state, reduced active service to two years and abolished practically all exemptions.

The army and the Republic definitively made peace with each other through the passage of the Three-years Law in May 1913, a measure long advocated by military professionals. Germany had steadily expanded its army by drafting a higher percentage of the available population. France, already conscripting virtually its entire cohort every year, could increase the size of its army in the short run only by increasing the term of service. The military impact of the law in August 1914 proved minimal. In fact, it probably weakened the French army in the last year before the war by further thinning the already sparse supply of trained commissioned and non-commissioned officers. The real importance of the law was political, in the way it heralded the national consensus that would carry France through most of the Great War.

On the surface, political conflict over the law seemed ferocious. *Troisannistes* (Three-yearists) battled opponents of the law, just as Dreyfusards and anti-Dreyfusards had battled each other fourteen years earlier, and using much the same language. The Russians made it clear that they saw the Three-years Law as essential to maintaining the alliance. Nationalist proponents of the law continually invoked dire concerns for national security. After the passage of the law, a number of anti-militarist demonstrations broke out, particularly in the Left-leaning south of France. There were also a few mutinies in units stationed in the south, supported particularly by young men who learned abruptly and to their considerable dismay that their release from military service would be delayed by a year. In the general election of May 1914, the *Troisannistes* lost some fifty seats, and hopes on the Left brightened for a reduction in military service. Yet the Center-Left government formed by René Viviani and approved by a large majority in the Chamber of Deputies comprised ten ministers who had voted for the law, only five who had voted against it, and two who had abstained. Machinations continued, virtually up to the moment when the diplomatic crisis silenced internal debate. But it was by no means clear that the law would have been overturned even if there had been no war.

In perhaps surprising ways, the rise of the doctrine of the offensive in France also reflected the evolving compromise between the army and the Republic. Two principles lay at the heart of the doctrine, known in France as "*offensive à outrance* (offense to the limit)" – the primacy of attacking over defending, and the primacy of moral over physical force. French planners believed that the best, indeed the only, defense was a good offense, and that the safety of France lay in bringing the war to the enemy. In 1903, the then Lieutenant Colonel Ferdinand Foch gave a famous series of lectures at the staff college, the École de Guerre, in which he observed: "War = Moral superiority of the victors; moral depression of the vanquished. Battle = the contest between the two wills."[5] Tactically, *offensive à outrance* meant simply getting as close to the enemy positions as possible, and then attacking as one man *à la baïonnette* (with the bayonet), and accepting whatever casualties would result. The doctrine did not, as is still often argued, ignore the increased killing power of heavy artillery, high-powered and accurate rifles, and the machine-gun. Rather, strategists and tacticians had seen the offense prevail in situations that seemed strongly to favor the defense, notably in the Russo-Japanese war of 1905–6. To be sure, most military historians today see the doctrine of the offensive as a dubious choice for a country whose main military problem was a substantial demographic inferiority to its most likely adversary.

Yet at the time, the "doctrine of the offensive" captivated military and civilian imagination on the political Right, Left, and Center in the last years before the Great War. It rendered respectable nationalist aggression, at least once a war was actually underway. Professional officers, monarchist, republican, or otherwise, could advocate the doctrine as a means of regaining collective self-respect after the Dreyfus debacle. Supporting the

---

[5] Marshal Ferdinand Foch, *The Principles of War*, first English edition, Hilaire Belloc, trans. (London: Chapman and Hall, 1918 [originally published in French in 1904], p. 287.

offensive even enabled triumphant Republicans to show that they held national ferocity no less dear than their rivals. Republicans also appreciated the emphasis the doctrine placed at the tactical level on the highly motivated individual citizen-soldier.

The Center-Right and Center-Left coalitions that ruled France in the last years before the war concluded that suitably "republican" generals devoted to the offensive could be invested with immense power. The government upgraded the post of Chief of General Staff with the appointment of General Joseph Joffre in 1911. Previously, one general had responsibility for preparing the army for war, another for actually commanding forces in the field should war break out. Now, one man became responsible for training, doctrine, strategy, mobilization, and, most importantly, the disposition of the French forces. Some historians have even suggested that Joffre had more authority than his German counterpart Helmut von Moltke, and had become more powerful than any French officer since Napoleon Bonaparte. Throughout his career, Joffre conveyed an impression of solidity and unflappability, not least because of his considerable physical girth. The War Ministry abandoned a scheme to enforce the retirement of any officer who could not mount a horse, for reasons clear from Joffre's photographs. He kept his views on politics, and much else, to himself. But all believed him to be a solid Republican.

Under the influence of the bright and energetic staff officers around him, known collectively as the "Young Turks," Joffre created Plan XVII, the last of the many French war plans before 1914 preparing for a general European war. Contrary to its historical reputation, the plan did not in itself require a French offensive into Alsace and Lorraine, which resulted from a decision made by Joffre himself in August 1914. Even his most senior subordinates had little discretion in the field. Army commanders, in charge of hundreds of thousands of men in some cases, could alter operations only in close cooperation with Joffre's liaison officers. These officers played a crucial role in the wholesale purge of field commanders that took place after the defeats along the frontiers.

The rigid centralization at the top of the command structure contrasted sharply with highly devolved authority at the bottom, above all at the moment of the attack. This thinning of command authority had been foreseen and even advocated by theorists of the offensive. Colonel Charles Ardant du Picq, one of the founding fathers of the doctrine of the offensive, had foreseen even before the Franco-Prussian War that discipline could no longer primarily be maintained vertically, through the physical and emotional intimidation of inferior by superior. Rather, discipline among large modern armies had to function first and foremost horizontally, through mutual surveillance among men who knew each other well.[6] The moral force that enabled the attack to prevail over superior defensive firepower, therefore, was highly democratic in nature. The last infantry regulations before the war, published in April 1914, prescribed attacks in which operational authority would devolve progressively from the regimental, battalion, company, and section levels. At the last stage of the attack, dispersed formations of highly motivated soldiers would descend as one man upon the enemy, bayonets fixed. Such a state of mind, of course, required extensive training and indoctrination, possible only after the Three-years Law was fully applied, and, equally important, fully funded.

Therein hangs the significance of a third area of compromise between the army and the Republic, over military funding. Given the stakes, the Third Republic prepared for a general European war frugally, not to say parsimoniously. To the end of its days, the Third Republic held dear its credentials as a middle-class regime. France would not create an income tax until January 1916, by which time the war had hugely strained public finance. To be sure, France allocated some 42 percent of all government spending to national defense by 1913, far larger than Germany's 20 percent, and huge by today's standards. But this was a large piece of a relatively small fiscal pie. As elsewhere in Europe, low and often regressive taxation supported low levels of governmental service of all kinds. German defense budgets drew from a far larger economy. France also spent far more than Germany on its empire, at the expense of defenses at home. While precise comparisons remain notoriously difficult, most contemporaries and historians agree that Germany spent much more per soldier. The professional command regained considerable operational and ideological autonomy in the last years before the Great War, but, for better or worse, it never had the means to effectively remake the army in the image of the doctrine of the offensive.

The gap between wish and fulfillment proved especially pronounced with junior and non-commissioned officers (NCOs), the very people who were supposed to bring the doctrine of the offensive from the Paris military *salons* to the conscripts garrisoned throughout France. French officers were always far worse paid than their counterparts in Germany. As the prestige of the army fell after the Dreyfus Affair, the number of talented young men interested in military careers fell with it, as shown by the number of applications to military academies and by deteriorating

---

[6] Charles Ardant du Picq, *Battle Studies* (New York: Macmillian, 1921 [originally published in French in 1868]).

admissions standards. The cautious reconciliation between the army and the Republic had barely begun to stabilize the situation before the war broke out. The situation was even worse for NCOs, ironically in part because of the Napoleonic tradition of promotion by merit. In Germany and Britain before 1914, men of modest backgrounds could only rarely obtain a commission. But they could achieve real if class-specific status as career NCOs. In France, talented NCOs were regularly siphoned off into the officer corps. German infantry companies in peacetime had eighteen to twenty career NCOs; French companies had eight or nine, in addition to a couple of draftees promoted after one year of service. The stereotype of the prewar French NCO was that of an ignorant brute unable to make anything of himself in civilian life.

The French army had serious material shortcomings as well. France had so few training camps that only one-third of active soldiers could expect to spend time there in a given year. The French had 2,500 machine-guns in August 1914, the Germans 4,500. The French had 3,800 of their soon-to-be-legendary 75mm artillery piece, but the Germans had 6,000 of their roughly comparable 77mm guns. The French had practically no heavy artillery, which contributed handily to their initial collapse before the German invasion.

Even the French uniforms of August 1914, dark blue jackets and red trousers, dated from the last century. By that time, all of the other Great Powers had abandoned uniforms that presented such obvious targets. Historians have often, but mistakenly, attributed the persistence of the colorful French uniform to stubborn myopia on the part of the French high command. But support for the anachronistic attire really spoke to a more broad-based and ancient notion that soldiers who go off to war should do so as beautifully appointed as possible. Heroes had to dress the part, most of all in a democracy, in which the army represented the sovereign people at war. Military practicality gained ground slowly over such powerful notions. Only on July 9, 1914, just one month before the war broke out, would the National Assembly pass a law providing for the grayish-blue *"bleu horizon* (horizon blue)" uniform, the one most identified with French soldiers of the Great War. French soldiers of August 1914 would face the Germans looking much like their fathers and grandfathers in 1870.

Denied the funds to do much else, conscripts before the war spent much of their military service in drill and menial work in garrisons strewn throughout France. The Republic used its army from time to time to break strikes, though by definition this never had much military utility. More often military ritual was the most common means of breaking the tedium of military life. Ceremonies constitute an important aspect of military experience anywhere, whether a given army is at peace or at war. In France before August 1914, ritual enabled the army and the Republic to display their reconciliation before the general population. Bastille Day, the French national holiday of July 14, provided much opportunity for such displays. Infantry, cavalry, and artillery would stage parades and mock military engagements in large public spaces. Martial music would precede patriotic speeches by local notables. The point of such displays was not lost on one Center-Left newspaper in Normandy, which commented in July 1913: "The greatest progress the army has made has been to become the image of the Republic, while at the same time becoming, as certain reactionary generals themselves recognize, 'the greatest army in the world.' " Military maneuvers, supposedly the most "realistic" approximation of warfare in peacetime, also had a highly ritualistic component. Armies would meet, brave charges would be first ordered then stopped at the crucial moment, bands would play, and generals would distribute praise liberally. Recriminations as to the unpreparedness of the French forces would follow only later, in newspapers and behind the closed doors of staff meetings.

In many ways, then, the French army was indeed "unprepared" for a general European war. The Third Republic had conceived an "immense plan," in Tocqueville's words sixty years earlier, to create a mass conscript army of citizen-soldiers. It had rehabilitated and given immense power to its high command, which had embraced a popular if militarily dubious doctrine. Yet France funded its twentieth-century doctrine on nineteenth-century budgets. This, plus the relatively recent nature of the reconciliation between the army and the Republic, limited the actual impact of the doctrine of the offensive on the soldiers who would face the Germans in August 1914. Of course, if the doctrine was as ill-advised as most subsequent historiography has argued, neglecting it in the training of the rank and file with it did not necessarily disserve them. French soldiers, raised in the schools of the Republic and some of the most literate soldiers in Europe, ultimately had more political cues than military ones.

It also bears pointing out that "preparedness" is always a relative rather than an absolute concept. Each army of 1914 could tell its sad tale of underfunding, political interference, and poor training – including Germany. In May 1914, Austro-Hungarian commander Conrad von Hötzendorf asked his German counterpart, Helmut von Moltke, what he would do if the Schlieffen Plan, the prewar German plan to invade northeastern France through Belgium, failed to produce a decisive result. In a famous response, Moltke replied vaguely: "Well, I will do what I can. We are not superior to the French."

August 1914 and the Union sacrée

In the summer of 1914, the "long nineteenth century" came to an end. On June 28, 1914, Serbian nationalists assassinated the heir to the Habsburg thrones, Archduke Franz Ferdinand, in Sarajevo. By early August, the murder had set a match to the power keg of European power politics. Austria-Hungary, backed by Germany, declared war on Serbia. Russia went to war with the Central Powers to back Serbia and preserve its credibility in the Balkans. The Schlieffen Plan drew France and ultimately Britain into what became the long-feared general European war.

But for most of the summer of 1914, internal rather than external crises dominated newspaper headlines in France. Charles Humbert laid the groundwork for a scandal following a speech in the Senate in July 1914, in which he laid out in scathing and accurate detail the material problems facing the French military, most notably its lack of heavy artillery. But as the wheels of secret diplomacy turned almost silently, the liveliest public scandal in France involved the trial of the wife of former finance minister Joseph Caillaux. Mme. Caillaux had shot the editor of the newspaper *Le Figaro* for publishing the Caillaux love letters, written before Joseph's divorce from his first wife. The "Affaire Caillaux" was the real "July crisis" up to July 28, when a jury (to general amazement) acquitted Mme. Caillaux. On that same day, Austria-Hungary declared war on Serbia.

As we have seen, the Franco-Russian alliance sought to deter Germany through the threat of an unwinnable two-front war against a superior alliance. The Germans formed a pessimistic military response to this diplomatic problem, which made the two-front war a self-fulfilling prophecy. The Schlieffen Plan called for an immediate invasion of France through Belgium. German planners reasoned that France could mobilize far more quickly than Russia, and thus had to be confronted first. Germany could exhibit a preponderance of force in the path of the invasion, particularly since (unlike France) it deployed reserve units in the front lines. The Germans hoped to knock out France before the Russian "steamroller" could be fully mobilized. With the Western Front secured, the German forces could be redeployed to the East. Germany thus had to invade France if Germany and Russia went to war, whether or not France played a role in the preceding diplomatic quarrel.

The determinism of the Schlieffen Plan did not mean that French politicians and diplomats lacked activity in the summer of 1914. President Poincaré played the central role in French crisis management. A native of the "lost province" of Lorraine, Poincaré was a conservative nationalist, elected president in 1913, the same year as the passage of the Three-years Law. Certainly, Poincaré proved one of the stronger presidents of the Third Republic, particularly in foreign policy. Through clever maneuvering behind the scenes, Poincaré saw to it that foreign ministers either shared his point of view or were so inexperienced that they needed to depend on him for guidance and support. Viviani, foreign minister as well as premier in August 1914, fell into the latter category. It was also widely assumed that Viviani was merely a place-holder for Caillaux, until the scandal over his wife died down. In his memoirs, Poincaré described himself as Viviani's tutor, particularly in affairs concerning Germany: "I showed him that I have never had serious difficulties with Germany because I've always used great firmness toward her."

On July 20, about three weeks after the assassination of Franz Ferdinand, Poincaré and Viviani arrived in Russia on a long-planned state visit. By that time, Russian diplomats knew in a general sense that Austria-Hungary, with German backing, planned a definitive show-down with Serbia. According to Poincaré's diary, the only record that survives of the meetings of French and Russian officials, Poincaré had made it clear that France intended to stand by its Russian ally, though it encouraged restraint on both Austria-Hungary and Serbia. The Austro-Hungarians delayed slightly the delivery of their ultimatum to Serbia, to make sure that Poincaré and Viviani did not hear of it before they left Russia. From July 23 to July 29, the two highest officials of France were quite literally at sea, and could receive only fragmentary and garbled radio accounts of developments. During a brief stop in Sweden on July 25, Poincaré advised the Russians to tell Serbia to accept as many of the Austro-Hungarian conditions as possible.

By the time Poincaré and Viviani arrived back in Paris, Austria-Hungary had declared war on Serbia, and Russia had begun its muddled mobilization. Events had reached a point of no return, and Germany began to put the Schlieffen Plan into effect. France no longer even had the option of abandoning its Russian ally. On July 31, German Chancellor Theobald von Bettmann-Hollweg sent a remarkable telegram to Baron von Schoen, German ambassador to France:

If, as is not to be presumed, the French Government declares its willingness to remain neutral, will Your Excellency [Ambassador Schoen] declare to the French government that as a guarantee for neutrality we must demand the fortresses of Toul and Verdun.

France at this point had two options. It could accept war, or the undoing of the whole great enterprise since 1871 of rehabilitating France as a Great Power. Most of the Great Powers made real choices in August 1914 – Austria-Hungary, Germany, Russia, even Britain. France had made plenty of real choices in the preceding decades – to form an alliance with Russia in 1894, to upgrade that alliance in 1899, and to clarify its military provisions in 1913. But realistically, by August 1914, France had no choice but to go to war.

On the same day as the telegram to Schoen, a driven, and most say crazed, nationalist named René Villain shot and killed Jean Jaurès, leader of the French socialists and arguably the most respected socialist in Europe of the day. One of the greatest orators of prewar Europe, Jaurès had worked ceaselessly to encourage working-class people to prevent a general European war by refusing to take part in it. But he had always made a delicate distinction between agitating against war before it broke out and supporting the nation once it did. As late as July 29, Jaurès had spoken to a crowd of 5,000 (with 10,000 waiting outside) in Brussels exhorting socialists throughout Europe to put pressure on their leaders to exercise restraint in the looming disaster. His death has often been interpreted as the murder of the last best chance to stop the Great War before it began, and indeed to transform Europe through peaceful means. Of course, we can never know just what Jaurès would have done once the German invasion began. But certainly Jaurès never agreed with Karl Marx and Frederich Engles, who argued in *The Communist Manifesto* (1848) that the workers had no country. "This is the sarcastic denial of history itself," Jaurès had once written, "the idea sacrificed to a whim." Certainly, his successors in labor unions and in the Socialist Party itself supported the defense of the nation.

President Poincaré coined the term Union sacrée (sacred union) in a letter addressed to the Chamber of Deputies and to the nation, in which he proclaimed that "nothing will break the Union sacrée in the face of the enemy." The term unified, among other things, civil and traditional religion. The term is perhaps best known through its more theatrical representations. In the Chamber of Deputies, Édouard Vaillant, who took part in the Commune, the Paris popular uprising that followed the defeat of 1870, shook hands for the first time with Albert de Mun, who had been an officer in the French army that suppressed it. Even Eric Satie felt motivated briefly to join a militia assigned to ensure public order in the Paris suburb of Arcueil-Cachan. More ominously, the term Union sacrée also conjures up images of thousands of chipper French soldiers marching on urban train stations en route to the front, and even of young officers from the military academy of Saint Cyr turned out to face the German machine-guns in their plumed hats and white gloves.

But the most prevalent reaction to the outbreak of war in France was not mindless, aggressive patriotism. The real character of the Union sacrée was more subtle, complex, and substantial. The French people in August 1914 faced war with shock, sadness, and consternation. On August 1, an automobile drove up to the mayor's office in the village of Saint-Lormel (with a population of 816) in the department Côtes du Nord in Brittany. A gendarme got out of the car and disappeared inside. A few minutes later, the church bells began to ring. The town's schoolteacher, Mme. Le Mée, heard an old woman mutter, "Here it is, the bell is tolling for our boys." But the national community from the outset showed great resolve to win a war forced upon the French by the invader. In the words of a schoolteacher from the Breton town of Glomel: "The men of all classes, from all careers and of all shades of opinion went forward, solemnly, but with great strength." Neither was the symbolism of the occasion lost on a teacher from the hamlet of Champsaur, in the mountainous Hautes-Alpes. Seven bells echoed across the valleys, each announcing the general mobilization. "It was not the first time I heard of all them all together," he remarked. "But it was the first time I heard them ring with one voice." Perhaps the greatest enterprise, and the one that Alexis de Tocqueville had found so lacking in the middle of the previous century, the creation of a unified and durable national community, at last actually existed.

The Union sacrée emerged through inclusion, through the integration of communities hitherto excluded from the configuration of forces that ruled the Third Republic. We have seen how this process began even before the war, with the reconciliation between the army and the Republic. Peace broke out in 1914 between the Republic and its other great foe in the Dreyfus Affair, the Catholic Church. Still overwhelmingly Catholic, the French in and out of uniform flocked to churches as mobilization began. Pope Pius X, with followers on both sides of the war, desperately sought neutrality and issued vain appeals to both sides to make peace. But French Catholicism rallied to the national cause from the outset. In August 1915, the Catholic clerical journal *La Revue du Clergé Français* captured the tone of the mobilization perfectly, by effortlessly uniting the cause of God with the cause of France:

France cannot lose. The world would be denied that of which she is the exquisite adornment, the Church that of which she is the tireless apostle, and God himself the service of a generous knight.

Clergy in France were not exempt from military service, yet only a small minority of the 25,000 priests mobilized served as chaplains. Most served in the ranks with their compatriots. Those often excluded from the mainstream for reasons of religion, Protestants and Jews, likewise flocked to the colors. The Republic returned these impressive gestures of loyalty. Poincaré spoke early and often of his thanks for the *foi patriotique* (patriotic faith) shown both by the organized religions of France and by individual believers.

Socialists, most often excluded from the Center-Right and Center-Left coalitions that formed prewar governments, likewise found themselves welcomed into the national community. Jaurès's funeral, held on August 4, showed that he had found some surprising friends in death. Viviani, himself an ex-socialist, led the mourners from the government. Maurice Barrès, virulent anti-Dreyfusard and president of the right-wing *Ligue des Patriots*, led mourners from nationalist organizations. Léon Jouhaux, secretary general of the socialist labor organization the Confédération Générale du Travail (CGT) likewise found an affection for Jaurès in death that he often lacked in life. In a fiery speech celebrating the murdered socialist, he reminded the assembled company that "we are all soldiers of liberty." But perhaps the most significant testimony to the incorporation of the political Left into the Union sacrée was a non-event. Minister of the Interior Louis Malvy decided *not* to round up the nearly 2,000 anarchists, syndicalists, and socialists whose names were inscribed in Carnet B, a list of persons drawn up as likely to disrupt a general mobilization. On August 26, Viviani enlarged the war cabinet, bringing in among others Jules Guesde and Marcel Sembat, two socialists who agreed for the first time to take part in a "bourgeois" government. Another socialist, Albert Thomas, would eventually run the ministry managing the production of armaments.

At the heart of the Union sacrée, its seriousness and its durability, lay national indignation at German aggression. Adolphe Thiers had remarked after 1870 that the French settled on a republic as the form of government that divided them the least. Now, the Third Republic had a cause that would positively unite them, as it turned out, more than would any other cause in the whole history of the regime. France could consider itself the most innocent victim of aggression, and conveniently forget or ignore the policy of Franco-Russian encirclement that had inspired the Schlieffen Plan in the first place. The operational brazenness and the brutality of the German scheme made the Russian alliance look like the most prudent of precautions. The time had now come, the French had concluded, to deal with the enemy across the Rhine, once and for all. The Schlieffen Plan handed France a huge moral and propaganda advantage, provided it could withstand the initial onslaught.

The fixation from the first days of the war on the long-dormant question of Alsace and Lorraine makes sense only in this context of renewed German aggression. Perhaps to a surprising degree, the French had heeded Léon Gambetta's advice on the question back in 1871 to think about it always, but to speak about it never. The large statue of a woman representing Strasbourg in the Place de la Concorde in Paris remained draped in black, and the life of France had gone on for more than forty years. French diplomatic and military policy throughout that time had been directed toward meeting the clear and present danger posed by the German Empire, not toward *la revanche* per se. But when Germany invaded France again in 1914, it suddenly became permissible not just to speak about Alsace and Lorraine, but to seize upon them as the supreme symbol of seeing off the German threat once and for all. A newspaper in Normandy captured most of what France wanted out of the war, from the first days to the last:

Our firm belief is that Germany will lose even on the battlefield and that our boys who depart so gallantly will return bringing, not the Victory of Berlin, which is a pretentious horror, but the piece of territory that was torn from France forty-five years ago, from which the scar is not yet healed.

Not having started the war, the French saw themselves determined to finish it, with the reconquest of the lost territories as the tangible sign that they had done so. Sarah Bernhardt drew from precisely this symbolism of Alsace and Lorraine in *Les Cathedrales* in November 1915. The French would continue to perceive the issue in more or less the same way in the grim years that followed.

Defeat, "victory," and stalemate: the battles of August–September 1914

The focus throughout this volume on the ways French society faced the trials and calamities of the Great War should not obscure the centrality of what happened on the battlefield. Military outcomes determined the parameters and even the purposes of national mobilization. War may be, as the nineteenth-century theorist Carl von Clausewitz put it, the continuation of politics by other means. But the politics of war by definition concerns winning and losing in a military sense. In strictly military terms, most of the first month of fighting in the Great War went very badly for France. What has come to be known as the "Battle of the Marne," in fact comprised a number of quite separate major pitched battles, several of which France lost. Joffre and most of the French high command completely misread German strategy. The French army embarked on a virtually foredoomed offensive into Alsace and Lorraine, and failed to see until the eleventh hour the German threat from the north through Belgium. Only the inherent flaws in the Schlieffen Plan and the timely decision by Joffre to recognize and take advantage of a retreat that soldiers in the field decided upon themselves spared France a disaster on the scale of 1870 or 1940. While the "Battle of the Marne" proper (September 6–8, 1914) indeed drove back the invader, by the time the fighting died down

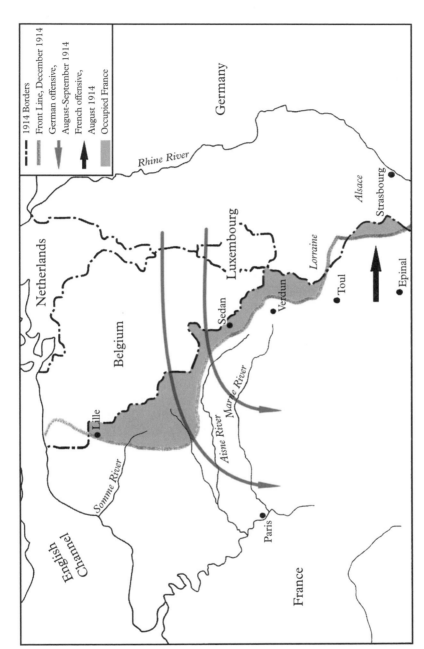

Map 1. The German invasion and occupied France

and stalemated in November, the Germans still held not only Alsace and Lorraine, but also most of northeastern France.

Plan XVII was not, in itself, a ridiculous scheme. As noted, it provided for the concentration of troops rather than a prescribed narrative for a campaign. This meant that Joffre could deploy anywhere the German threat presented itself. He had complete autonomy over how to use his forces once assembled. Plan XVII placed three of the five major French armies in the center of the French line, where the Belgian, Luxembourg, German, and French borders all met. But the doctrine of the offensive, so zealously propagated by Joffre, called in the abstract for France to bring the war to the enemy *somewhere*. Civilian leaders had prohibited invading Germany through Belgium, what would have amounted to a Schlieffen Plan in reverse, out of concern for traditional Belgian neutrality. An invasion of Germany could only take place through "French" territory, meaning Alsace and Lorraine.

In the event, Joffre made a number of operational errors that nearly cost France the war. Most importantly, he stubbornly refused to believe that the Germans would use reserve units alongside regular army troops in an invasion, though there was a mountain of evidence provided by French intelligence to the contrary. Other errors followed from this. Although Joffre was aware in general terms of the Schlieffen Plan, he believed that the Germans would not be able to muster enough regular army troops to invade through Belgium *and* resist a French offensive in Alsace and Lorraine. While the plan did not require Joffre to invade the lost territories, he would have been politically and professionally hard pressed to do otherwise, given what they had come to symbolize. Prudence and indeed any defensive posture were at odds with espoused French doctrine.

Joffre insisted on believing that the most important concentration of German forces lay between Metz and Thionville. He planned to encircle the enemy from the north and the south according to a three-pronged operational strategy reminiscent of Napoleon's great victory at Austerlitz in 1805. The French 1st and 2nd Armies, as well as the smaller Army of Alsace, would attack in the lost territories, which in addition to the obvious objective would seek to cut off the bulk of the German forces from the rear. They would be supported by an offensive by the Third and Fourth Armies toward Sedan, where the French army met disaster in 1870 and would again in 1940. The 5th Army on the French left, combined with the six infantry divisions sent by Britain, would support the offensive by the French center, as well as support whatever German units crossed into France from Belgium. In combination with the anticipated success of the Russian offensive into East Prussia, which dutifully began on August 17, Germany would quickly sue for peace. None of these scenarios played out as planned.

The attack into the lost territories, a rough and heavily wooded country that strongly favored the defense, went deceptively well at first. On August 8, only one week after the general mobilization, the 7th French Army Corps occupied Mulhouse after a brief engagement with small German forces. Joffre's communiqué set the tone: "Children of Alsace, after forty-four years of waiting in sorrow, French soldiers march again on the soil of your noble countryside. They are the first workers in the grand enterprise of *la Revanche*." Yet the commanders on the ground took no meaningful measures to secure the city, and failed even to cut the telephone lines to Strasbourg. The Germans counterattacked, and forced the French to evacuate the city barely twenty-four hours later. The 7th Army Corps commander, General Bonneau, proved the first of many generals to lose his command. The main French effort beginning on August 14, an attack by the First and Second Armies toward Saarbrück and Château Salins, likewise failed with more serious results. The German commanders had been ordered to let the French advance a certain distance, then encircle them in a flank attack. Prince Rupprecht of Bavaria actually sprang his trap earlier than advised by his superiors, which enabled the French forces to escape, if with heavy casualties. But by August 25, they had been pushed back past their starting line.

The news was no better in the center of the French front, where Joffre gave the Third and Fourth Armies the mission of attacking north into the Belgian and Luxembourg Ardennes, a region even rougher and more heavily wooded than Alsace and Lorraine. But here, the terrain did not necessarily favor either side, given that both the French and the Germans were attacking in foreign territory. The Schlieffen Plan did not call for an advance into this region until the invading armies to the north had gotten deep into French territory. But inspired by their success in defeating the French in Alsace and Lorraine, the Germans advanced first, thereby affording themselves some limited opportunity to gain familiarity with the terrain and, crucially, to move in heavy artillery. The French and German forces ran into each other on August 22, between Longwy and Neufchâteau. Two days of confused but deadly fighting followed, by the end of which the French, as in Alsace and Lorraine, had been driven back behind their original positions. Casualties in the 3rd French Colonial Division, comprising white troops raised from the empire, totaled 11,000 men – killed, wounded, or missing – out of the 17,000 who entered the battle. The division commander and one brigade commander were killed, the other wounded and taken prisoner. Most of its artillery was lost as well. So heavy were the losses that the French high command ceased to count the division in its order of battle.

The battle in the center of the French line swept over both soldiers and civilians. "The battle was lost," wrote Paul Lintier of the 44th Campaign

Artillery Regiment. "I knew neither why nor how. I saw nothing."[7]
Corporal Jean Galtier-Boissière of the 31st Infantry Regiment took cover
in a dense wood during a ferocious German bombardment. He wrote of
his comrades: "Protecting themselves as best they could, the soldiers
jumped from trunk to trunk in small groups, lined themselves up in
ditches, bent over in two, falling into pot holes, dazed by the thunderous
explosions that followed them from clearing to clearing."[8] There had
been no time to evacuate non-combatants. "Escaping civilians mixed
in with the flood of soldiers," wrote Galtier-Boissière, "carrying their
trunks on their shoulders, terrified women leading their children. They
wore their most beautiful dresses and their flowered Sunday hats to try
to save them."[9] Sometimes civilians could not escape at all. The ten-
year-old Yves Congar, later a cardinal and a famous Catholic theologian,
could only watch and secretly mock the invaders as they marched by his
home in Sedan: "They pass by the window, we hear a guttural command:
'aarrarrrncharr'. . . ."[10]

Yet civilians not at the front remained remarkably uninformed into
the third week of August. Fantastic stories circulated in the French press,
which set the pattern for chronic credibility problems throughout the war.
Worried loved ones read that German shells and bullets caused no harm,
and that German soldiers had surrendered for a *tartine*, a slice of bread
and butter. The Russians were reported to be closing in on Berlin when
in fact they were on the verge of being routed and captured by the tens of
thousands at Tannenburg and the Mansurian Lakes. Nor was misinfor-
mation confined to civilians. As late as August 25, Second Lieutenant
Maurice Genevoix was told that his 106th Infantry Regiment would
march into Mulhouse and protect it against possible enemy counterattack. "This prospect appealed to me," he wrote, "to go into Alsace and
stay there. It was less glorious than to have gotten there first, but pretty
fine all the same."[11] In fact, the Germans had retaken Mulhouse nearly
two weeks previously. The French in and out of uniform found it a rude
shock when the true gravity of their situation became known.

France, in fact, had been in serious danger from the moment the
German army crossed the Belgian frontier on August 3. The Germans
had three armies assigned to the invasion, the French just one to defend
against it. The invaders had a numerical advantage of about 3:1 (about

[7] Paul Lintier, *Ma Pièce* (Paris: Plon, 1916), p. 44.
[8] Jean Galtier-Boissière, *En Rase Campagne, 1914; Un Hiver en Souchez 1915–1916* (Paris: Berger Levrault, 1917), p. 48.
[9] *ibid.*, p. 54.
[10] L'Enfant Yves Congar, *Journal de Guerre, 1914–1918*, ed. Stéphane Audoin-Rouzeau and Dominique Congar (Paris: Cerf, 1997), p. 30.
[11] Maurice Genevoix, *Ceux de 14* (Paris: Flammarion, 1950), p. 12.

750,000 men facing about 250,000 men) and an overwhelming preponderance of heavy artillery. Joffre envisaged the principal mission of the
5th Army (posted along the Belgian frontier) as defending the flank of
the French offensive in the Ardennes. However, 5th Army commander
General Charles Lanrezac believed (correctly) that the principal threat
lay to the north. He argued vigorously at the time and even more so after
the war that Joffre had left his forces in limbo. The 5th Army, he maintained, had not been allowed to advance far enough into Belgium to link
up with the Belgian army, then engaged in a heroic if doomed defense
of the Belgian homeland. Yet neither had the French 5th Army been allowed to set up adequate defenses, on the assumption that it would soon
be attacking in support of the French forces to its right.

As if this were not enough, some corps and divisional commanders,
whose professional talents varied widely indeed, interpreted the doctrine
of the offensive and its emphasis on the moral over the physical in a
disastrously literal manner. In the 5th Division posted along the Sambre
River, for example, two battalions from the 74th Regiment were ordered
to recapture the village of Roselies in a night attack in the early hours of
August 22. They had neither artillery support nor meaningful intelligence
as to how many Germans were in the village. The Germans used rifles and
machine-guns in effective defensive positions, with the result that about
half of the attackers ended up killed, wounded, or missing. At the tactical
level, the doctrine of the offensive offered little help as to what soldiers
should do should an attack fail. According to the infantry regulations
of April 1914, battalion commanders were supposed to commit their
troops to the last man, up to and including themselves. Few did so in the
event, if only to avoid annihilation and a resulting battalion-sized hole in
the French lines. In the 5th Division and elsewhere, effective command
authority disappeared, leaving soldiers in the field to escape as best they
could. Lanrezac's orders to retreat given late the night of August 23, and
Joffre's acquiescence to those orders, only ratified a decision made in the
field. One officer complained to a recently promoted brigadier general
about the lack of direction from the senior command. The brigadier,
named Philippe Pétain, responded: "What do you want? Everything we've
learned has become false. We have to relearn our calling from top to
bottom."

The situation in the last days of August provided good reason to believe that the Germans would repeat their crushing victory of 1870.
The French offensives in Alsace and Lorraine and in the Ardennes had
gained nothing, while the Germans, seemingly unstoppable, poured into
northeastern France. The wartime alliance with Britain got off to an
unpromising start. The British had landed some 120,000 soldiers in

France, about 80,000 infantry and 40,000 cavalry, posted to the left of the 5th Army. Though not very numerous, they were some of the best-equipped and best-trained soldiers in Europe. Lanrezac had not informed the British of his retreat after August 23, leaving them to disengage in their famous retreat from Mons on their own. According to legend, the "Angel of Mons" appeared with a fiery sword, to hold back the Germans and to guide the British to safety. The success of the legend spoke volumes about the lack of coordination between the French and British armies. So confident had Moltke become that he shifted two army corps to the Eastern Front – the only immediate military benefit to the French of the Franco-Russian alliance. The French army revealed, blandly, in a communiqué on August 28 that the situation "remained unchanged from the Somme to the Vosges." Most of the French public was stunned to learn that the Germans had reached the Somme at all. Some 500,000 Parisians fled the capital, Sarah Bernhardt among them. On September 3, the government itself relocated to Bordeaux, on the southwestern Atlantic coast of France.

Yet through it all, Joffre maintained a remarkable calm, which contemporaries reported had a soothing effect on his subordinates. At least according to legend, he never missed sleep or one bite of his ample meals. Yet he remained actively in charge. Even Joffre's fiercest critics give him credit for his response to the dire situation he had done so much to create. He began a thorough purge of the command structure. He removed some 100 generals and colonels commanding brigades, and replaced them with commanders of proven ability under fire. Joffre added insult to injury by sending many of the displaced officers to the distant city of Limoges in central France. To this day, *limogé* remains a colloquial French term for getting sacked.

Joffre began to develop an alternative to the failed Plan XVII that responded to the inherent flaws in the Schlieffen Plan. German victory depended on a quick and complete encirclement of the French forces. If the French and British in Belgium could simply disengage, they could trade space for time. It is important not to forget how much more slowly the battle for France proceeded in 1914 than in 1940. To be sure, railroads could deliver troops to the front with great speed, just as they did for the Prussians in 1870. But with the automobile still in its infancy, soldiers in 1914, once they disembarked, could move no faster than soldiers in Roman times. The Schlieffen Plan assumed that the invaders could march for more than twenty miles a day for weeks on end in what turned out to be the blazing heat of late August. Any invading army has what military historians call the problem of the "rubber band" effect. The invaders' supply lines become more and more stretched, while the defenders fall back on theirs. Even the German advantage in artillery diminished. Their heavy artillery could not keep up with the infantry, while the light, mobile, and accurate French 75mm gun began to achieve what became a legendary reputation.

The Schlieffen Plan also called for taking the city of Paris from the northwest. But doing so would thin still further the already wearying German forces. And everyone remembered from the Commune of 1871 that the city could cause a great deal of trouble to anyone trying to occupy it. Yet swinging east of Paris left in place a large armed camp on the exposed German flank. Joffre deepened the German conundrum by ordering the 5th Army to attack at the city of Guise along the Oise River on August 29. Although the French retreated immediately after this riposte, it provided an unsettling reminder that the French and smaller British armies were bloodied, but still standing. They had little choice but to abandon the Schlieffen Plan entirely and pursue the retreating French and British south. In his deliberate, not to say plodding, manner, Joffre had begun to prepare for the Battle of the Marne proper.

The Germans also played into the hands of the Allies in the propaganda war. The image of the *francs tireurs* (guerrilla fighters) behind the German lines in 1870–1 remained very much alive in August 1914, particularly among the older men in the German command. The Germans vowed that they would not have such problems again. They killed at least 5,500 Belgian and 500 French civilians and burned tens of thousands of buildings, the most famous of which the Louvain Library in Belgium, with its irreplaceable collection of medieval manuscripts. Stories of German atrocities, numerous as they were, got better with the telling throughout the fall of 1914. The invaders, it turned out, especially favored cutting off the hands of young children, particularly girls. Nothing was beyond the Germans – using priests as clappers in church bells, crucifying prisoners (see Plate 1), and roasting children's feet. Rapes of French women were held to be so commonplace that a lively debate ensued over whether the children produced by these unholy unions would pollute the French race.

Disentangling fact from fiction remains difficult even today. It seems clear that the Germans killed large numbers of civilians with dubious cause, though cruelty toward the civilian population did not approach that of World War II, or even that of the Turks toward the Armenians later in the Great War. Clearly, however, the perceived viciousness of the invasion reinforced the image of the Germans not just as aggressors, but also as beasts. The Germans developed an active propaganda machine of their own, yet it never achieved a comparable effect, particularly in neutral countries such as the United States. As British historian A. J. P. Taylor once put it, the Allies "managed to give the impression that

Plate 1. Anonymous French painting: "The Crucified Canadian."
Reprinted with the permission of the Historial de la Grande Guerre.

they acted brutally or unscrupulously with regret; the Germans always looked as though they were enjoying it."[12]

From August 30 to September 5, the French and British forces retreated more or less due south, crossing the Marne River and then almost as far as the Seine. Although Joffre had originally ordered General Maurice Sarrail to abandon the forts around the city of Verdun, Sarrail had declined to do so. Deciding to use this insubordination to his advantage, Joffre employed the series of forts around Verdun as a point around which to pivot to his right. This seemed like a good idea at the time, but it set the stage for the traumatic German siege of Verdun in 1916. He also created two new armies out of units withdrawn from the unsuccessful effort in Alsace and Lorraine – the 6th Army northeast of Paris, and the Ninth Army positioned between the Fifth and Fourth Armies to the south and led by a promoted corps commander, Ferdinand Foch. General Joseph Gallieni had been made military governor of Paris, as the city braced for attack or defense. For the troops in the field, the long retreat without fighting proved the most dispiriting phase of the whole battle. "What was happening? We knew absolutely nothing," wrote Great War veteran Marc Bloch, later a famous medieval historian and Resistance hero in World War II. "I stand bad news better than uncertainty. . . . Oh, what bitter days of retreat, of weariness, boredom, and anxiety!"

Joffre told his troops in his famous orders for September 5: "We are about to engage in a battle on which the fate of our country depends and it is important to remind all ranks that the moment has passed for retreating; all our efforts must be directed toward attacking and driving back the enemy." His plan called for simultaneous attacks to the south and the west of the German armies. Every motorized vehicle in Paris was requisitioned to carry troops to the front, including the entire taxi fleet. The "taxis of the Marne" transported only a few thousand of the two million or so men taking part in the battle, but they provided one of the more enduring anecdotes of French determination to expel the invader. Four days of desperate battle among exhausted troops on both sides took place from September 6 to September 9. Heroism never completely conquered fear, in September 1914 or thereafter. Genevoix wrote of his soldiers during these days: "It seemed to me that one thought lived in them, to get out of there, quickly, no matter where, as long as there weren't any more bullets whizzing past. Nearly all of them seemed to me like children, who you want to console, protect." Yet the invaders, it turned out, were even more spent. Moltke, approaching some sort of nervous collapse, issued

---

[12] A. J. P. Taylor, *The First World War: An Illustrated History* (London: Hamish Hamilton, 1963), p. 57.

no orders at all between September 5 and September 9. Finally, following a fateful meeting of the German high command on September 8, he ordered retreat. The "miracle of the Marne" had rescued France, for now.

A "miracle" the Marne might well have been, but a complete victory it was not. The Germans retreated far enough fast enough to be able to choose their ground where to stop. They did so with considerable skill, particularly along the heights of the Aisne River. The positions chosen by the Germans in September 1914 would remain fundamentally unbroken until 1918. The "Race to the Sea," a series of attempted movements of enveloping each other as both sides worked their way north through the fall of 1914, served principally to confirm the exhaustion of both sides. It remains difficult to see how either side could have taken strategic advantage of an envelopment of the enemy, even if it had occurred. The French, British, and Germans began to dig trenches in order to protect their forces as they began the task of regrouping and resupplying. The war of movement had ended and the stalemated war of the trenches had begun.

In military terms, it is tempting to see the first month of fighting in the Great War as an avoidable near-catastrophe for France, almost a latter-day illustration of French national character as described by Tocqueville in the 1850s. The French army had suffered some 329,000 deaths in August and September 1914, by good measure the most deadly period of the war. Not even at Verdun would France suffer so many dead, or perhaps kill so many of the enemy in such a short time. Paradoxically, we still know very little about how violence actually functioned in this most lethal episode of the war. And the outcome was at best ambiguous. The enemy still held nearly all of Belgium and thousands of square kilometers of French territory, and would do so until 1918. A negotiated settlement had become impossible for France, for the simple reason that it had nothing to negotiate. France had nothing it could give up, and much it had to get back. To some extent, the greatest miracle of the Marne was that Joffre came out of it with his reputation enhanced.

Yet contemporaries in France construed these results very differently, in ways that reflected their ability to adjust to a long war. "Papa" Joffre became an adored father figure by the fall of 1914. The Battle of the Marne, which in the minds of the French eclipsed the defeats that preceded it and a good many that followed it, provided the first confirmation of the resilience of the Union sacrée. The French army itself became the emblem of abiding national commitment. As General Alexander von Kluck, commander of the German First Army, put it after the war: "That men who had retreated for ten days, that men lying on the ground half-dead from exhaustion were able to pick up their rifles again and attack at the sound of the bugle, that was something we had never reckoned with; that was a possibility that had never been discussed in our military colleges."

Perhaps the most famous French literary casualty of the first month of fighting was the poet Charles Péguy, who died on September 5, 1914 as a soldier in the 6th Army. Péguy, much drawn to the mystical traditions of Catholicism, wrote in a 1913 poem: "Blessed are those who died in a just war,/ Blessed is the wheat that is ripe and the wheat that is gathered in sheaves." Péguy's many friends apotheosized him almost instantly, a symbol in his way as powerful as Joffre of the continuing national determination to win the war. "This dead man is a guide," wrote Maurice Barrès on September 17. "This dead man will continue to serve, this dead man more than anybody is alive today." Throughout the war, Barrès would do his best to efface aesthetically the line between life and death, in the name of cultural mobilization of the country. Such lyrical expressions of war and death would come to ring hollow, in France as elsewhere, though the intensity of the national commitment to winning remained. But winning meant accepting a different kind of war and a different kind of national struggle. In the nineteenth century, an indecisive outcome on the battlefield would have pointed the way to a negotiated peace. In contrast, the outcome of the first month of fighting in the Great War paved the way for the totalization of the conflict.

The victory of the Marne and the "race to the sea" left France triumphant, but gravely weakened. In stark contrast to 1870, the armies of the Republic had thrown back the invader in the greatest feat of French arms since Napoleon. But all or in part, the departments of the Nord, the Pas-de-Calais, the Somme, the Aisne, the Ardennes, the Marne, the Meuse, and the Meurthe et Moselle, had fallen into enemy hands, and with them hundreds of thousands of French citizens. France had lost some of its most productive agricultural lands and its second most industrialized region. The occupied territories set the stage for the "totalization" of the war. For those living under German rule, deportations, forced labor, and martial law quickly blurred the line between soldiers and civilians. Northeastern France and Belgium became virtual German colonies, governed by repressive regimes directed toward economic extraction rather than production. In the rest of France, expelling the invaders and making the nation whole came to justify unprecedented and open-ended national mobilization. As the war totalized, the French confronted the shift from "the imaginary war," dreamed of and feared before August 1914, to the real war, here and now. They had to face up to an extended confrontation and to the immense war effort that it engendered.

"Total war" became the order of the day, rooted in the suffering, day in and day out, endured by an entire society during these four-and-a-half years. Why did the French nation face such an ordeal? How did they cope with the sacrifices demanded of them, what the French historian Jean-Baptiste Duroselle went so far as to call "the incomprehensible"?[1] The massive and desperate national struggle permeated all aspects of daily life for the French, in and out of uniform. This is where the concept of "war culture" may be useful, as we attempt to understand how the French represented the conflict to others and to themselves, and discerned what

[1] See the subtitle of Duroselle, *La Grande Guerre des Français, 1914–1918* (Paris: Perrin, 1994).

they saw as its true meaning. This meaning in turn defined the range of their attitudes, behavior, and habits between 1914 and 1918.

Occupation: living with the enemy

Memory of the Great War has focused almost exclusively on the violence suffered by the soldiers, at the expense of the violence suffered by the unarmed populations. Yet from the beginning of the war, murder, rape, and pillage were committed against civilians who happened to be in the path of the invasion, whether the Western Front, the Eastern Front, or in the Balkans. We have long known that the invaders of 1914 committed atrocities, such as the Russians in East Prussia and Galicia and the Austro-Hungarians in Serbia. And yet into the 1990s, historians in the cases of France and Belgium continued to refer to "German atrocities" in 1914 only in quotation marks. As the war continued, myths replaced real atrocities, most notoriously the many tales of children whose hands had been cut off by the Germans. But once the various propaganda services had instrumentalized atrocities real and imagined, few mentioned them again. Over time, general opinion on both sides came to discount all atrocity stories of the Great War, the true as well as the false. Consequently, the victims of genuine mistreatment became silenced.

People who lived in what became the battlefields of 1914 in Belgium and northeastern France initially experienced the devastation of armed attack, but did not benefit from the "miracle of the Marne." They remained prisoners of the initial German advance. The Western Front ran through eight departments, some of them completely occupied, others battlefields or militarized zones directly behind the front lines. After 1914, civilians living under German rule regularly referred to unoccupied France as "free France."[2]

French civilians endured a war ancient in its cruelty and very modern in the ways it regulated and extorted from the subject people. For the duration of the war, the occupied populations thought of themselves, quite accurately, as living at the front. For French civilians cut off from their national community – now fighting for its very survival in this most just of wars – daily life was further burdened with the moral and physical brutality imposed by the occupying forces. Civilians in occupied France endured two wars at the same time: the war between Western Allies

---

[2] Today, the term is more commonly associated with the French resistance movement operating out of London during World War II. This movement was led by Charles de Gaulle, himself a native of Lille, in the department of the Nord.

and the Central Powers; and their own, unique, civilians' war. Civilians everywhere faced burdens of the death of loved ones, extra work, and ideological mobilization. But the inhabitants of occupied France faced the ongoing threat of military operations. Indeed, these people knew that they could rejoin their compatriots one day only through renewed fighting where they lived. In the meantime, atrocities (minus the quotation marks) were facts of daily life for civilians in occupied France, through the misery, distress, and grief imposed on them by the occupier. Their identification as people both invaded and occupied took on great significance.

For a long time, the invasion itself seemed the most terrible period. The invasion marked the beginning of hostilities, the transition from peace to war, from normal social, economic, cultural, emotional life to breakdown and total transformation. There were also the atrocities committed in the ferocious panic of the invasion – civilians shot, women raped, homes and public buildings burned. In a sworn statement made to a French board of inquiry in December 1915, Mademoiselle G–, aged twelve, recalled an incident during the invasion in which she, her aunt, and several others were taken hostage and placed in front of the advancing Germans. The hostages found themselves caught in the middle when the two armies opened fire. A bullet in the heart killed her uncle, and Mlle. G and her aunt survived only by pretending to be dead until the Germans left the scene.[3]

After the invasion came the extended static period, the occupation proper. Although it lasted for four years, this time remains less studied than the three months of invasion in 1914. Paradoxically, part of the reason for this silence lay in a long refusal to accept that occupied France had in fact been occupied. For the French on both sides of the German lines continued to consider *all* the invaded territory still part of the war zone. Consequently, down to 1918 contemporaries rarely described the eight departments as "occupied," a term that indicated an accomplished fact. Rather, they used the term "invaded," which indicated a temporary state destined to disappear with the victorious advance of the French soldiers.

The material conditions under which the occupied populations lived, the way the Germans treated them, as well as their patriotism, convinced them that they lived at the military front. The moral drama of defeat (at least in their part of France) and the terrible feeling of being excluded from their own country was made worse by the financial and economic

---

[3] See Margaret Higonnet, ed., *Lines of Fire: Women Writers of World War I* (New York: Plume, 1999), p. 151.

pressure of the occupation. Requisitions affected industries and individuals. In some cases, industrial machinery was simply packed up and sent across the Rhine. Cities, towns, and villages found themselves subject to large and unpredictable special levies in money or goods – whether to support the cost of billeting soldiers, as some sort of reprisal, or simply to inflict terror. Often, the Germans took hostages to make sure levies were paid. In May 1915, the family of the eleven-year-old future cardinal and Catholic theologian Yves Congar in Sedan preferred to have the beloved family dog killed rather than pay a new and spiteful tax on pets.

The regulation of daily life knew few limits. "German time," differing from French time by one or two hours depending on the time of year, governed the very schedules of people in the occupied territories. French people needed passes for the most minor trips. Germans forbade any public gatherings, and took the trouble to surround even cemetery burials with armed soldiers. People lived between an economic "scissors," in which the price of bread and other food rose steeply even as quality fell. Living conditions were harsher in the cities than in the country, for it was often impossible to find work, and often even enough to eat. The textiles and sugar-refining industries, very active throughout the region before 1914, also suffered severely from deliberate destruction or requisitions. Even describing daily life in writing became an act of resistance. Maria Degrutère, a young schoolteacher, risked criminal prosecution for keeping a diary, in which she wrote in November 1916: "Our town is sorely tried; we are alive today, but we don't know if we will be half an hour from now. It is worse than for the soldiers."

Broadly speaking, Germany's war aims against French civilians were the same as those against French soldiers – the destruction of the ability of France ever again to make war against Germany. In occupied France, the Germans established a true reign of terror in 1914 and continued it throughout the war. This paradigm of imposed brutality adhered to the true meaning of terrorism, designed to humiliate and thus dominate the civilian population by keeping it in a state of shock through the systematic use of emergency regulations and violence.

French civilians suffered collective reprisals, most of the time resulting from difficulties encountered by the Germans in enforcing requisitions of labor, food, or materiel. The most extreme reprisal involved sending forced laborers or prisoners of war to work at the front itself, fortifying enemy trenches or burying enemy dead. While there, they worked in constant danger from shells fired by their own compatriots. They became, in effect, human shields, cruel defensive weapons that mocked centuries of effort to protect civilians from the violence of combat. Requiring civilian workers to labor in the enemy lines brought the horror of their condition to its logical conclusion, and essentially effaced the line between military and civilian prisoners.

The Germans waged a kind of interior siege warfare against civilians in the occupied regions. For war became totalized, both through the spatial extension behind the battlefields and through the intensification of violence and even cruelty. The occupier and the occupied mobilized each other through hatred. By the end of 1914, French civilians described the occupiers as *barbares* (barbarians) and *savages* (savages) as a matter of course. In occupied France, the demonization of the enemy evolved spontaneously and owed nothing to propaganda. When this demonization of the enemy turned into open resistance, it perpetuated and deepened the cycle of repression.

As the occupation dragged on, it drew the inhabitants of northeastern France into a trap. In Germany, as elsewhere, the demand for labor increased enormously, just when millions of men previously in the workforce had been sent to the front. But Germany had brought under its rule hundreds of thousands of French civilians, who needed somehow to be fed. Requisitioning French labor and later deporting French workers to Germany enabled the occupier to solve two problems. First, the Germans found workers, particularly for difficult and sometimes dangerous construction tasks close to the front lines. Second, they could empty the great occupied cities of their inhabitants, who became unemployed as economic activity there gradually came to an end, and who otherwise would have needed public assistance. Necessity, coercion, and punishment blended into the practical requirements of the war.

Europeans had previously set up civilians internment camps in their colonies on at least two occasions – the Spanish in Cuba during the Spanish-American War of 1898, and the British during the Anglo-Boer War of 1899–1902. The authorities "concentrated" people, meaning that they assembled them in congested conditions, preferably behind a fence of barbed wire or stakes, where they could be disciplined and punished as necessary. These sites soon became known as "concentration camps," enclosing men, women, children, and old people, and mixing them with common criminals. But "concentration" did not mean "organized." Concentration camps in the Great War were created through improvisation and muddle. But these camps spoke to a particular aspect of the totalization of war at the beginning of the twentieth century – the practice of confining enemies, whether soldiers taken on the battlefield in formal combat or civilians who happened to be in the path of the invaders. No international convention had anticipated the status of interned civilians, still less that of civilians occupied/deported/interned and set to forced labor. We must therefore look closely at the two very different categories of "civilian prisoners."

The first group comprised civilians interned in enemy territory, both men subject to military service (between the ages of eighteen and forty-five) and others. Internment of all civilians (men, women, and children) was universal practice, not just inside the territories of the belligerent nations, but in their colonies as well. France, like Germany, interned enemy nationals. Paradoxically, internment in a concentration camp in the Great War saved some men from death on the battlefield. German men interned in Vendée and Frenchmen interned in Saxony had no need to fear death at Verdun. In this respect, they resembled prisoners of war, protected in some seemingly arbitrary way by their captivity.

The second category of civilian prisoner was much broader and covered far more people in occupied France. All civilians not immediately interned remained subject to various forms of sequestration and confinement, from isolation from their compatriots to deportation to concentration camps, where they might be set to forced labor. Indeed, from the first weeks of the occupation, the Germans requisitioned men, women, and adolescents of working age to restore part of the railways and roads, sometimes even fortifications damaged by fighting. This directly contravened the Hague Conventions of October 18, 1907, which forbade requiring civilians to work in direct opposition to their own country's war effort. Elsewhere, faced with the lack of labor, the Germans called on volunteers to work in the fields or to reopen businesses to serve the occupying forces.

Theoretically, the Germans divided governing authority between the *Kommandantur* (the military command established in each large town), charged with military affairs, and an *Inspection des Etapes des affaires économiques*, the civilian inspectorship for economic affairs. But the need to use military force to coerce the inhabitants to work for the occupiers inevitably confused this distinction, for contemporaries then and even for historians today. By playing on the semantic ambiguity between requisitioned labor/volunteer labor, and between military affairs/economic affairs, the occupiers claimed to comply with the Hague Conventions, which authorized requisitions by the victors to help in the tasks of occupation. But legalistic distinctions made by the Germans to assuage international opinion tended to be lost on the conquered, humiliated, and terrified inhabitants. When they rejected volunteering en masse, the military authority soon turned to coercion.

In 1916, the Germans created a category of civilian forced laborers, the *Zivil Arbeiter Bataillonen* (ZAB). They became known as Brassards rouges, after the red armbands workers had to wear. This "uniform" marked their conscription into an army of civilian workers. The Germans deported ZAB workers to labor camps in occupied France or Belgium. When most mayors in the occupied territories refused to provide lists of the unemployed, the Germans responded simply by rounding up men in the streets for deportation. They gave those rounded up, often young men who came of military age after August 1914, a dubious choice between working for the Germans "voluntarily" or explicit deportation to a labor camp. The resulting choices sometimes pitted the French against each other. A young man from Lomme near Lille wrote plaintively to his prefect, the senior French official in the department of the Nord: "I am 21 years old, and I am thus under military authority, and the mayor of Lomme knowing this very well sent me an invitation to work for the Germans and they tell me that I have to. What should I do?" Rounding up workers with the help (under duress or otherwise) of local officials, all in an atmosphere of vagueness as to just what would happen to them, fostered the most alarmist rumors, which often were proved after the war to be accurate.

From the time the German occupation began in October 1914 until the Allies pushed the Germans out of most of France by October 1918, the resources and the strategic position of the occupied territories placed them at the center of the German war effort. The civilian prisoners at the epicenter of that war effort discovered what it meant to live under a policy of "concentration": very long working hours, severe living and nutritional conditions, and lengthy separations from home, all under military discipline. As civilian prisoners had been concentrated not just to work but also to ease the burden of feeding the great occupied cities, there was no question of feeding them as well as German soldiers. And this in fact meant eating very little given the terrible conditions brought about by the Allied naval blockade, which sealed off German imports from outside Europe. Food aid from neutral countries had great moral significance, but could not in itself meet the needs of the inhabitants.[4] There is little difficulty in believing the grim accounts by civilian prisoners (mostly adolescents during their fastest growth period) of their rations and physical conditions.

Outside France, the best known episode of the mistreatment of civilians involved the forced evacuation of some 20,000 people, in large part women and young girls, from the Lille region beginning at Easter 1916. Probably not by coincidence, the deportation took place during a

---

[4] Most notable were Hispanic and American supply committees, which became Hispanic and Netherlands bodies after the United States became belligerent in 1917. The most important organization was the *Commission for Relief in Belgium*, run by future American president Herbert Hoover, and its French adjunct, the *Comité d' alimentation du Nord de la France*.

particularly ferocious phase of the German offensive at Verdun, that vast battle of attrition that weakened the attackers as much as the defenders. The stated reasons given by the Germans involved the difficulties feeding the civilian population caused by the blockade, and their own lack of success in attracting "volunteers" to work for the German war effort. "Because this is an irrevocable order," the proclamation published in the *Bulletin de Lille* on April 23, 1916 read, "it is in the interest of the population itself to remain calm and obedient." All females, including young girls, had to submit to a gynecological examination, in the manner of officially tolerated prostitutes. As if to emphasize the arbitrary character of the episode, many were simply sent off to different parts of occupied France, mostly to rural areas such as the Ardennes or the department of the Aisne.

Why did the occupiers choose this particular means of repression at this particular time? Did they see women and young girls as particularly useless mouths to feed? Did the Germans seek a special way of humiliating the enemy by undermining the "honor" of their womenfolk? Did the occupiers wish to head off any movements of revolt, by deporting enemy wives? All witnesses emphasized the flouting of usual conventions of gender and class. Women worked like men, including digging trenches and burying corpses. Middle-class housewives were treated like prostitutes, young girls like mature women. Behavior towards these people highlights the importance of gender in the totalization of war. By systematically humiliating and deporting women and young girls, the Germans acted out their status as victors by arbitrary right. Like many others in similar situations in the twentieth century, they made women the chosen target in total war.

It seems likely that in part, the deportations of Easter 1916 had a connection to rising discontent within Germany. Beginning in 1915, German women began to demonstrate in Berlin and other large cities against the irregular supply and high cost of food. Perhaps the wartime regime in Germany, having lost part of its legitimacy at home by no longer being able to guarantee food supplies, could not allow even the possibility of trouble in the occupied territories. In addition, civilians always saw food supplies in moral terms. The malnourished people of Berlin might have resented the similarities between their own situation and that of the people of Lille. Both, in effect, were being fed by the same inefficient German military bureaucracy. Deportations served to illustrate the inferior position of the occupied peoples. The Germans served notice that they would not be spared as women, in a war that demarcated new imaginative boundaries. By deporting the women from the large cities of occupied France, perhaps, the German authorities sought to assure the women of

Berlin and elsewhere that the regime was not wasting the vast effort demanded of them. The women of Lille paid the price of reestablishing some degree of civilian confidence in Germany.[5]

Evacuations, forced and voluntary, threw into stark relief the contradictions that overtake societies in a desperate national war. To the few who could afford the enormous sum of at least 500 francs per person, the Germans offered the possibility of repatriation to France through Switzerland. Given the choice, many French people refused evacuation despite their suffering, in part out of patriotism, and in part because they feared losing all their possessions if they left their homes. Various types of indigent people unable to work, such as old people in hospices, children, and those completely impoverished and debilitated, could be deported involuntarily, simply to get them out of the way. Deportations and forced labor had the same objective. Simply put, the occupied civilians had to take part in the war effort of the occupier, or disappear. Ultimately, it is difficult to distinguish clearly between evacuations and deportations. Both evacuees and deportees most often traveled by cattle cars – a grim harbinger of the mass deportations of World War II.

The French government protested before world opinion the forced evacuations of the indigent, though not without a certain degree of cynicism and hypocrisy. Few would have been able to contribute to the French war effort in any event. Moreover, since the Germans would never have let the indigent go had they been able to work, the French saw a certain propaganda advantage in adding to what had become a long list of German cruelties. At the same time, civilians in unoccupied France treated the exhausted refugees, whose strange journey they did not understand, as "*Boches du Nord,*" or "Huns from the Nord." Discrimination against returned refugees illustrated the complexity of the situation. Their compatriots accused refugees of taking work away from the very people who welcomed them, despite the obvious shortage of labor in France throughout the war. Moreover, by definition, impoverished refugees who could not work had to live on public assistance, largely at the expense of municipalities living in straightened circumstances themselves. Civilians in unoccupied France contented themselves with viewing the enemy as a torturer who drove the refugees from their homes, even as they resented the burden of caring for the new, and French, "other" in their midst.

---

[5] To make its case to neutral countries, particularly the United States, the French Foreign Ministry saw to the publication in English of *The Deportation of Women and Girls from Lille, with Extracts from Other Documents, Annexed to the Note relating to Germans Breaches of International Law During 1914, 1915, 1916* (New York: George H. Doran Company, 1916).

In short, the occupied territories became a vast prison in which several ages of war existed simultaneously. Ancient practices of extraction and slavery were administered through the most modern bureaucratic techniques of coercion. The departments finally returned to France in 1918 had been drained of their people and their economic resources. As the Allied armies advanced, the Germans forced most civilians remaining in occupied France to evacuate to Belgium or Germany. The retreating German army systematically destroyed remaining businesses, mines, and communication routes behind them. The war radicalized against civilians as well as against soldiers. What happened in the occupied territories between 1914 and 1918 speaks of the totalization of war in the twentieth century. The concentration of enemy civilians would be carried to racial extermination, its logical conclusion, in the next war.

Also "occupied" in a different but equally profound sense were prisoners of war (POWs). By 1917, some 600,000 French soldiers were confined in Germany, out of over 1.8 million Allied prisoners in all. Some of the issues of captivity in the Great War, the desire to escape versus the odd protection from the war offered by a prison camp, as well as broader issues of nineteenth- versus twentieth-century "total" warfare, were brilliantly portrayed in Jean Renoir's 1937 film *La Grande Illusion*, to many still the best film about the Great War. Most of the time, the Germans followed the Hague Conventions on prisoners of war. But most soldiers lived lives rather more grim than those portrayed by Renoir. As early as 1915, representatives from the Red Cross began to worry about how the Germans would feed prisoners, given that food imports had been cut off by the Allied blockade and priority would be accorded to German soldiers and civilians. Thanks in part to the efforts of the Red Cross, food packages from France generally arrived. French soldiers did not have to contend with starvation, as did Russian or Italian prisoners. But clearly hunger became a serious issue in POW camps. "There are among us stealers of bread," wrote schoolteacher and prisoner Georges Leroy in October 1918, "and its extraordinary to see the dexterity with which they operate. It pains me greatly to see Frenchmen who have come to this, to giving our enemies such a spectacle to see."

Captured enlisted men were often put to work, mostly in ghastly but familiar nineteenth-century working conditions in mines and factories, or as hard labor in drainage projects. Unlike the Allies, the Germans did not have a large population of colonized non-Europeans from which to draw labor during the war. As a result, they used prisoners heavily. The Germans maintained severe discipline among POW workers. One soldier from Brittany who tried to call a strike in a munitions factory was tied up under a lit coke furnace, where the heat and the lack of air shortly obliged him to plead for mercy. In 1917, as a collective punishment, the Germans sent some 10,000 French prisoners to work in the rear German lines. Prisoners dug and maintained German trenches within range of French artillery. "What an assault on dignity and honor to see ourselves so forced," wrote Robert Senecaut in February 1917 to the president of the Red Cross, "even though we are under the protection of an international convention, to carry out work like this against our own country."

Whether prisoners were harshly treated or not, many suffered a profound sense of alienation, of being forgotten in the war, not just by the enemy, but by their own compatriots. The poet André Warnod found himself in a train car designed for farm animals bound for Germany, mixed in with the wounded and with civilians. "We have the atrocious impression," he wrote, "that no one will ever let us out of this wagon, that we have been forgotten." Some felt sadness and were full of guilt at not being able to contribute further to the war. Captain Charles de Gaulle had been taken prisoner at Verdun in 1916. As an officer, he was exempt from work duties. But in December 1917, he wrote a remarkable letter to his parents from the camp in Ingolstadt explaining his emotional state.

A sorrow that will end only with my life, and which I thought could never encounter so deeply or so bitterly, afflicts me now more directly than ever. To be so totally and irremediably useless as I am in the times we are going through, when every bit of me wants to strike out. Moreover, to be in such a situation as I find myself, as a man and as a soldier, is the most cruel one you can imagine.

Yet memory of the Great War came to revolve around the suffering of soldiers at the front. The French remembered the living and the wounded, but most especially the dead. The national narrative placed the combatant at the center, supported and commemorated by the national community in life and in death. It tended to exclude the suffering of those who fell outside that narrative, whether civilians in the occupied territories or prisoners of war. Indeed, the very intensity and resilience of the Union sacrée helped cast, practically into oblivion, the experience of the occupied in the construction of memory in France. The civilians who returned to broken homes and broken families after the war took part in this amnesia, whether out of a sort of "survivors' guilt" at having lived with the enemy for four years or out of a will to include themselves in the national narrative of the Union sacrée. As a result, neither the deported women of Lille, nor the forced laborers, nor the POWs, nor indeed the grinding daily distresses of the Great War, have been truly remembered.

Propaganda and cultural mobilization

It is not a straightforward matter to understand how the French national community as a whole managed to accept the war, above all of its extension over a period of nearly four-and-a-half years. Part of the difficulty lies in the complexities of constructing (in an intellectual, moral and psychological sense) and thus "mobilizing" French public opinion. To some extent, the construction of a war culture through propaganda between 1914 and 1918 helps us explain the colossal human and material sacrifices accepted by French society. But propaganda itself provides only a partial answer.

In France, as in other combatant nations, the Great War undoubtedly marked the birth of modern propaganda – whether through the written and spoken word, through songs, or through fixed and moving visual images. Wartime cultural mobilization through propaganda became the first attempt on a vast scale to structure societies at war. In so doing propaganda in the war of 1914–18 opened the way to methods used by democratic as well as dictatorial regimes throughout the twentieth century. In France as elsewhere, the scale of war propaganda was vastly greater than in previous conflicts, and directed itself toward every member of society, soldiers and civilians, adults and children. Over forty years of Republican education policy had made France more or less universally literate by 1914. Reinforced by such factors as the growth of cities, the popular press, and universal male military service, French society had become more culturally homogeneous than ever before. Although France remained largely rural, far more so than its enemy Germany or its ally Britain, urban culture had become widely diffused.

The cultural infrastructure for a new type of propaganda thus existed from the earliest days of the war. For example, the production of newsreels, a new medium closely controlled by the military authorities, expanded spectacularly after 1915. The French produced over 600 newsreel films of various lengths over the course of the war. Initially an urban media, the cinema proved highly portable, not just to the villages of France but also to the front itself. Powerful images, spectator numbers, and the production of an effective message combined to produce a breakthrough in the practice of framing public opinion in wartime.

Yet the very term "propaganda" suggests a vertical and authoritarian pattern of influences, operating within spheres of management. We are tempted to think that producers of propaganda developed the material, and cultural consumers at lower socioeconomic levels of society accepted it without further mediation. Certainly, through means of effective (if imperfect) censorship, the state could forbid the dissemination of certain facts or ideological positions. But censorship by definition is essentially negative; it cannot in itself drive public opinion in a positive sense. Ultimately the French state created a censorship bureaucracy of nearly 2,000 people, an enormous staff for the day. But while this bureaucracy effectively kept some forms of reticence toward, or opposition to, the war out of the public sphere, it was never in itself a creative force. It could not give meaning to the war.

In the end, the "war culture" of 1914–18, resulted from a vast and extraordinarily diverse creative activity, whose origins lay in individuals and not in governmental institutions. Tens of thousands of people created the images that mobilized the French between 1914 and 1918 – journalists, teachers, writers, actors, popular singers, photographers, painters, designers, film directors, artisans, industrialists, and many others. A surprisingly broad cross-section of the French population developed and disseminated the themes constructing the war, themes then interiorized by their compatriots.

Further, for deeper exploration of the mechanisms of this system of representation in wartime, we must also understand those who served as intermediaries between national institutions and everyday people. For example, in rural France, we still know little about the important role played by representatives of the Catholic Church, by schoolteachers, or by mayors. In the world of industrial labor, issues of class and nation were debated in complex ways we still do not completely understand in government and trade union offices and on the shop floor. Only relatively recently has it become possible to consider in a more positive light the intermediary role of the bourgeoisie. Jean-Jacques Becker once observed that if the rural masses provided the foundation of French society, the middle classes constituted its backbone.[6] Diffused and perhaps even invisible, the unflinching will of the French bourgeoisie to win the war probably proved crucial.

We may never fully understand the precise modalities according to which French society constructed its own system of representations in the Great War. But it seems clear that the authorities and the instruments of state played no more than a secondary role in this largely spontaneous creation of a national war culture. French society during the Great War reconfigured itself primarily through a horizontal and decentralized process rather than through passively accepting orders.

French intellectuals unquestionably played a key role in crystallizing the body of ideas and representations underpinning the war culture.

[6] Jean-Jacques Becker, *La France en guerre. 1914–1918, La grande mutation* (Bruxelles: Éditions Complexe, 1988), p. 92.

Though many intellectuals, notably university professors, were employees of the state, they drew their legitimacy from a national tradition dating at least from the Enlightenment that esteemed intellectuals as autonomous public figures. No nation takes its intellectuals more seriously than France. Intellectuals and artists (such as the painter Fernand Léger, and even foreigners in France such as writers Guillaume Apollinaire and Blaise Cendrars) showed their commitment to the necessity of the war by volunteering. As a group, no one in France believed more strongly in the justice of going to war in August 1914 than the intellectual and artistic elite. The mobilization of French intellectuals was never total. Figures as important as André Gide, Marcel Proust, and Paul Valéry remained silent from the beginning of the war to the end. But the fact that figures as diverse as the writer Henri Barbusse, the historian Albert Malet, or the philosopher Alain, joined the army as volunteers when they were above the age of active duty showed how effectively the Union sacrée could draw the French into the war.

Throughout the Great War, intellectuals fought with the pen as well as the sword. Right-wing author and member of parliament Maurice Barrès wrote a newspaper article about the war every day from its beginning to its end. While we can see Barrès as the archetype of the "mobilized intellectual," the term is actually a bit misleading. For Barrès, as for so many others, mobilization came first and foremost from within.

The role of Barrès in the success of the story of "Debout les Morts!" (Arise the Dead!) illustrates the role of intellectuals in articulating but not determining war culture. In April 1915, Lieutenant Jacques Péricard, an obscure journalist in civilian life, submitted a report to his peacetime employer, the news bureau Agence Havas. He told the story of being surrounded in a trench by advancing Germans, when a badly wounded comrade stood up and cried "Debout les Morts!" Several wounded men lying on the ground got up and helped drive the Germans off. After a version of it appeared in the *Journal des Débats*, Péricard attracted the interest of public intellectuals like Barrès and Victor Giraud. In the version of the story that became famous in Barrès's newspaper *L'Écho de Paris*, Péricard himself assumed center stage. The timely help to the defenders came not from the wounded, but from the dead themselves. Whether spiritually or somatically, the dead not only rose, but provided grenades to help the French. By the end of 1915, practically everyone in France knew the "Debout les Morts!" story. In part, the story achieved the status it did because it combined the "authentic" experience of an actual combatant with the literary and political power of intellectuals like Barrès. But in the end, the story succeeded because, however peculiarly from the point of view of readers today, it spoke to deep anxieties about death, the afterlife, and a national yearning for miraculous intervention to win the war. The French people raised "Debout les Morts!" to the status of national myth, not Barrès by himself, and even less so Péricard.

Intellectual and academic institutions lined up to support the war. The Centrist Comité d'Etudes et de Documents sur la Guerre (Committee of Studies and Documents on the War) played a pivotal role, both inside France and overseas. Under the leadership of the Republic's quasi-official historian Ernest Lavisse, flanked by the sociologist Émile Durkheim as secretary, the committee included names as prestigious as philosophers Henri Bergson and Émile Boutroux, historian Charles Seignobos and the literary specialist Gustave Lanson. Subsidized by the Paris Chamber of Commerce, the committee published pamphlets on various issues of the war with a huge distribution, both in French and in seven foreign languages. After 1917, La Ligue civique (The Civic League), chaired by Hubert Bourgin, represented mobilized intellectuals from further to the Left and counted among its members some front-line combatants, such as Gustave Bloch. Prominent patriots among members of the Académie Française, which through its dictionary arbitrated the French language itself, included Henri Lavedan, Jean Richepin, Pierre Loti, and Jean Aicard.

The greatest names of the academic world also publicly proclaimed their support of the war – in addition to Bergson, Lavisse, and Durkheim, renowned professors such as Émile Boutroux, Émile Mâle, Victor Bérard, Charles Andler, and many others. *Les Lettres à tous les Français*, edited by Lavisse and Durkheim beginning in 1915, illustrated the public role played by the academic world in mobilizing the nation. Initially published in leaflet form (of three million copies each!) and compiled in 1916, these were short and deliberately simple texts. They sought to inform through putting academic "objectivity" at the service of the nation. The very title of the complilation expresses the moral majesty, the "Ministry of the Word" that French intellectuals sought to construct during the Great War.

The Union sacrée among intellectuals even transcended the split created by the Dreyfus Affair. Catholic intellectuals such as Léon Bloy could take their place alongside not just secular nationalists such as Barrès, Charles Maurras, or Léon Daudet, but alongside intellectuals of the Left such as Lanson, the former antimilitarist Gustave Hervé or author Anatole France. Indeed, very few Leftist intellectuals maintained their prewar pacifism after August 1914. One exception was Romain Rolland, who remained in Switzerland throughout the war and who, in September 1914, published a famous essay entitled "Au dessus de la Mêlée" (Above the Fray), in which he denounced both French and German intellectuals for supporting the war. More common was the path of Anatole France, who wrote a book in 1915 entitled *Sur la voie glorieuse* (Along the Glorious Path). Only later would he choose silence on the war and ultimately describe his 1915 book as the worst deed of his life. The most famous French war novel, socialist Henri Barbusse's *Le Feu* (Under Fire, 1916) came to be read after 1918 as a devastating indictment of war, militarism, and capitalism. But during the war, Barbusse – both in the novel or in his many newspaper articles and speeches – never advocated anything but the most ferocious prosecution of the national struggle. Paradoxically, he sought to remobilize the French war effort as such by turning it into a crusade for international socialism. Barbusse, like most intellectuals on the Left, rejected the war only after 1918.

The late-twentieth-century notion of the conflict of 1914–18 as part of a thirty-year civil war within a single European civilization did not exist at the time. Rather, the French viewed the war in universal terms. "The war has pitted two different concepts of God and Humanity against each other," wrote Ernest Lavisse in 1915. War in the nineteenth century had been read and lived largely as a classic confrontation between nations or coalitions of nations. But virtually from the day it began, the French, almost unanimously, interpreted the Great War as a struggle of civilization against barbarism. They saw, lived, and represented the German enemy as a barbarian. Not just a threat to the nation, the soil, the families of France, he endangered civilization itself. German victory would be a defeat for the whole of humanity. In this way, the war became a radical confrontation posed in terms of the survival of a certain concept of humanity.

To some extent, this reading of the war originated in the defeat of 1870 and the determination of the Republican regime to instill patriotism in the populace through national institutions, by such means as education and conscription. But the idea of the war as a crusade was based more immediately on the particular circumstances preceding the 1914 invasion, which as we saw left France no alternative to going to war. By the beginning of 1915 the idea of the enemy as barbarian had firmly taken root. French opinion learned very quickly about the atrocities, either directly from refugees' accounts or indirectly through the earliest press reports. From the beginning of 1915, the publication of a succession of official reports published by a commission of inquiry comprising mostly lawyers deepened convictions of German bestiality. These reports attracted widespread comment in all French newspapers. Pamphlets published by the Comité d'Etudes et de Documents sur la Guerre chronicled German atrocities in gruesome detail. Among the most influential of these was a piece by philologist Joseph Bédier of diaries from captured or killed German soldiers that sought to prove the veracity of reports of atrocities in the invasion of 1914. The concept of a war of civilization against barbarity remained at the heart of French war culture.

This reading of the war brought together republican and Catholic messianism. Given the previously poisoned relationship between the Republic and the Catholic Church, this meeting of visions proved one of the more remarkable cultural achievements of the Union sacrée. Both forms of messianism attributed to France a unique mission to the whole of humanity. Republicans saw the war in terms of the 1789 Revolution and the Declaration of the Rights of Man, which conferred on the Great Nation the role of universal beacon, the torch of humanity. Republicans of a Jacobin bent, among them Georges Clemenceau in 1917, could see the war as a return to the Year II (1793–4), in which the mobilized and free people of France astounded Europe with the victories of Valmy and Jemappes. French Catholics could recall the eminent position of France in Catholic Christendom as the "the eldest daughter of the Church," thanks to the baptism of Clovis at the turn of the sixth century. In short, we cannot overlook the eschatological dimension of French war culture, its sense of the war as a redemptive trial with implications for all of humanity. Civilization itself would progress through a French victory. Civilization would decline and probably fall through a French defeat.

Along the margin of this broadly dominant construction of the war as a crusade on behalf of civilization lay the notion that the war would regenerate the French race through reviving its vital creative spirit. Overtly racist conceptualizations of the struggle between France and Germany, born largely of Right-wing ideological nationalism, brought to fruition ideas of social Darwinism discussed widely in France since the 1890s. This representation saw international relations in terms of a struggle for life, through a deformed version of Charles Darwin's theories of evolution.

Racist interpretations rested on the idea of incommensurable physical differences between the French and Germans, and were not at all confined to the less educated members of French society. Captain Augustin Cochin, was a son of one of the most distinguished academic families in France and himself a historian of some reputation. He wrote that the Germans "have a special odor, very strong, and that you can't get rid of," as well as their own species of fleas, much larger than those that afflicted the French. Psychologist Edgar Bérillon suggested in a lecture in 1917 that the population of Alsace and Lorraine could never really be assimilated into Germany because they would always find the smell of Germans too disagreeable. French racial integrity was threatened by German blood, seen as corrupt and corrupting. Josephine Barthélemy, a twenty-year old domestic servant repatriated from occupied France, was acquitted of infanticide in 1917 because she convinced a Paris jury that she had been raped by a German. Her explanation, "I did not want to have a child born of a Boche father," appeared in every major Paris newspaper. As the Union sacrée gradually drifted to the Right the longer the war continued, views of the war as a racial struggle became increasingly respectable. This particularly radical aspect of war culture pointed ominously toward attitudes in subsequent conflicts among European nations.

Patriotic rhetoric in French war culture perhaps had more aggressive and brutal connotations than elsewhere. This ferocity of language was particularly evident in speaking to French children during the war through specially designed books, magazines, games, and toys. Even very young children were read stories that preached martyrdom for the French and hatred for the Germans. A whole genre of children's literature flourished telling tales of the *enfant héroïque* (heroic child), miniature guerrilla warriors who killed Germans almost as cheerfully as they accepted their own death, by firing squad or, preferably, by bayonet. Teachers assigned arithmetic calculations of shell requirements and casualties as an everyday part of their lessons. The systematic integration of children into the adult world of war shows that no age group, however young, could escape ideological mobilization.

In short, the war culture of 1914–18 resulted from what historian Pierre Chaunu once described as "the immense emotional investment, on a national scale, of the French in France."[7] Wartime propaganda was the effect of this investment on the part of the men, women, and children of France, as well as its cause. This war culture remained dynamic, in ways historians understand only in its broad outlines. The national commitment of 1914–15 drew from outrage at the German invasion and the atrocities that accompanied it. By 1916, in the wake of the immense but indecisive battles of Verdun and the Somme, this war culture began literally to deconstruct, to fall apart through its internal contradictions. The more the nation mobilized, the less likely it seemed that France would ever be able to expel the invader. If the crises of 1917, the subject of Chapter 4, marked the military and political turning points of the Great War, 1916 marked the cultural turning point. The cultural remobilization of the second half of 1917 prepared the French for renewed German invasion in 1918, and the gradual turn of the tide thereafter. While there remains much to be learned about French war culture in the Great War, it is clear that unifying, consensual, and highly dynamic ways of understanding the conflict helped the French to continue to accept the material and emotional sacrifices required, even at the worst moments of the war.

[7] Pierre Chaunu, *La France* (Paris: Robert Laffont, 1982), p. 20.

Plate 2a. Images of the German enemy. Photograph by the authors.

Plate 2b.

Economic and social mobilization

Before 1914, the expectation of a short war precluded planning for a large-scale war economy. It was assumed that current industrial production could replace losses in the event of war. In August 1914, three-quarters of military production came from state arsenals. A few companies specializing in armaments, such as Creusot, Saint-Chamond, Firminy, and Schneider, supplied the remainder. Private firms tended to focus their attention on the export market. Mobilization and then war in August 1914 brought all industrial activity virtually to a halt. Most firms retained on average only one-third of their pre-1914 workforce. Only the railway workers, responsible for transporting the French army to the front, escaped mobilization. Initially, the *impôt du sang* (literally "blood tax," a colloquial term for conscription) affected even the armaments industry. The near-depletion of supplies in the first months of fighting, coupled with the loss of occupied France (the most heavily industrialized part of the country after Paris) and the prospect of a long, drawn-out war following the stabilization of the front in the autumn of 1914, forced the French state to take its first steps towards establishing a war economy.

War Minister Alexandre Millerand assembled the leading French industrialists at the Bordeaux Conference of September 20, 1914. The overriding priority in the evolving strategic plan involved the production of the 100,000 shells per day, which the General Staff required to restock. Every French company available was to be enlisted, and new factories to be built through enormous advances provided by the state. The other goal involved vastly expanding the production of artillery pieces – both the now-legendary *Soixante-quinze* (75mm cannon), and heavy artillery, the lack of which had badly hurt the army during the German invasion. The vast and growing needs of the artillery, already revealed as the predominant armament on the battlefield, largely determined French industrial mobilization at this stage of the war.

The industrial mobilization that began in the autumn of 1914 involved nothing less than the conversion of the entire industrial structure of France to war manufacturing. Yet two serious bottlenecks impeded the establishment of a true war economy – the shortage of labor (made worse by the conscription of much of the male workforce), and the loss of industrial infrastructure in occupied France. The agricultural economy, on the other hand, continued to function remarkably well. Even though the general mobilization occurred in the middle of the harvest season, rural France proved capable of mobilizing impressive reserves of labor (older workers, women, and children) and of operating highly effective village systems of mutual aid. The people of the countryside somehow managed to bring in the 1914 harvest, and so averted the serious food shortages in the winter of 1914–15.

As the military front stabilized, the state authorized industrialists to recall essential workers mobilized into the army in the summer of 1914. The Dalbiez Law, passed in June 1915, eventually enabled 500,000 workers to be released for industrial work. These men remained under military discipline, and in effect could be sent back to the front at the discretion of their employers. Even during the labor unrest of 1917–18, this threat proved an effective means of managing male workers' discontent. Within a month after the passage of the Dalbiez Law, by July 1915, the metallurgy industry regained over 80 percent of its 1914 labor force (and 100 percent by January 1916). The chemicals industry regained two-thirds of its workforce by July 1915, (and more than 90 percent six months later). One consequence of this redeployment of male industrial workers was that this social group suffered proportionally fewer casualties at the front than either agricultural workers or men from the middle classes.

Yet the number of mobilized industrial workers never exceeded 518,000 men, the figure attained in August 1917. The French army could not send more men home without seriously undermining the principle of equality of recruitment, according to which all male citizens had an equal obligation to bear arms for the country. Consequently, firms could fulfill the enormous orders placed by the state only through recruiting additional workers such as foreigners and colonial workers. The French also used prisoners as workers, though to a lesser extent than the Germans. But most importantly, employers recruited women, who gained access to forms of work from which they previously had been pointedly excluded. This marked an enormous turn for French society of the day. But the image of women flooding into the workforce during the war should not be overdrawn. Although the female percentage of the workforce in metallurgy increased from about 5 percent to about 25 percent, this industry proved the exception. The total number of women in factories increased by only about a third during the war, rather a small figure given the scale of the changes in the French economy. In 1918, the industrial labor force was made up of 42 percent unmobilized men, 39 percent mobilized men, 3.7 percent foreigners (European and colonial) and 15.3 percent women. Taking the economy as a whole, the proportion of women in paid employment rose only from an estimated 35 percent to 40 percent of the labor force during the war years.

The loss of the occupied territories proved a serious blow for French war industries – nearly 50 percent of coal production, 64 percent of iron and 58 percent of steel. Clearly, France could win the war only through establishing an effective means of importing strategic materials. Import planning began in November 1915. The Minister of Trade (Étienne Clémentel from 1916), the Comité des Forges, and the Chambre Syndicale du Matériel de Guerre (respectively the Heavy Industry Committee, and the Syndical Chamber of War Materiel, both powerful employers' organizations) played an essential collaborative role in establishing import monopolies for heavy industry and in managing the distribution of essential materials among various firms. Unique among the countries that fought the Great War, France managed the supply of its metallurgical industry through a private employers' organization. As early as 1915, armaments production in the private sector had overtaken production in the state arsenals. Given the strategic nature of this industry, the cartel of the great armament manufacturers, generally in close collaboration with the state, played the leading role in managing the war economy.

French industry as a whole gradually organized itself along similar lines, directed by the largest companies under conditions of considerable autonomy, even though the state continued to play a role in industrial decisions and still exercised powerful pressure over industrial organization. Industry became divided into "manufacturing groups," subordinate to a leading company. This company received orders from the state and distributed them among companies within the group. The first manufacturing groups were formed as early as September 20, 1914, around the companies of Le Creusot and Saint-Chamond. Eventually, three groups directed the manufacture of guns and fifteen the manufacture of shells. These eighteen groups supervised the production of 375 companies in all. Only firms in the Paris region worked outside the group system and had a direct relationship with the representatives of the state. By 1918, some 17,000 companies employed 1.7 million people in armaments manufacturing, the great majority around Paris and in the Loire basin. For better or worse, the Great War made France one of the world's most important producers of weapons, a tradition to which it returned after World War II and which continues today.

French industrial mobilization achieved spectacular results. Shell production ultimately increased ten-fold from its level at the summer of 1915, and the production of powder and explosives six-fold. By 1918, French industry produced 1,000 artillery pieces per month, and 261,000 shells and 6 million cartridges per day. France became the "arsenal of democracy," the chief arms supplier for the Allies, even the United States. Of course, such success relied on massive imports of primary strategic materials (mainly of American origin) and on a huge return on capital at no risk guaranteed to the industrialists by the state. New methods of work management resulted in spectacular advances in labor productivity (if at the expense of rising labor discontent) in industries such as mechanical engineering, steel manufacturing, and chemicals. That French industry could redirect itself so fast under such difficult conditions illustrated the tremendous growth potential of the French economy at the beginning of the twentieth century. The military victory of the French and the Allies in 1918 rested on an economic victory over the industrial system of the Central Powers (aided, of course, by the British and French naval blockade). As we will see, after the war, the French vowed to extend this hard-won superiority over Germany into the peace.

The French chose a unique way of coordinating relations among the state, industry, and the military command by incorporating all three into the making of policy. In Britain, the state negotiated directly with industry and excluded the military, while in Germany the key dialogue took place between industry and the military High Command. But in France, the Viviani government set up the Direction de l'Artillerie du Ministère de la Guerre (Artillery Management of the Ministry of War) in May 1915. Under the direction of socialist Albert Thomas, the Artillery Management was founded as an independent under-secretariat of state. It became its own ministry, the Ministry for Armaments, in December 1916. This ministry coordinated production through to the end of the war, though after Thomas left the government in September 1917, his successor Louis Loucheur had a smaller sphere of influence.

Under the direction of Thomas, who had been a disciple of Jean Jaurès, the new administration heralded the birth of modern technocracy in its flexibility, pragmatism, and willingness to introduce unconventional solutions. Thomas brought into his ministry some of the most talented minds in the country, such as sociologists François Simiand and Maurice Halbwachs. The Ministry of Armaments combined market principles with centralized planning, both within France and at the international level, through its organization of trade with Great Britain and the United States. It established a new type of state intervention, clearly a break with prewar liberalism yet far from the *dirigisme* of a state-directed economy. In the interest of efficiency, Albert Thomas sought to retain private initiative, with profit as its driving motivation, under economic conditions as close as possible to those of peacetime. He saw war profits, in short, as a necessary evil. Indeed, as the war continued, the state became willing to assist private initiative, to the extent of giving direct grants for industrialists to build new factories. In return, the state insisted on working closely with the leading companies of industrial groups, and on retaining strict control over prices and the effective implementation of production plans.

Even though Thomas came to prefer more state planning after 1916, he generally promoted war industry to a position of partnership with the state, in a relationship based on collaboration and encouragement rather than on formal control. He was known to shower employers with praise. "Yesterday," he told a joint meeting of workers and managers at Creusot in April 1916, "there was competition between industrialists, or at least an absence of union and sometimes open struggle. [Today], in wartime, all of this finds itself regulated by the common will." But even after his departure and the rise of the "Jacobin dictatorship" under Clemenceau, industry remained free to accept or to refuse state orders. The Left never raised the issue of the ownership of the means of production, and avoided any notion of factory requisition.

But in his way, Thomas remained a Socialist visionary. He continued to address workers as "comrades," and believed that the war had given France "the concrete possibility of integrating the working class into the nation." In addition to his undeniable patriotism, something Thomas certainly shared with Jaurès, Thomas believed industrial mobilization could create a "collective economy" that combined socialism and capitalism. He believed that class collaboration forged in wartime could build a new France once peace returned. But in the short run, no politician in France contributed more than Thomas to making the Union sacrée a matter of practical politics. His perspective and policies legitimized the reliable participation of millions of French workers in the national war effort.

The state intervened massively in the economy through wartime finance. Like its allies and enemies, France financed the war by borrowing on a vast scale and by monetary inflation through increasing the money supply. The amount of cash in circulation multiplied 500 percent over the course of the war. Gold reserves backed 69 percent of cash before the war, but only 21.5 percent in 1918. Direct taxation remained fairly restrained, so as not to make worse the difficult position of French families. Although France finally imposed an income tax in January 1916, it brought in only 1 billion francs in total by the end of the war. A tax on war profits brought in only 1.5 billion. In the meantime, state expenditures (running only about 5 billion per year in 1913) averaged 38 billion francs per year by the end of the war.

To make up the difference, France borrowed more than any other country, both internally and externally. Foreign loans, subscribed mostly on the American market, reached the sum of 43.5 billion francs by the end of the war, making France one of the main debtors to the United States. Long-term bonds, launched on the home market with a great fanfare of patriotic publicity, brought in 24 billion francs. Most important were short-term Bons de la Défense Nationale (National Defence Bonds), which replaced the old Bons du Trésor (Treasury Bonds). Short-term war bonds brought in 76 billion francs between 1914 and 1918, and financed most of the French war effort. To some extent, the French state proved able to raise such sums thanks to its remarkable legacy of financial prudence in the nineteenth century, across long periods with many episodes of political unrest. But more importantly, the success of war borrowing spoke to public confidence that France in the end would win the war. Consequently, financing the war economy had cultural implications, and spoke profoundly to the question of acceptance of the war effort by society as a whole.

As we saw in the case of occupied France, the war made very different demands on civilians, depending on where they lived. The price paid by civilians should be evaluated in the context of a greater or lesser degree of exposure to the enemy and to the direct effects of the war. Civilians living in a militarized zone some fifty kilometers behind the front lines running from the North Sea to Switzerland suffered more severely than their compatriots through the chronic disruption of social and economic life – the threat of enemy offensives, extensive bombardments, forced evacuations ordered by the army, and the constant and, at times, oppressive proximity to soldiers passing through. Even the population of Paris was not completely safe, as demonstrated by civilian casualties from German shells in the spring of 1918. People who lived close to the front, particularly if they were old enough to remember the invasion of 1870, experienced the war quite differently from people who lived further south and had no family or local memory of the presence of the enemy in their town, their village, or their own homes.

France proved able to manage material difficulties more effectively than the Central Powers. Several factors helped ward off a prolonged social crisis, even in 1917. Among the rural population, more than half the French nation at that time, military allowances introduced from the beginning of the war (1.25 francs per day, plus 0.50 francs for each child) provided cash support for daily needs. Though the sums involved seem tiny, this program played a decisive role in sustaining peasant acceptance of the war. Wartime inflation actually often enriched people in the countryside. As food producers, they also avoided the food supply difficulties suffered by the cities from 1917 on. Their urban compatriots sometimes expressed astonishment (and not a little resentment) at increased prices for agricultural goods. The most serious economic problem faced by rural people was the labor shortage. But by mobilizing the labor of old people, women, children, and ultimately German prisoners, the rural population managed largely to compensate for the absence of their men folk.

The consent of the rural population remained a decisive stabilizing element in the French nation accepting the prolongation of war, particularly after 1916. The rural world, considerably more hesitant about going to war in August 1914 than the urban world, proved perhaps more steadfast in waging it, down to the Armistice of November 1918. Certainly, weariness deepened as the war dragged on, gradually transforming acceptance into sad resignation. But overall, the idea of a rupture in the national consensus never took root in the countryside. The rural world thus proved something of an anchor for the French people as a whole.

The world of industrial labor, in which people felt the initial economic effects of the war far more severely, to some extent presented the opposite case. Although military allowances and a moratorium on rents declared in August 1914 mitigated the catastrophic effects of the departures of millions of heads of families, these solutions never came near to providing full compensation for the financial consequences. Certainly, conditions for many working-class families began to improve as early as the fall of 1914. As noted, the government recalled from the front some 500,000 men for key jobs in industry. More women also joined the labor market, many eventually moving toward better-paid jobs hitherto reserved for men.

But without direct access to food or fuel like their compatriots in the countryside, workers in the cities had to suffer the full force of shortages and inflation. Between 1914 and 1918, prices rose from an index of 100 to 211 in Paris, and from 100 to 235 in the provinces. Only workers in the armaments industries kept ahead of inflation. Their wages rose from an index of 100 in 1914 to 240 in 1918, against 100 to 175 for industry as a whole. For most workers, the increase in the cost of living outpaced the increase in wages. We should note, however, that these indices exclude mitigating factors such as the disappearance of unemployment among working-class people, and thus the positive impact of having more people able to contribute to family income. Nor do they indicate additional income from overtime, a considerable factor at a time of labor shortage. Problems of supply for basic commodities such as coal or sugar became serious only in 1917, and thereafter were managed by rationing.[8] Indeed, perhaps we should evaluate the most difficult material aspects of working-class life during the war not so much in terms of income, but in terms of overwork, physical exhaustion, and unhealthy or dangerous working conditions, particularly in shell-making factories.

The working classes also benefited from new forms of state intervention. For example, the government set up an employment office at the beginning of the war to counteract the massive unemployment caused by the temporary halt in economic activity. The state provided pensions for men disabled by the war, and introduced a system of care for orphans. In January 1917, Albert Thomas introduced obligatory arbitration in war factories, followed by the establishment of minimum wage rates. Also in 1917, Thomas established a system of workshop delegates to mediate

---

[8] In a remarkable testimony to the success of agricultural production in France, the government had to issue food ration cards only in June 1918, just five months before the end of the war.

disputes and began to bring in worker representatives in the ministry's consultative commissions. The state intervened, often decisively, particularly in disputes between capitalism and labor, in order to guarantee continued production.

The success of the French war economy should be appreciated in its many social contexts. These could be highly differentiated according to sector or trade, to rural or urban setting, or to proximity to the front lines. Such factors shaped how acceptance of the war endured or weakened in various settings. Overall, very favorable economic conditions in the rural world worked to support consent for the war, even as that consent became increasingly weary and resigned. By 1917, problems of purchasing power and supply made the urban working population more volatile, as we will explore further in Chapter 4. But even in the cities, difficult conditions never defeated the essential consensus to continue the war.

Waiting, death, and mourning in wartime

Of course, the most acute and chronic form of stress for those millions of French left behind in August 1914 entailed the anxious wait for news – from the fathers, husbands, sons, grandsons, brothers, cousins, sons-in-law, brothers-in-law, or friends exposed to mortal danger. We cannot hope to understand the home front without appreciating this aspect of civilian experience. During lengthy periods of quiet between pitched battles, most men wrote home every day, which indicates the strength of the bond created by correspondence between soldiers and civilians. Any break in the stream of letters from soldiers generally meant a period of intense military activity, even the launch of a major offensive. If the interruption proved protracted, families had good reason to fear that their men folk had been wounded, captured, or killed at the front. As the war continued, fighting it inevitably became incorporated into the rhythms of everyday life, But beneath the "banalization" or "normalization" of the war in the apparently sheltered world behind the lines lay a pall of constant waiting, in anguish and sometimes in torment. Primice Mendès wrote what turned out to be his last letter to his mother on April 15, 1917. He died on April 23, and his mother received notice of his death on May 8. Jane Catulle Mendès recalled later: "Hour by hour I can recall them, those sixteen days of waiting. Those days were of another existence, of another world."

This anxiety took many forms. As in the case of the mother of Mendès, and despite the best efforts of the military and the Red Cross, families might have to endure a long wait before finally hearing that a loved one had been killed, wounded, or taken prisoner. Advances in military medicine notwithstanding, nearly any wound was serious. Anguish over the survival of the wounded and the future of the mutilated afflicted much of the country. More than 40 percent of the eight million Frenchmen in uniform were wounded at least once. Worst of all, an increasing number of French people, especially French women, had to face the death of a loved one and the wrenching experience of grief and mourning.

The social consequences of mass death and generalized mourning appeared well before the end of the war. Never before had war caused so many deaths in France, particularly in so short a time. Fully 50 percent of the 1.3 million Frenchmen killed during the war lost their lives in a seventeen-month period between August 1914 and December 1915. Frenchmen killed in battle totaled more than 300,000 men in the last five months of 1914 alone, an average of 2,000 deaths per day. The rate of losses diminished thereafter, although it still remained extraordinarily high: nearly 935 deaths per day in 1915, 677 in 1916, and 419 in 1917. When the more deadly war of movement returned in 1918, the toll rose to 800 deaths per day. Overall, the average over four-and-a-half years came to the stunning figure of 890 men killed per day, with three or four times that number of wounded.

Within the figure of 16.8 percent of mobilized Frenchmen killed, certain classes (cohorts) and categories of men suffered particularly heavily. The classes of 1911, 1912, and 1913 (on active duty at the outbreak of war) suffered losses of 25 percent or more. The classes of 1914 and 1915, who reached the front lines for the great battles of 1916 (Verdun and the Somme), suffered losses of 22.3 percent and 27.8 percent respectively. Casualties among junior and non-commissioned officers were consistently much more than among private soldiers, particularly in the infantry, where casualties averaged 25 percent. In France, as in other countries, many middle-class and upper-class young men had leadership positions that put them at great physical risk. Consequently, their losses were higher than for other socioeconomic groups. The seriousness with which certain elites viewed the war showed itself in their casualty rates. Young officers from the Saint-Cyr military academy and students from the École Normal Supérieure in Paris generally suffered nearly 50 percent losses.

Very early in the war, hundreds of thousands of French families were plunged into mourning. By the end of the war, few families were completely spared. The term "circle," used by modern demographers to describe the sphere of relationships in which an individual lives has great relevance here. When a given individual died, grief from that one death could affect a large number of people depending on the ties that person had created during his lifetime. The concept of "circles of mourning" brings home the depth of the catastrophe and helps define the scale of the disruption and the damage that casualties caused as they shattered the emotional worlds of millions of people.

It may be impossible to precisely determine the number of French people plunged into mourning because of the Great War. Official statistics recorded only the parents and descendants of the dead, only a part of that person's circle of relationships. The only figures we have are misleading, because they evolved from rules established by the state for indemnification. For example, a widow who later remarried lost her widow's pension, though this certainly did not necessarily efface her previous grief. Conversely, a woman who after 1918 married a war invalid who later died prematurely became a war widow. Yet emotionally, her grief differed from that of a woman whose husband died at the front. Similar complexity emerged in the case of orphans. When the children of soldiers killed reached the age of 21, they disappeared from the statistics. This explains why the number of "orphans" diminished rapidly after 1919. Nevertheless, they would feel the loss of their fathers to the end of their lives.

How then to assess the number of French people in the inner circle of mourning, that of the closest relatives of the deceased? The simplest way is to count the number of French widows and orphans first of all: 600,000 war widows[9] and 760,000 orphans.[10] Estimates for parents were more complicated. We have a reasonably reliable picture of the situation at the end of the 1920s, though the figure was of course greater in the immediate aftermath of the war. Most of the 1.3 million soldiers killed at the front left at least one parent behind, which meant as many parents in mourning as dead men. In total, this inner circle of mourners comprised more than 2.5 million people. But this figure greatly underestimates the full impact of the losses. It excludes an unknown number of other close relatives, such as grandparents and siblings. Those killed also left behind uncles, aunts, nephews, nieces, cousins, and various in-laws. Beyond the circle of blood and legal relatives lie additional circles of male and female friends, surviving comrades, and persons more distantly connected who felt the loss.

---

[9] Accounting for later deaths, this number had increased to 700,000 in 1933, including 262,500 who had remarried. See Antoine Prost, *Les anciens combattants et la société française*, 3 vols. (Paris: Presses de la fondation des Sciences Politiques, 1977): vol. I: pp. 11 et seq.

[10] This is a low estimate of the number of orphans, which has gone as high as 1.2 million. Recently, Olivier Faron arrived at a figure of 1.1 million people legally defined as "wards of the nation." But not all of these were orphans, since the children of war invalids could also claim this title. See *Les Enfants du deuil: orphelins et pupilles de la nation de la première guerre mondiale (1914–1941)* (Paris: Éditions de la Découverte, 2001).

Given the limits on what we can know about how many people the dead left behind, it seems reasonable to extrapolate from figures used by present-day demographers to describe the circles around a given person in France – at least ten people in the immediate family, and a maximum of twenty other people connected to the deceased in less close social relationships.[11] Consequently, if each of the 1.3 million Frenchmen killed in the Great War left thirty people in various degrees of mourning, we arrive at a figure of 39 million people – practically the whole of French society.

The reality of a whole nation in mourning, of a community of grief that comprised everyone but a small and extremely fortunate minority, did not have precedent in modern times. Some of the smaller belligerent countries suffered proportionately greater losses than France, and therefore experienced even more extensive mourning. But among the Great Powers, the French were certainly the most affected: 3.4 percent of its population was killed in the war, against 3 percent for Germany, 1.9 percent for Austria-Hungary, 1.6 percent for Great Britain and Italy, and 1.1 percent for Russia.[12] In a surprising number of cases, recurrence of loss deepened the pain of bereavement. General Edouard de Castelnau, a senior commander at Verdun, lost all three sons in the war; politician Paul Doumer lost four sons. The war memorial at La Forêt du Temple, in the north of the Creuse department, bears the name of a mother, Emma Bujardet, who, according to her death certificate, "died of grief" in 1917 after she lost her three sons.

Beyond the scale of mourning lies the question of just how people mourned. In many ways, war-related mourning has very little in common with mourning in times of peace. War-related grief always has specific causes and effects. In the Great War, the death in combat of so many men at the very beginning of their adult lives reversed the normal order of generational succession, with the young dying before the old. This reversal inverted the pattern of customs linked to death in peacetime. Consequently, it helps explain feelings of guilt among generations too old to fight themselves and forced in this way to witness the deaths of their children. "It is my fault," wrote Jane Catulle Mendès of the death of her son, "why did I so need to talk to him so much about honor, duty, beauty, for him to want a soul so right, so elevated?" Forms of "survivors' guilt" may also help explain why so many women in the interior

---

[11] E. Lelièvre, C. Bonvalet, X. Bry, "Analyse biographique des groupes," *Population*, July-August 1997, pp. 822–3.

[12] Serbia lost 5.7 percent of its population, and Turkey 3.7 percent. J. -C. Chesnais, *Les morts violentes en France depuis 1826. Comparaisons internationales* (Paris: Presses Universitaires de France, 1976), table 58, p. 183.

volunteered to serve as nurses, so as to experience at least the consequences of combat, if not combat itself. Similarly, did not the greatest intellectuals in France so completely serve wartime propaganda in part as a response to a visceral need to help their children carry the weight of the future of the nation? Barrès, Lavisse, and Durkheim all had sons at the front. Their commitment to the war spoke of their guilt at seeing their own children exposed to death while they themselves remain sheltered.

Even if, in the end, survivors outnumbered the dead, the reversal on this scale of the normal order of generational succession stunned contemporaries to a degree that we can appreciate only with great difficulty today. The shock was all the greater, moreover, because a general reduction in death rates in the nineteenth century had made it increasingly unusual for the young to die before the old. There is some evidence that older people, consciously or unconsciously, have hastened their own deaths. In Paris, as in London or Berlin during the war, there was a high mortality rate among the old which cannot entirely be explained by material conditions. To find a satisfactory explanation, we must therefore look at the psychological shock and the unprecedented suffering that the death of the young created among their elders, particularly grandparents facing the death of their grandsons.

It was not uncommon during the war for parents to die, apparently of psychosomatic causes, shortly after the death of their son. André Durkheim, son of famed sociologist Émile Durkheim, was killed in the Balkans in December 1915. Émile Durkheim wrote to his nephew Marcel Mauss, who Durkheim had raised after the death of Mauss's father, to tell him the news. "When you respond," the elder Durkheim wrote, "speak as little as possible of the irreparable. It is the images of what happened that make me suffer. Everything that they bring up makes me recoil."[13] Thereafter, Durkheim appeared to be able to cope with his grief. But he had a stroke around the first anniversary of the death of his son, which Mauss always attributed to the death of André Durkheim.

Present-day psychology, which has developed alongside the conflicts of the second half of the twentieth century, makes it possible better to understand the mental suffering of the parents of French soldiers who were killed. We now understand the permanent effects on parents of the death of their children, at whatever age. The pain of the loss can be even greater, and can frequently become pathological, if the child has reached adulthood. This was precisely the situation of a huge and increasing number of parents and grandparents of soldiers killed in action. Similarly, we

---

[13] Émile Durkheim, *Lettres à Marcel Mauss* (Paris: Presses Universitaires de France, 1998), pp. 501–2.

understand today how serious it is for a child to experience the death of his or her father. This, of course, was the experience of an enormous number of French children. The French state itself recognized the gravity of the situation of war orphans by according them special rights and appointing them *pupille de la nation*, or "wards of the nation." The term literally translates as "pupils of the nation," meaning the very center of the nation's eye. The plan, unachieved and perhaps unachievable, involved treating the *pupilles de la nation* as a future knighthood, an elite carefully groomed by the nation to lead it when they became adults.

Only in rare cases could families be with the dying in their final moments. Soldiers often died alone and in agony. Sometimes they died surrounded by their friends, but almost always without the support of their own families. For the survivors, this meant that the steps preparing for bereavement could not take place, nor could the rituals immediately accompanying the first moments of loss, such as closing the eyes of the deceased. The inability to locate the bodies of the dead caused special anguish for the bereaved. Typically, identified bodies were buried in military cemeteries established quite near the front lines. Despite the immense efforts of some families to break the rules and travel to the Zone of the Armies in order to dig up by night the bodies of their loved ones, the return of the bodies of the men who were killed remained essentially impossible during the war.

To be sure, the laws of July 31, 1920 and the governmental decree of September 28, 1920 gave French families the option of requesting the return of the bodies of their dead for reburial in family vaults. But the movement of bodies under this legislation did not actually begin until the summer of 1922 and after several years resulted in the return only of about 240,000 coffins. This figure represented only about thirty percent of the more than 700,000 of the identified dead whose families had the right to request repatriation. This relatively small percentage, perhaps, is suggestive. Return of the body of the deceased was possible only several years after his death. Of course, it was not an option at all for the families of more than 300,000 of the dead, for whom there did not exist identifiable remains. Life had to go on, whether grief had been resolved or not. Many families, perhaps, preferred letting their dead lay where they were to reopening severe and recent emotional wounds. As Durkheim suggested in his letter to Marcel Mauss, repression could prove less immediately painful than remembering.

It was typical of the Great War for survivors to lack precise information as to how their loved one died, particularly if the death occurred in the incredible confusion of an offensive. The unprecedented scale of the fighting and the fact that two-thirds of those who died were killed by the artillery meant that many of those killed could never be identified. Hundreds of thousands of families therefore never had a grave at which to gather, a specific tomb as the focus for their mourning. Symbolizing death by a tomb, in whatever form, seems fundamental to the grieving process. Through gradually transferring meaning from the body to the tomb, survivors reposition their grief on something that replaces the body of the dead. This metonymy was precisely what was lacking for millions of French people within their circles of mourning.

The extreme agony that often accompanied death in combat added a particularly cruel element to grief in the absence of a body. Comrades often repeated official lies, with the intent of not adding to the suffering of the bereaved families. But it was not difficult to imagine the pain and the loneliness their loved ones had endured before death. In *Là-bas avec ceux qui souffrent* (Out There, with Those who Suffer, 1917), Second Lieutenant Guy Hallé of the 74th Infantry Regiment described an episode in November 1916, in which a women inquired as to the specific fate of her husband, who had been reported missing. Somehow, she knew that mines had exploded in his sector of the front. Hallé, rather brutally, chose silence in not responding, even though he knew that the man had been buried in a mine explosion. But since no body or other physical evidence of his death had been discovered, he would forever remain officially classified as "missing." He recalled with remarkable candor: "When all's said and done, I think that sometimes it's better not to respond. This unhappy women will understand that he is dead. It is useless to tell her in so many words what has happened. No, truly, it is better not to say."

For people such as the wife of this dead man, how could a general knowledge or even the simple intuition of how men died in battle have failed to add to their emotional suffering? We can understand why in their letters to the comrades or the superiors of the deceased their questions always turned to the final moments, the exact circumstances of death, the wounds received and sufferings endured. They wanted to know whether he died alone and, if he had been buried, the exact location of his grave. Survivors within the circles of mourning thus attempted to fill in terrible gaps in their knowledge. After the fact, they tried as well to compensate for not having been able to be with the dead – from his wounding to his agony, from his agony to his death, from his death to his burial. Whether this process and their absence from it had been just a few hours or, more often, a few days, the absence of any companionship for the dying seems to have added to the grief of the survivors and to have made wartime mourning so difficult and closure so elusive.

Sometimes, in fact, closure seemed impossible. For Francoise Vitry, mourning seemed to tear apart her very identity. She now had two souls:

The one that loved movement and life is dead. She has gone to live over there, next to a tomb in Lorraine. Sometimes she tries to revive; she makes prodigious efforts; like a little child she tries to laugh, to sing, to love; she succumbs to the violence of the effort, sinks, and leaves the other soul alone.

That is the dreamer soul, who often returns from distant and unknown countries, and keeps something like nostalgia for them. How sad and tired she is! Whatever she sees, she sees too well. Before her eyes, the closest friend, the best thing, drops its mask and exposes an empty carcass.[14]

There were as many ways of articulating the experience of mourning as there were mourners. But Vitry captures just how deeply mourning scarred the lives of those whose loved ones were killed. Ongoing mobilization of the national community must be considered in this context, and mourning as part of wartime experience itself. The resilience of the national community as a whole notwithstanding, the task of mourning the dead of the Great War proved extremely arduous for French people, both during the war and after 1918. If we look closely, we can still see its traces today.

[14] Quoted in Higonnet, *Lines of Fire*, pp. 409–10.

3   The front and the soldiers' war

The stalemate produced by the battles of August and September 1914 transformed the character of warfare in Europe, for generals as much as for common soldiers. Throughout the nineteenth century, military theory had rested on the assumption of decisive battle. Battle had been conceived as having a definite beginning and end. Most importantly, it had long been held that battle produced clear winners and losers. Certainly, the war plans of 1914 rested on the assumption of battles that would prove nasty and brutish, but also decisive and short. But as the war on the Western Front descended into the trench system, the very meanings of "battle" and "the front" changed. Pitched battle in its conventional sense proved relatively rare in the conflict of 1914–18, mostly because of its horrendous cost in men and materiel when it did occur. But in the trenches, a grinding and inherently indecisive form of "combat" was supposed to be constant. The spatial configuration of warfare changed radically as well. Millions of men fought for four years along hundreds of kilometers of trenches, a far longer front than had ever existed in European military history.

Between the congealing of the Western Front in the fall of 1914 and the resumption of the war of movement in the spring of 1918, Frenchmen in uniform struggled to understand the new war, and to find a way to win it. In the generals' war, French strategy became a matter of diminishing expectations, and of an increasingly unconvincing insistence that stalemate would one day produce victory. Soldiers in the trenches faced new weapons, new rhythms of life and death, and constant danger. They became known as the *poilus*, or "hairy ones." With unruly hair and beards or mustaches grown at the front, soldiers and civilians alike embraced a term that connected the defenders of the country to Samson from the Bible, who likewise drew his strength from his hair. The *poilus* created their own world, with its own rules and strategies of survival, separate from yet intimately connected to both the generals' war and the war of the civilians in the interior. Yet in their great majority, and in much more dire circumstances, French soldiers maintained the same fierce commitment to the nation and the war held by those behind the lines – their generals, their loved ones, and their compatriots.

Strategy: from *Percée*, to *Grignotage*, to *Tenir*

By the end of 1914 the front line between the opposing armies was stabilized along more than 700 kilometers, from the North Sea to the Swiss border. In 1915, the British army and the small Belgian army gradually took over an increasingly lengthy section of the front line between the North Sea and the Somme. The French held the rest of the front, from the Somme to Switzerland. The role of the British and Dominion forces proved crucial during the four years of war, for the Western Front remained the decisive front – the setting for the victory or defeat of both combatant coalitions. For their part, the French had a clear military objective on the Western Front, from the first days of the war to the last – expelling the invader where he stood, from northeastern France and from Alsace and Lorraine.

The Allied and German armies had achieved stability through the gradual digging and constant improvement of vast networks of trenches. In itself, trench warfare was nothing new – it had been part of siege warfare for centuries. The reinvention of mining, particularly in 1915 and 1916, emphasized the similarity to the most traditional forms of siege warfare. Miners would attempt to dig under the enemy position and place explosives there in an attempt to effect a breakthrough of the enemy lines. Trench systems eerily prescient of World War I had emerged late in the American Civil War and in the Russo-Japanese War of 1905–6. What was new about the trench warfare along the Western Front in the Great War was its scale and its duration.

The "front" comprised thousands of square kilometers, organized as two dense networks of ditches between one and two kilometers wide on each side. "No man's land" (so called in French as well as in English) separated the protagonists, sometimes by several hundred meters, sometimes by only a few dozen. As early as 1915, each side had three lines of trenches in most places. By 1917 and 1918 they would often have five or six. The front lines, with their protective parapets and firing points, were guarded by small advanced look-out posts. The trenches provided for movable, protected, and concentrated fire from infantry, one characteristic that made them so difficult to conquer. Communications trenches connected the front line to the second line, as well as to support positions established still further back. Units rotated among these successive lines of defense. Dense curls of barbed wire protected each line of trenches. The trenches were dug in a hatched pattern, so that even if enemy soldiers got into a given trench, they could not fire down its entire length. Much of the Western Front was located on relatively flat terrain in a wet climate, with the water table quite close to the surface. The ever-present mud, the regular flooding of the trenches, and the general confusion of physical space profoundly shaped soldiers' experience.

Militarily speaking, the heart of the problem of trench warfare lay in the strength of the defense. For most of the war, all the defenders had to do to stop an offensive was to slow it down. Paradoxically, the attacking artillery barrage often helped the defenders as much as the attackers. The attackers launched the artillery barrage to destroy the defending trenches, and particularly the machine-gun nests and the barbed wire protecting them. But most of the artillery used in the Great War fired shells with a relatively flat trajectory.[1] Shells hit the ground at an angle. They made a horrendous, deafening noise, threw a great deal of earth into the air, and certainly frightened and often traumatized soldiers on the battlefield. But particularly on the German side, defenders could emerge from deep dugouts with surprising speed, to deliver deadly machine-gun and rifle fire. Worse, the attacking barrage jostled barbed wire more often than it destroyed it, and turned no man's land into a sea of mud. Wire not destroyed by artillery had to be cut by exposed infantry. Conventional wisdom before 1918 had it that the barrage should begin days before the infantry assault – in the case of the offensive along the Somme in 1916, a full week. This gave the enemy plenty of time to bring up reinforcements. Military leaders, not just in France but throughout Europe, believed the key to victory lay simply in increasing the amount of force deployed by the attackers – in other words, more guns, more shells, and more men. This contributed to the "totalization" of the war, not just on the battlefield, but also in the war economies mobilized to support it.

As in Britain, some in France advocated circumventing the stalemate on the Western Front by an "eastern strategy." Such a strategy involved invading the Balkans through Greece, to help Serbia and threaten Germany's relatively weak allies, Austria-Hungary and Bulgaria. In the summer of 1915, some French strategists also worried that the British and Dominion attempt to force the straits of the Dardanelles at Gallipoli could prove successful, and thus increase British influence in the Mediterranean. The wartime alliance did not erase prewar rivalries.

In the event, Gallipoli turned out to be one of the great Allied disasters of the war, and concerns about increased British influence in the region

---

[1] Trench mortars, which came into wide use after 1916, had a much more steep trajectory, and could send shells directly into enemy trenches. But the higher the trajectory, the shorter the range. To the end of the war, most firepower on both sides came from conventional artillery.

proved unfounded. In September 1915, France landed a small force at Salonika in technically neutral Greece. Joffre had stridently opposed the enterprise. He plotted to send General Maurice Sarrail there, as a form of exile. Sarrail had been an ardent Dreyfusard, whose career flourished thanks to excellent political connections on the Republican Left. Sarrail and his patrons (notably Premier Aristide Briand) advocated sending a huge force to Salonika of up to 700,000 French and British soldiers. Ultimately, Joffre accepted sending 150,000 Allied troops, four French and five British divisions, joined by another 150,000 Serbians. Joffre's power over French strategy was never absolute, even at his zenith. The Balkan strategy was probably never a good idea, and little came of it before the closing weeks of the war in 1918. The Balkans, then as now, combined rough terrain with venomous ethnic hatreds – an unpromising part of Europe to seek an Allied victory. Salonika functioned mostly as a huge internment camp for Allied soldiers until the very end of the war.

But on the Western Front, the French found themselves caught between an irresistible force, the desire of the national community to expel the invader and win the war, and an immovable object, the trench system and the stalemated war that resulted from it. The General Staff insisted on huge assaults with virtually no chance of strategic success, and tried to compensate for the many imponderables of such attacks with scrupulous and absurdly detailed forecasts of timing, troop movements, and objectives. As one offensive after another failed, French generals changed the terms they used to describe just how they were winning the war. The year 1915 began with great hopes. A personality cult had developed around the phlegmatic and portly "Papa" Joffre, now hailed as the greatest French military genius since Napoleon for effecting the "miracle of the Marne." Joffre promised to complete the miracle by achieving a *percée*, a rupture of the German position in France. But when this failed to occur despite two major offensives, in the Spring of 1915 in the Artois and in the Fall in the Champagne region, he insisted that France was still winning the war, through *grignotage*, "nibbling" of the enemy forces through attrition. The Germans themselves applied the strategy of *grignotage* beginning in February 1916, by attacking at Verdun, a battle that would last in one form or another for nearly ten months. At Verdun, the French came to equate victory with the verb *tenir*, to "hold on."

In the spring of 1915, Joffre believed he had found a place where a *percée* of the German position on the Western Front could be exploited strategically, along the Vimy Ridge in the Artois. This meant attacking at an enemy strong point, since the Germans had chosen carefully where to end their retreat back in September 1914. But Joffre and many of the soldiers he commanded remained confident that the French army could prevail in the first great "over the top" offensive against entrenched German positions. The French offensive in the Artois lasted from May 9 to June 18, 1915. "All the trenches were full," remembered Roland Dorgelès of the 39th Infantry Regiment, writing about the beginning of the Artois offensive in his best-selling novel *Les Croix de bois* (Wooden Crosses, 1919). "To feel yourself that close, side by side, with hundreds, thousands, you felt a vicious confidence. Bold or resigned, you were no more than one grain of this great human mass. The army, that morning, had victory in its soul."

The French never came close to a *percée* of the German position. Beyond this strategic non-result, what actually happened in the Artois offensive, and in most of the great attacks of the Great War, does not exactly match the literary image best known through Erich Marie Remarque's *All Quiet on the Western Front* (1929). Eighty years of literary tradition have handed down an image of soldiers of the Great War as lambs sent in the greatest innocence into slaughter, with the story more or less ending there. Certainly in the Artois, French soldiers had some agency of their own. They left the trenches, in great fear and more or less in good faith and simply stopped moving forward when they perceived their efforts as no longer likely to result in anything but their complete massacre. The command structure then found itself obligated to accept results essentially determined in the field as adequate, and to reconstruct continued stalemate into victory.

But thousands died all the same. Even allowing for a generous interpretation of the territory gained, the 10th Army, the key French army involved in the offensive, took more than 4,000 casualties (men killed, wounded, or missing) for every square kilometer gained. The French high command pronounced itself satisfied with these gains, and insisted that huge numbers of Germans had been killed or wounded, though no one on the Allied side had any meaningful way to determine this at the time. "How sad is this panorama of victory," wrote Dorgelès wryly. "The fog still hides certain corners under its winding sheet, and I can no longer recognize anything on this vast map of torn-up earth."

Confusion lay at the heart of the second French offensive in the Artois, in September and October 1915 – not just in its outcome, but even in its intention. The specific plans called attacks at both ends of the huge bulge into France seized by the Germans in 1914 – a French-British attack in the Artois, coordinated with a French attack in the Champagne. But beyond these broad goals, senior French commanders no longer agreed whether the objective was a *percée* or *grignotage*. Foch directed the attacks in the Artois, and advocated simply attrition, until the French had such means that they could push back the Germans in methodical, sustained attacks. But General Edouard de Currières de Castelnau (a devout, conservative Catholic known to his enemies as the "booted Capuchin") still believed in the *percée*. In the event, Joffre let each commander go his own way, though in the debate he leaned toward de Castelnau. Alliance politics figured heavily in the offensive. The British army, bloodied that summer at Gallipoli, would be kept active by helping the French, while their mass volunteer armies (named the "Kitchener Armies," after War Minister Lord Kitchener) prepared for action in 1916. Even more important, a major offensive on the Western Front would assist the hard-pressed Russians, who had been defeated in Habsburg Galicia and much of Russian Poland in the summer of 1915.

The results proved as challenging to construe as victory as those in the spring. The French achieved neither a *percée*, nor *grignotage* at a level that would end the war anytime soon. De Castelnau persisted in the Champagne offensive long after it became clear that no rupture would take place. The French 10th Army, again attacking in the Artois, would suffer nearly 2,700 casualties per square kilometer gained, again without significantly weakening the German position. The British attacking at Loos would suffer more than twice the number of casualties as the Germans. Robert Desaubliaux, a cavalry sergeant who had volunteered to join the 129th Infantry Regiment, wrote of the fall attacks: "This war will finish like this battle. There will be neither victory nor defeat. The two parties will both claim themselves the victors, and both will be the vanquished."[2]

In February 1916, the Germans began their nearly ten-month siege of the collection of forts around the city of Verdun, their grand attempt at a strategy of attrition. General Erich von Falkenhayn, who replaced Moltke as head of the German armies in September 1914, saw an offensive at Verdun as an alternative to the stalemate of space that had emerged on the Eastern Front, where territorial gains that would have been decisive in the West never seemed to bring Russia closer to defeat. Falkenhayn reasoned that following a decisive battle of attrition, France would sue for peace and Britain would leave the European continent for good. Russia would not last long after victory in the West, and German security, equated with German hegemony, would at long last become accomplished.

The key lay in setting a trap for the French, some objective the French would feel obligated to defend to the last man. Verdun was located in a small piece of Lorraine kept by the French after 1870. After 1918, much was made of Verdun as a site of ancient conflict between Gaul and Teuton. Indeed, a treaty had been signed there in 843, dividing up Charlemagne's empire into what one day would become France and

---

[2] Robert Desaubliaux, *La Ruée: étapes d'un combattant* (Paris: Bloud & Gay, 1919), p. 197.

Germany. But Verdun assumed its place in the pantheon of national symbolism *because* of the battle of 1916. After 1914, Verdun posed a peculiar salient in the southern sector of the French line, and could be bombarded around a wide perimeter by German artillery. It remained in French hands in 1914 only because General Sarrail had defied orders from Joffre to retreat. Verdun had been generally a quiet sector since that time, its heavy artillery nearly stripped to shore up the French armies to the north. Colonel Émile Driant, a deputy serving in the army, used his political connections to have a stern memo sent by War Minister General Joseph Gallieni in December 1915 to warn Joffre of French weakness in the Verdun sector. Joffre's annoyance at what he saw as political interference (by a colonel supposedly his subordinate, no less) only hardened his resistance to reinforcing Verdun, which he believed could only happen at the expense of his own plans for 1916, a major offensive alongside the British at the Somme. Driant's death on the first day of fighting at Verdun rendered him a martyr as well as a prophet.

While the fighting was not entirely continuous, Verdun was the longest battle of the Great War – from late-February to mid-December 1916. As in August 1914, fortune at first favored the German armies. The attack, under the direction of Crown Prince Wilhelm, began on February 21 after only an eight-hour artillery barrage. The huge fort at Douaumont, one of the key positions, fell with relatively little fight on February 25. Joffre originally intended to retreat from the entire Verdun salient. But Premier Aristide Briand knew well the political consequences of surrendering yet more of France, above all in what remained of French Lorraine. He took the extreme measure of having Joffre awakened in the middle of the night, to inform him that he would be sacked if he tried to abandon Verdun. Joffre changed his mind, as the French took the bait offered by Falkenhayn. General Philippe Pétain, allegedly tracked down while enjoying himself with a prostitute in a hotel near the Gare du Nord in Paris, was summoned on February 26 to take command of the 2nd Army, in charge of the defense of Verdun. He organized a new line of defense, supplied by nearly 4,000 trucks along a road eventually designated the *Voie sacrée* (sacred way). Pétain used a system called *Noria*, of rotating troops in and out of the front lines every few days, so that units could be moved out of what quickly became known as "the furnace" before they were completely destroyed. The *Noria* system, combined with the duration of the siege, made Verdun an exceptionally generalized experience throughout the French army. Of the eighty-five divisions in the French army in 1916, fully seventy served at Verdun at some point in the battle.

On April 9, after the French repulsed a particularly ferocious series of attacks, Pétain issued his famous order of the day, which concluded

"*Courage, on les aura!* (Courage, we shall have them!)" But the most grim days of the defense of Verdun were still to come. A quixotic effort on the part of the 5th Division to retake Douaumont failed completely, and over 40 percent of the division became casualties. In June, the Germans took the fort at Vaux, and by July threatened to break through the whole French position through Souville. At about this time, General Robert Nivelle included in an order of the day the other great phrase made at Verdun, "*Ils ne passeront pas!* [They shall not pass!]" The French ultimately prevailed, in part because the Germans needed to reinforce their positions against the Allied offensive along the Somme. At about the same time, the Germans concluded that *grignotage* worked no better for them in 1916 than it had for the French in 1915. A series of French counterattacks beginning in October 1916 regained the most critical parts of the French position. But only in 1918 would the French, attacking with the Americans, regain the position of February 1916. Through the course of the battle the village of Fleury changed hands sixteen times. The French suffered nearly 380,000 casualties, the Germans some 330,000. *Grignotage* came to look like an early version of mutually assured destruction, put into practice.

The Allied offensive along the Somme began on July 1, 1916 and ground on in one form or another until November. The Somme was in many respects the "greatest" battle of the Great War. Some four million men from Britain, France, their empires, and Germany fought along a front of only forty kilometers. Yet the Somme is most often associated with the British, and most particularly with the 60,000 British and Commonwealth soldiers who became casualties on the first day. But France actually contributed about one third of the divisions used in the offensive. The British, flush with the new "Kitchener" divisions, continued to hope for a *percée*, a hope supported but not shared by the French. The Somme proved another huge and costly battle of *grignotage*. The British suffered some 420,000 casualties, the Germans about 400,000. The French suffered about 340,000 – nearly as many as at Verdun. The Allies never got close to a rupture of the German lines. The Somme achieved only secondary status in French national memory, perhaps because it was an "offensive" rather than a "defensive" battle, perhaps more likely because it was an Allied rather than a French undertaking.

For the French, 1916 would remain the year of Verdun, which thereafter became the supreme symbol of French sacrifice and of the enmity between France and Germany. It was no coincidence that President François Mitterrand and Chancellor Helmut Kohl would meet at Verdun in 1984 to join hands and honor the dead, to commemorate the battle and to salute the friendship that had grown up between the old enemies after World War II. Historians have written about the Battle of Verdun as a turning point not just in the history of the Great War, but in the history of France. Some have argued that Verdun showed the unshakable nature of French resistance. The national community that won by holding on at Verdun could withstand anything – victory in 1918, the bitter peace that followed, defeat in 1940, and rule thereafter from Vichy, a regime that collaborated with the Nazis and was led by none other than the hero of Verdun, Philippe Pétain. To other historians, Verdun proved a classic pyrrhic victory, a prophecy of what would follow. Events proceeded in a straight line of causation from the alleged decay of the French army after 1916, to the decay of the Third Republic in the interwar years, to the collapse of first the army and then the Republic in 1940. According to this interpretation, it was only fitting that Pétain should lead at Vichy, and preside over a regime he had unintentionally prefigured by his stand at Verdun.

But in the short term, the failed war of attrition in 1915 and 1916 on both sides meant that the French no longer had a strategy worthy of the name. "Victory," which meant breaking through the German lines at the beginning of 1915, meant only killing Germans by the end of that year. By the end of 1916, "victory" meant simply being able to hold on. Stalemate and failing to lose became equated with winning. Along the way, the distinction largely disappeared between the offense and the defense. Defending at Verdun meant attacking for months on end with horrendous casualties to regain pieces of the position that lacked real strategic significance. The Allies could not win the war on the Western Front, and the useless adventures at Gallipoli and Salonika showed that they could not win it anywhere else. The French in 1917 would turn to a new military commander, General Robert Nivelle, in a desperate attempt to resolve their strategic muddle.

The face of battle

Military history has gradually become less oriented toward a didactic explanation of why battles are won and lost and more oriented toward examining armies as social and cultural organisms that shape and are shaped by the societies that raise them. The four-year stalemate should not obscure significant changes that took place in the French army across that period. The army that went to war in August 1914 had deep roots in the nineteenth century. Infantry still made up two-thirds of the army. Railroads had long played a crucial role in war plans in transporting troops to the front, but in 1914, trucks and other motor vehicles played virtually no role at all. Soldiers moved on foot, carrying their shelter and equipment on their backs, much as they had done in the middle of the nineteenth century. Soldiers in the earlier period required only about eight kilos per day of supplies. But over the course of the Great War, uniforms and equipment had been entirely transformed to suit trench warfare. During 1915, the famous blue-gray *horizon bleu* (horizon blue), further darkened by omnipresent mud, replaced the extremely impractical red trousers. By the end of the war, only about half of the French army comprised infantrymen, though infantry continued to play the determining role on the ground. The development of other branches (artillery, armored units, aviation, administration, logistics) had transformed the make-up of the army. The needs of a vastly more complex army transformed logistics. By 1918, during a period of attack the army required thirty kilos per man per day at the front. The changes in the soldiers' war and in the civilians' war proceeded in tandem.

New approaches to military history also employ a different approach to violence and danger on the battlefield. John Keegan's path-breaking book *The Face of Battle* (1976) called for writing military history from the point of the view of those at physical risk rather than that of those who commanded them. Such an approach implies an examination of the specific forms of weapons in use on the battlefield, of how soldiers responded to them, and of how the death and damage done to human bodies accomplished by these weapons shaped soldiers' experiences. The physical perils faced by French soldiers in the Great War closely resembled those of their allies and their enemies, though even the world of trenches had national variants. At the heart of danger in the trenches lay unprecedented effectiveness of the two most deadly forms of weapons in the Great War, artillery and machine-guns.

By 1914, artillery had become ten times more deadly in its explosive power, its range, and its accuracy, than at the beginning of the nineteenth century. Artillery inflicted more than two-thirds of wounds in the Great War, compared to only one-third as recently as the Franco-Prussian War. Artillery bombardment therefore constituted by far the worst trial that combatants had to endure. Shells also posed the most constant threat, not just before major attacks but in sporadic harassing bombardments between them, and during rotations in the front lines. Accidental or "friendly" fire was by no means rare, given chronically uncertain communications between artillery and infantry. "Half of our casualties," wrote Charles Delvert in *Histoire d'une compagnie* (1918), "were the deeds of the French artillery. The 'glorious 75 [mm gun].' Bravo!" Before an offensive, shelling could continue uninterrupted for several days and nights. At Verdun, approximately one shell fell on each square meter of front. In such extreme circumstances, the bombardment destroyed all tactical links within units. The shelling cut soldiers off from their leaders, reducing units to tiny groups, isolating individuals, and leaving them deprived of all forms of support.

At its worst, shelling produced a feeling of total helplessness among soldiers, who could only wait until it stopped. Often, cessation of the bombardment meant an impending attack from enemy infantry. Even in an "ordinary" barrage, it became impossible to move or to sleep. Eating and drinking became difficult, for food no longer reached the front lines. Thirst became one of the best-remembered tortures of life at the front. Evacuation of the wounded became impossible. The trench system offered only limited protection, and essentially none at all against the small steel balls from shells exploding above the ground (shrapnel), or direct hits. Parapets were designed principally to offer cover for rifle fire, and provided inadequate protection if a shell landed nearby. The shelters and saps dug by the soldiers rarely survived a direct or near-direct hit from heavy-caliber percussion-fuse shells, unless they were lined with concrete or dug to great depth. And of course, the deeper the trench or dugout, the greater the chance that an explosion could bury the occupants alive. Veteran and literary critic Jean Norton Cru told an audience at Williams College in 1922 that "no section of trench, long or short, can be held, if the enemy chooses to use enough artillery against it . . . There is a fatality about it which never existed in past military history."

For the soldiers in the trenches, the only measures they could take to protect themselves were reactive rather than active. Combatants developed an increasingly professionalized sense of how to read a bombardment by listening to it. As the shells approached, soldiers could often identify their direction, caliber, and probable point of impact, often in time to take cover accordingly. But sometimes, soldiers could take only the simplest measures, such as clinging to the parapet so as to expose to the shell burst the smallest possible body surface, or even more simply, just flinging themselves to the ground.

Machine-guns in the Great War remained relatively immobile, and hence were used primarily as defensive weapons. "Our machine-gun is a delicate instrument," advised 10th Infantry Brigade commander Colonel Viennot in July 1915, "which you must recognize has a completely French mentality. She possesses a temperament unique to herself. She must be treated with a certain concern, and unlike the German machine-gun, cannot support brutal treatment." But the firepower of machine-guns – up to 600 rounds per minute with a 180-degree field of fire – proved deadly serious. Even the most dispersed formations of attacking infantry could rarely escape machine-gun fire. Machine-guns were also clearly industrialized weapons, whose methodical factory-like sound terrified attackers. "Clac clac clac clac clac, there was no mistake . . .," wrote Jean Bernier in

Plate 3. Exploded shell. Reprinted with the permission of the Historial de la Grande Guerre.

La Percée (1919), a novel culminating in the death of the main protagonist in a doomed infantry assault. "Next two, three, four machine guns opened fire with the identical German cadence. They were mixing together, overlapping, weaving an abominable fear." Consequently, destroying enemy machine-guns became the primary artillery objective before the infantry assault. As the war continued, infantry became more adroit at destroying machine-guns, thanks to tactical innovation, improved use of the famous Lebel rifle, and new forms of ammunition, particularly grenades, which acquired a growing importance in trench warfare. Barbed wire proved a more intractable problem, never really resolved until tanks became more practical after 1918. Any soldier's nightmares included being mortally wounded and caught on enemy barbed wire, dying there exposed and alone.

Theoretically, the use of poison gas had been outlawed by the Hague Conventions of 1899 and 1907. But from 1915 on, gas added a further element to the horrors of the battlefield, one particularly associated with the Great War. Contrary to conventional wisdom, the French and not the Germans first used gas, in experiments with tear gas in early 1915. The Germans first used chlorine gas as a lethal weapon on April 22, 1915, in the form of thousands of gas bottles opened along a front of eight kilometers at Ypres. Thereafter, several other types of gas came into use – phosgene in 1916, followed by the most notorious gas of the Great War, mustard gas, or Yprite, in 1917. At the same time, the means of delivering the gas changed from containers simply opened into the prevailing wind to gas artillery shells, which proved much more reliable. By 1918, one quarter of the shells fired by the artillery contained poison gas. However, chemical warfare in the Great War took the same basic course as other forms – for most of the war, the defense proved stronger than the offense. Increasingly sophisticated gas masks limited casualties due to gas to a mere 1 per cent of total losses.

But poison gas had a far greater cultural impact than the number of casualties suggests, both on the combatants and on the historical image of the Great War. The author of an article in the trench newspaper *Le Filon* wrote in 1917: "With the wave [of gas], death enveloped us, it impregnated our clothes and our blankets, it killed everything around us that lived, that breathed...."[3] Simply breathing while wearing a mask proved so difficult that it became a form of agony in itself, above all in moments of physical exertion. By preventing comrades from recognizing each other and sometimes even from speaking, the use of gas masks

---

[3] Trench newspapers were written by and for combatants at the front, and provide some of the most important sources in understanding daily life in the trenches.

combined physical danger with a total anonymity and alienation, the nadir of battlefield experience. Poison gas also created intense memories because it introduced a new way to die in war, by suffocation. This sort of death overthrew a long tradition in Western warfare, which linked death on the battlefield to the loss of blood.

The Germans appreciated the superiority of the defense earlier and more completely than the French. Of course, the Germans understood the strategic importance of occupying such a vast amount of enemy territory on the Western Front, and from the beginning settled in for a long war. They employed remarkable ingenuity in the task of making life in their trench networks as secure as possible and with the least possible discomfort. They employed the most advanced building and mining techniques to create deep shelters, often lined with concrete, some with ventilation and heating systems – amenities unheard of on the French side.

The French, in contrast and over-optimistically, saw the descent into trench warfare as a transitional necessity, imposed by an almost cowardly refusal on the part of the enemy to meet in open country. Consequently, the French maintained their trenches as horrible places to live, particularly in the long winters and protracted periods of rain that characterize the climate of northeastern France. Rain became an acute and chronic form of torture for the French infantry, as it turned the trenches into channels of mud. The trench newspaper *Le Bochophage* in March 1917 described how each soldier faced mud as a personal enemy: "It throws its poisonous slobber out at him, closes around him, buries him . . . For men die of mud, as they die of bullets, but more horribly. Mud is where men sink and – what is worse – where their souls sink." Philippe Barrès (the son of Maurice Barrès) recalled advice on trying to sleep in the trenches in the rain in *La Guerre à vingt ans* (War at Twenty-years Old, 1924): "Don't stretch your legs outside your niche, because it's raining; don't raise your eyes, because the water will seep into them; don't budge your arms, because the freezing water will get into your blanket; but shiver because the cold will make you numb. Don't sleep."

Other chronic afflictions included omnipresent vermin (lice, fleas, and especially rats), very uncertain sanitary conditions, lack of sleep, wretched food (or complete lack of it), and the general disruption of any sense of time and space. Sporadic combat in the form of harassing artillery and machine-gun fire, and work details in maintaining the trenches made it difficult to establish regular sleep patterns in the trenches. Soldiers in the trenches suffered a high death rate beyond casualties inflicted by the enemy. The French army recorded five million cases of sickness during four years of war, though this figure includes soldiers reported ill on several occasions.

Although pitched battle remained a relatively rare event in soldiers' lives, it held a unique form of terror in their minds, perfectly expressed by the French word *échafaud*, or scaffold. Literally referring to the ladders set out along the trenches to enable the men to climb over the parapet, the term also clearly spoke of a fear of combat as a form of execution. Men prepared for death before an attack in various ways. Believers prayed, often intensely. Soldiers wrote final letters to their families, letters to be kept with them or given to a close friend to be sent "in case of misfortune." They sought assurance that their families could learn of their death by some means other than the famously sterile official telegram. Comrades exchanged promises to go find the body of whomever was killed in no man's land. Some soldiers envisaged their death in grisly detail. Guy Hallé wrote in *Là-bas avec ceux qui souffrent* (Out There, with Those who Suffer, 1917) of his thoughts just before his company attacked at Verdun: "There will be a huge flame, a cry, then I will have smashed legs, my chest all torn up and bloody, eyes open wide and my face completely white." Others pointedly refused to imagine their death, or so they claimed. In *La Guerre 14–18: Tragédie Bouffe* (The War of 14–18, Comic Tragedy, 1964), René Arnaud wrote that at Verdun: "Even though death whirled all around me, I felt in myself the will, the certitude of surviving."

Many accounts by combatants simply stop at the moment the attackers climb out of their trenches, suggesting that the experience of crossing no man's land resists verbal representation, no matter how many years after the fact. Accounts that do describe this experience report the immediate disappearance of fear once soldiers climbed over the parapet. But this feeling does not appear to have come from courage as conventionally conceived, as it existed alongside a feeling of nakedness, and a sense of the unreal appearance of bodies that dropped during the race forward, or effectively folding in two, so as to offer the smallest possible target for the bullets. Acute stress during the advance heightened all the senses: hence the sensitivity to the sound, the dull thud, of bullets penetrating the flesh of those hit nearby.

It often happened that the enemy barbed wire had not been destroyed, and that enemy fire became so intense that retreating became as dangerous as advancing or staying still. In such situations, soldiers could only burrow down in a hole and wait for nightfall before trying to return to their own lines. Even taking the enemy position did not necessarily mean safety, or the end of the engagement. The trench system was so complex that it was often difficult to tell what had been taken and what had not. Attackers also had to anticipate the inevitable counterattack. Those who had survived the ordeal of an attack "over the top" of the trenches have described the unbelievable joy they experienced in accomplishing the simplest actions of life, the exaltation of feeling one's body intact when death had brushed so close against it. In this peculiar way, survival could serve to legitimize the war. Dorgelès, hardly one to glorify fighting in the Great War, wrote in *Les Croix de bois* of an episode in which a general, military band in tow, came to salute his regiment after a modestly successful attack in the Artois in 1915: "The rousing music made us drunk, and seemed to take us into a Sunday holiday. We had advanced, ardor in our guts, our tears against our pride as male conquerors."

Generally speaking, the terror of the front line remained anonymous. Since artillery inflicted most of the casualties, death and mutilation originated far from the afflicted bodies. Even in no man's land and in the first line of trenches, soldiers rarely knew who they killed, or who killed them. Soldiers' accounts from all countries emphasized the impersonal character of mass death, a feeling of overwhelming personal insignificance on the battlefield. In a world of violence in which death came from metal and explosives sent from hundreds or thousands of meters away, the soldier's skill and training counted for little. Once a soldier learned and internalized essential measures of protection and prudence, only chance good fortune offered escape from mutilation or death.

Yet battle did not always take place among groups of men who never saw each other. More direct forms of combat also existed, such as sniper fire or grenade duels. And there might be hand-to-hand fighting, such as during surprise raids or in night patrols, or when a trench was captured before all its occupants could escape. At such times, the *nettoyeurs des tranchées*, or "mopping up" crews would come into action. Paradoxically, surrender also offered opportunities for individualized violence. The Tirailleurs Sénégalais, black African light infantry, had a particular reputation for not taking prisoners, though there is little evidence they deserved this reputation any more than white troops. Because it was often difficult to tell which parts of a position had been taken and which remained in enemy hands, surrender became a difficult and high-risk procedure. Soldiers who threw down their weapons in an attempt to surrender invited their own execution. Combatants often killed unarmed men, either as a precaution or as a cruel protest against the omnipresent and impersonal violence that had governed them and had threatened their lives.

When violence became personal at such moments of absolute brutality, regulation weaponry proved of little use. Rifles and bayonets, if used at all, became clubs and knives, joined by picks, hand knives, any physical object at hand that could harm the enemy. War itself rests on the notion, and perhaps the fiction, that killing is not always murder. Personal combat strained this notion to the breaking point. The brutality of the battlefield led soldiers to commit acts they wished to forget after the war. Not surprisingly, few soldiers wrote about episodes of cruelty or personal combat. One who did was the avant-garde poet and novelist Blaise Cendrars, a Swiss national who fought in the French Foreign Legion. In *J'ai tué* (I Have Killed, 1919), he described an individual encounter with a German in which Cendrars's only weapon was a knife: "I jumped on my antagonist. I gave him a terrible swipe. The head was nearly cut off. I killed the Boche. I was more nimble and quick than he was. More direct. I struck first. I have the sense of reality, me, a poet. I have acted. I have killed. Like one who wishes to live."

Never before the Great War had soldiers seen such damage to their friends' bodies or to their own. This mass corporeal destruction, caused particularly by shell explosions, effected an anthropological transformation, a fundamental and terrifying change in the ways soldiers, doctors, and nurses imagined physicality. Dr. Joseph Vassal, a physician in the colonial army, described an evacuation of wounded colonial soldiers in the Dardanelles in 1915: "All human miseries were brought together on this cluster of soldiers laid out on the bridge of the ship. How much longer can he moan, this poor little thing whose skull has a bullet furrowed into it? When you raise his head, blood and brain matter run out, and he just groans. This one over here is very pale, he begs us not to move him; a shell fragment has gone through his chest. That one over there, a Senegalese, has had both legs broken. His comrade, a Black from Saint-Louis or Dakar, had a lot of his face blown off, and his chin is gone. From a bloody crater he emits unintelligible sounds while splashing us with blood."[4] Soldiers' accounts record no spectacles more poignant than foredoomed efforts to save horribly wounded comrades. In *Nous autres à Vauquois* (1918), André Pézard wrote of a soldier with a fractured skull and a huge wound that opened up his chest. The stretcher-bearers evacuated him to the cellar of a house, which was so crowded that they dropped him in the confusion: "The wounded man opened his enormous and hard eyes, unable to cry out," wrote Pézard. "We put a bandage on his head. As for the chest, we wasted ten individual bandages without being able to close his horrible wound. Moreover, his blood was no longer flowing. We let him die in peace, his eyes wide open and fixed, looking at the vault of blackened stone."

---

[4] Joseph Vassal, *Dardannelles, Serbie, Salonique: impressions et souvenirs de guerre (avril 1915–février 1916)* (Paris: Plon, 1916), p. 66.

Hundreds of thousands of such horrifying stories had tended to occlude substantial improvements in the medical services of the French army during the Great War. These services had been no better prepared for a major war in 1914 than had the French heavy artillery. In the first battles of the war, the military health service found itself overwhelmed by a flood of men far more numerous and far more seriously wounded than anticipated. Most had been evacuated to hospitals in the interior without having received in the field the immediate surgical care that they needed. But thereafter, infrastructure for evacuation and battlefield surgery, combining anesthetics and antiseptics, improved rapidly. Medical services in 1914–18 benefited from advances of the nineteenth century (such as the use of disinfected surgical instruments) and also from genuine scientific breakthroughs directly linked to the needs imposed by the new types of war wounds. Certain therapies underwent extraordinary advances, such as blood transfusion (invented before 1914 but not widespread until the end of the war), the excision of damaged tissue (introduced in 1915 and reducing risks of gangrene), and systematic exploration with X-rays. New techniques were developed for washing wounds with disinfectant fluids under the skin. While such treatments must have been excruciatingly painful, they proved highly effective. Amputations were much less common at the end of the war than at the beginning.

But the number and gravity of wounds inflicted overwhelmed considerable advances in the health services. The struggle of the medical staff against suffering and death proved wholly unequal, from the beginning of the war to the end. Despite medical innovation, mortality among those wounded was probably higher in the Great War than it had been at the beginning of the nineteenth century, because of new and extremely complicated wounds. Only 1 per cent of injuries were caused by a bayonet or knife. Most wounds came from shell explosions, shrapnel balls, or modern bullets (high-velocity, conical, and twisting, they lacerated flesh and burst bones). Never before had human bodies been so severely torn apart, even on the battlefield. Many wounds were life-threatening by nature, particularly those to the stomach, the abdomen, or the head.

Thousands of soldiers died of wounds not intrinsically fatal, because of delays in receiving proper medical care. Wounded soldiers could lie near death for hours or even days in no man's land. Even individual dressings that soldiers carried in their equipment were of use only if the wounded soldier could either dress his wound himself, or could find a helpful comrade. Soldiers generally had to get to first-aid posts by their own efforts, alone, or supported by a friend. Sometimes a tacit truce would take place in no man's land, to give the stretcher-bearers on both sides the chance to evacuate the wounded. But such truces were never more than tolerated by the command structure, and by definition were fragile and short. Even when stretcher-bearers were able to collect the wounded, taking them across the trench-lines was slow, uncertain, and dangerous. Aid posts, or casualty clearing stations, were immediately overwhelmed during attacks or bombardments. Evacuation behind the lines was often very slow, first aid sometimes disastrous.

The prognosis for severe facial wounds had been highly pessimistic at the beginning of the war, and soldiers wounded in the face sometimes had to wait for a week before receiving the first serious attention. But in thousands of cases, the human body proved able to withstand great disfigurement, in the face as elsewhere. As the war continued and military medicine became more efficient, many thousands of horribly wounded men survived. Those wounded in the face acquired their own name, the *gueules cassées* (the men with broken faces). Reconstructive surgery became an entirely new specialty, and included experimental procedures attempting to graft bone and cartilage. But such operations were not only painful but also potentially dangerous; many soldiers refused them and chose to live as the war had marked them. The *gueules cassées* found their own forms of sociability, both in hospitals and after the war. Hénriette Rémi volunteered as a nurse during the war. In *Hommes sans visage* (Men Without Faces, 1942) she recalled that some would circulate a mirror around the ward, and would remark wryly: "Still, I'm not as ugly as Y or Z," this sort of remark always coming from the most disfigured. *La Greffe générale*, a bi-monthly for soldiers wounded in the face, argued philosophically early in 1918: "In this life, everything passes, beauty is only a toy."[5] Veterans founded *Union des blessés de face* (the Union of Those Wounded in the Face) in 1921. As late as 1953, it still had over 10,000 members from the Great War. The *gueules cassées* lived on for many decades after the war, a source of reverence and horror for the national community, and a constant reminder of the cost of the conflict.

The brutality suffered and inflicted by soldiers of the war also produced millions of men psychologically wounded or mutilated. They too provided a living reminder of the war long after 1918, though often invisibly and in ways still poorly understood by historians. But the continuous violence marked individuals to their deepest core with mental damage, and was a major cause of hospitalization during the war. Some cases proved incurable, and victims had to spend the rest of their lives in an asylum.

---

[5] The title means literally "The General Graft." But *greffe* can also refer to something that shields or protects.

The English language developed a straightforward term for these forms of psychological trauma – shell-shock. The French tried several terms with obvious English cognates – such as *commotion cérébrale, congestion cérébrale, accidents nerveux.* Another French term was simply *obusite,* or "shell-itis." But the most general term became the one used most often, *commotion.* The French military command, like their counterparts elsewhere, only slowly appreciated the effects of psychological attrition. Survivors and the wounded deemed fit for combat would be returned to the front, again and again, sometimes to the same sectors where they had been wounded.

Traumatic shock in the Great War raised delicate issues, in France as elsewhere. Nothing, of course, has been more natural throughout history than fear on the battlefield. "I would very much like to know," remarked Marshal Ney, who had fought with Napoleon, "who is the total idiot who has never been afraid." Like other armies, the French army had formidable means of engineering the mastery of fear – small-group dynamics that exist in any army, courts martial, as well as appeals to the abstract but powerful attachment to the national community. But for some soldiers, wrote André Léri of the University of Paris medical faculty in *Commotions et Émotions de guerre* (1918), fear of the shells became "instinctive and irresistible, invincible. The soldiers can give only one explanation, invariably: 'It was stronger than I was.' " A medical explanation of involuntary physical resistance to the war emerged, though suspicions remained of cowardice or lack of patriotism.

Treatments for shell-shock in the French army had a profound effect on the subsequent history of military psychiatry that is still little recognized. French and the far better-known British practices differed greatly. The British tended to treat men far from the front, most often back in Britain. Officers such as the famous war writer Siegfried Sassoon were treated with the innovative techniques of Freudian "talking" therapy. Enlisted men more often received coercive treatments. Some, such as electric shocks applied to the ears, the neck, or the scrotum, must surely have recalled the brutality of the war itself. Certainly, such strategies had their advocates among French psychiatrists. But coercive treatments were relatively rare, in favor of more gentle measures, such as extended warm baths and plenty of regular rest. The French began treatment immediately, as close to the front lines as possible, so as to minimize separation between the afflicted soldier and his comrades. French techniques for treating shell-shock were adopted by the Americans in World War II, and became the foundation for treating nervous disorders on the battlefield thereafter. Yet it cannot be said that the French "solved" the problem of shell-shock, any more than the other protagonists. It remained a serious if manageable problem.

Psychiatrists seem to have made little attempt at follow-up of particular cases even during the war, let alone after 1918.

In short, the 8.4 million Frenchmen mobilized between 1914 and 1918 experienced a war without historical precedent, in the duration of various forms of combat, and in its brutality. Fully 16.8 percent of all the men France mobilized died in the Great War, the highest figure among the Great Powers. But this already high figure conceals even higher losses among particular groups. Among troops actually engaged in some form of fighting, 18 percent of the enlisted men died, and 22 percent of the officers. In the infantry proper, by far the most exposed branch of the army, one officer in three was killed and one soldier in four. The total number of wounded is likewise enormous, though more difficult to establish. The French army recorded 3,594,000 wounded, though this included many men wounded more than once. An estimated 40 percent of soldiers were wounded at least once, or 2,800,000 men out of 8.4 million mobilized. Half of these were wounded twice, and 100,000 three or four times. By the end of the war, the French government had officially designated some 300,000 men *mutilé de guerre* (or war disabled) and some 2 million men as suffering from at least a 10 percent disability.

Consent and the national community

Even as coldly presented as in the conventional forms of military history, a quantitative description of the French army in the Great War helps illuminate the predicament of soldiers in the trenches. More than the other powers fighting on the Western Front, the French operated under a "crisis of manpower" from the first months of the war. As we have seen, the fighting was by far the most deadly during the war of movement. Only in 1918 would casualty figures approach those of the beginning of the war. Before 1918, deaths in the French army actually decreased with each year of the war.[6] But the effect was cumulative, both in the trenches and in the country as a whole. As the number of dead approached one million in 1917, France seemed farther away from winning the war than ever. And the supply of additional manpower looked increasingly fixed. Of the 8.4 million men who would serve in the French army between 1914 and 1918, 7.3 million were already in uniform by January 1916. With essentially the entire eligible population serving, men could be added only through the new cohort of young men coming of military age – some

[6] The French army suffered some 430,000 deaths in 1915, 361,200 in 1916, and 189,200 in 1917. Calculated from Colonel Guinard, Jean-Claude Devos, and Jean Nicot, *Inventaire sommaire des archives de la guerre, Série N, 1872–1919* (Paris: Service Historique de l'Armée de Terre, 1975), p. 213.

250,000–300,000 men per year. This was fewer than the number of men killed in 1915 and 1916. The French army found it increasingly difficult simply to remain the same size.

The 8.4 million Frenchmen mobilized were never all in uniform at the same time. At the time of mobilization in August 1914 the army on active service consisted of three-year classes (1911, 1912, and 1913), conscripts aged between twenty-one and twenty-three. The mobilization of the reserves brought the number of troops under arms to the unprecedented figure of 3,400,000 men. During the four years of stalemated war, a smaller number, fewer than 2,500,000 men, held the Western Front. But the enormous casualties of the first battle of the war resulted in lowering the age at which young men were incorporated into the army, previously fixed at twenty-one. By September 1914, the high command called up the class of 1914 (twenty-year-olds), and by December the class of 1915 (nineteen-year-olds). Likewise, the high command called up early the classes of 1916, 1917, 1918, and 1919, thus incorporating into the army hundreds of thousands of men aged eighteen and nineteen. The cumulative losses also required a near-total mobilization of each class. The number of exemptions became so low that fully 95 percent of the class of 1917 was mobilized. The infantry absorbed the great majority of men (for example, 91 percent of the class of 1915). Consequently, most of the men who went over the top of the trenches were quite young, increasingly so as the war dragged on. But it was not only the young who served. Men were mobilized in the Territorials and in the Territorial Reserves up to the age of forty-seven. By the time of demobilization, the oldest French conscripts were fifty-one years old.

Even when phrased in the anonymous terms of demographic statistics, the scale of the hecatomb poses an important problem of historical interpretation. What kept so many men in the trenches under such deadly conditions for so long? Wartime propaganda provides a one-dimensional and simplistic explanation. According to this propaganda, the tenacity of the French soldier spoke simply of his unlimited and unquestioning patriotism, his unconditional willingness to sacrifice himself for his endangered France. But combatants often rejected this image during the war in letters, personal journals, and trench newspapers. This rejection became more profound in accounts written in the 1920s and in the 1930s, and evolved into a diametrically opposite explanation. Rather than out of patriotism, this view maintained soldiers "held on" for very limited reasons – loyalty to friends, force of habit, a spirit of resignation, an almost self-denigrating sense that soldiers had a thankless job to do that no one could or would refuse. They fought, this explanation claimed, without hatred for the enemy. Historians for many years largely accepted these explanations at face value, and have reproduced a discourse created by combatants after the war as exclusive arbiters of their own experience.

But today, an adequate explanation of soldiers' persistence in the trenches of the Great War must include an examination of soldiers' war culture, the broad-based system of representations through which soldiers shaped and were shaped by the war. For the question goes beyond simple *acceptance* of more than four years of suffering. The tenacity of the soldiers of France, and for that matter the soldiers of the other protagonist nations, rested on myriad forms of *consent* to an ordeal that, in effect, their nations imposed on them. Soldiers' war culture developed alongside civilian war culture, while remaining distinct from it. But like civilian war culture, soldiers' war culture was engineered only in part by the superstructures of authority. War culture proved so resilient precisely because its organization was primarily horizontal rather than vertical. Particularly for soldiers, war culture rooted itself in shared practices of representation, and in shared created experience.

To some extent, the basic solidarities of small groups of soldiers explains the endurance of the French army as a whole. The terrible conditions of trench warfare gave what sociologists call "primary groups" a fundamental significance. Binding men closely together, these tiny components made up the true structure of the large units. This configuration of relationships most affected the private soldiers. The duties and greater freedom of officers and non-commissioned officers, sometimes, though not always, placed them in connected but distinct social groups that separated them from their men.

Primary groups, to some extent, carried on their own war, often at the fringe of official authority. They maintained some autonomy within larger units, such as the company (up to 250 men), the battalion (up to 1,000 men) and the regiment (up to 3,000 men). As a rule, the French army did not cultivate the strong regional regimental identities so prominent in the British army and in some units of the German army. For the French, units as large as the regiment often proved too large, too abstract, and too remote to arouse a powerful feeling of belonging. Primary groups lived together according to their own rules and hierarchies, and could have their own rites of initiation. Roland Dorgelès in *Les Croix de bois* wrote of an episode in which Sulphart, a battle-hardened veteran, carefully inspected a white imitation-leather haversack brought to the front by a new recruit. He told the neophyte: "If you're afraid that sometimes the Germans won't be able to spot you easily enough, you could bring along a little flag and play a trumpet." But after the new comrade blushed appropriately, Sulphart took him under his wing and became his mentor.

Primary groups could not guarantee the survival of each member, but could have a real impact on any given soldier's odds. Contact, human warmth, and above all the assurance that if a man was wounded someone would come, no matter what, to find him in no man's land – these factors improved a soldier's chances of emerging alive from the ordeal of the war. In the pitiless world of trench warfare, an individual soldier without friends saw his chances of survival considerably diminished.

The primary group established itself around a very specific sociability, based on sharing. In *De Charleroi à Verdun dans l'infanterie* (1934) J. La Chausée wrote that men "formed small communities, in which it was not rare to see each one giving what he could, food, drink, tobacco, etc., and sometimes money." Meals taken together were the most frequent and the most important feature of this sociability. Sharing also concerned letters, photographs, newspapers, as well as the organization of duties, such as the rotation of guard duty, or going out on patrol at night under the barbed wire. Daily life in the trenches also required pooling the skills and aptitudes of each individual – clearing the ground, digging a stretch of trench, setting up a shelter. Even letter writing could become a group activity, particularly for soldiers literate or barely illiterate.

Primary groups also suffered bombardments and mounted assaults together. They promoted and sustained the memory of those who had left it, through wounds, a change of posting, or death in battle. A soldier on leave had a self-imposed duty to visit the family of a severely wounded or dead comrade. Even at the front, close comrades tried to provide for decent burials. Soldiers honored the graves of their dead whenever possible, particularly if they remained in the same sector. Even if not, they noted the site of the grave, and told the family of the final moments of the dead man, recounting the esteem in which they had held him. Through providing the first circle of mourning of the lost comrade, the primary group continually faced the most fundamental experiences of the war. Within the group, a whole series of cultural practices flourished that produced much of the evidence of soldiers' war culture – such as trench newspapers and hundreds of songs.

Soldiers who in civilian life would not even have exchanged words because of class barriers became soul mates in the trenches. Such intense bonds could efface or greatly diminish socioeconomic, generational, professional, or geographical differences, even differences in rank. In *Le Carnet sublime* (The Sublime Notebook, 1916), Paul Gsell described how Lieutenant Lucquiaud of the 68th Infantry Regiment died after having most of his face and part of his neck blown away by shrapnel. As his horrified men gathered around, his sergeant handed him his cheap notebook, in which he had written the names of his men and who he should contact if disaster befell them. Gasping for air and with a tortured hand, the lieutenant wrote "Thanks to all those who fought alongside me, you will tell my parents that I always did my duty." Just before dying he wrote, "500 francs for Poupard. 500 francs for the poor of my village." Gsell had the notebook deposited at the Musée de l'Armée in Paris, where it remains today.

There seems little doubt that fidelity to one's *copains*, to close comrades within the group, mattered more than the military justice system in enforcing obedience in the trenches. To be sure, some notorious examples existed of soldiers shot "for example." Perhaps the best-known case involved soldiers from the 336th Infantry Regiment, court martialed and shot for refusing to leave the trenches in a hopeless assault near the village of Souain in March 1915. The incident provided the inspiration for Humphrey Cobb's 1935 novel *Paths of Glory*, in turn best known through Stanley Kubrick's 1957 film. To this day, the French army itself has helped perpetuate the historically received image of ferocious military justice through granting only sporadic access to court martial records. But the research that exists suggests that after 1915 very few soldiers were shot for individual infractions, even recidivists. Nevertheless, desertions never became rampant in the French army, even after the cost of deserting had clearly become very low. Comrades saw to it that soldiers in their vast majority did not leave the trenches, that they returned from leave when they were supposed to, and even that relatively few sought safer jobs behind the lines. No greater insult existed than to be called an "*embusqué*," or shirker. So fierce a critic of the war as Corporal Louis Barthas was aware of this, when he wrote late in 1916 that "our commanders do not deceive themselves. They understand very well that it is not the flame of patriotism that inspires this spirit of sacrifice, it is only the spirit of bravado so as not to seem more chicken than your neighbor."

But it would be a mistake to explain the tenacity of the French army in the Great War solely by primary groups. Many intense friendships existed between individuals rather than among groups. Such friendships, homoerotic if seldom overtly homosexual, have helped hold armies together throughout history. Nor did individual or collective friendships eliminate a fundamental egotism hardened by the daily spectacle of suffering, a simple and fierce determination to save one's self. Nor were the primary groups among French soldiers of the Great War a wartime invention. Links of solidarity and mutual assistance had long played an important role in managing the precariousness of life in the countryside or in the industrial city. Primary groups, in short, do much to explain acceptance of the war among French soldiers. But we need more to explain the complex phenomenon of consent.

Much of the traditional historiography of the soldiers of the Great War emphasizes a simple dichotomy between coercion from above and resistance from below. This dichotomy has left aside the central issue of consent, and has made it difficult to read the myriad forms of evidence soldiers left behind to represent how they interpreted the meaning of the war, the defense of the nation, and their obligations to it. Soldiers never stopped expressing themselves in a vast range of ways. They sculpted blocks of earth, pieces of chalk, and wood. They carved hundreds of bas-reliefs in every cave and underground quarry used behind the front lines. They drew sketches by the thousand in letters and personal diaries. They painted on every material imaginable, on caps, shells, leaves from trees, and on animal bones. From the very metals produced to kill them, their friends, and their enemies, soldiers fashioned rings, crucifixes, miniature weapons, pendants, and cigarette lighters.

At a certain level, historians today might find this varied cultural production at once fascinating and disappointing in its conventionality. Soldiers' art used primarily conservative and conventional idioms rooted in prewar conformities. Some of this art spoke to less-revealed deprivations of the front, such as bas-reliefs carved into the chalk walls of some shelters showing nude women, usually with one hand over the pubic area. But more often, soldiers' art expressed conventionally acceptable material, that in one way or another showed how the war had become part and parcel of the way they perceived their world. Soldiers turned bullets and twisted metal into crosses and into sculptures of the Sacred Heart. They turned stone, wood, and metal into altars for celebrating the mass. They painted landscapes and pictures of the war, identical to those they could observe in the popular press every day. Many objects drew directly from life at the front, such as models of tanks and aircraft, regimental flags and insignias, pictures of the prestigious war cross medal, the *Croix de guerre*. Some presented calculations of the number of months or years spent at the front.

Soldiers also wrote a great deal, frequently under precarious conditions – often in pencil, on their knees, using their kit bags as writing pads. They created songs, poems, prayers, and kept personal diaries in daily contravention of (widely ignored) military regulations. These diaries made up a large part of the documentary basis for hundreds of literary works created by the veterans after the war. Others edited or illustrated the trench newspapers which began to appear as soon as the front stabilized at the end of 1914. Through various forms of expression, soldiers both recast and managed to retain some of their humanity.

Great literary works, on the other hand, appeared only slowly. "High culture" literature in France never played the role it did in Britain in

Plate 4. Crucifix made from munitions. Reprinted with the permission of the Historial de la Grande Guerre.

shaping the general understanding of combatants' experience. Bestsellers of the time, such as Dorgelès's *Les Croix de bois* and Henri Barbusse's *Le Feu* (Under Fire, 1914) were praised for their "realism." But critics did not really accept them as great literature even at the time, and much less so subsequently. Two of the greatest French novels of the war appeared only in the 1930s, Jules Romain's multivolume *Les Hommes de bonne volonté* (Men of Good Will, 1932) and Roger Martin du Gard's *L'Été 14* (Summer 1914, 1936). Both authors had served in the army, though neither in a combatant role. Some authors, such as Roger Vercel, the author of *Capitain Conan* (1934), only later found a way to examine his earlier fear, the absolute humiliation produced by the loss of human dignity and personal integrity as the war brutalized him. In the 1930s, some writers not only confessed cowardice and rejection of the war, but also transformed into "true" courage the rejection of the Great War and the national community that had fought it. Some of the most sophisticated and enduring French literature of the Great War was also some of the most negative, such as Jean Giono, *Le Grand Troupeau* (The Great Herd, 1931) and Louis-Fernand Céline, *Voyage au bout de la nuit* (Journey to the End of the Night, 1932). Another great war writer, less embittered by the war than Giono or Céline, was Blaise Cendrars, who lost an arm at the front in 1915. Cendrars wrote most of his best work on the Great War during and after World War II, perhaps most notably *La Main coupée* (The Severed Hand, 1946). Only many years after the conflict of 1914–18 could he fully articulate the enduring presence of having fought the war in his everyday life.

Combatants writing without literary aspirations only very rarely expressed trauma and even more rarely disgust with the war. Letters and trench newspapers remain the most important sources. Thanks to the success of the Third Republic in achieving nearly full literacy before 1914, the French soldiers could write to their families and friends on an unprecedented scale. Extended and unedited extracts from these letters, and often whole letters themselves, survive through the records of postal censorship, established by the end of 1915. Although trench newspapers were subject to censorship and were edited by a better-educated elite, their audience was soldiers themselves, rather than civilian society in the interior. They thus offer considerable insight into soldiers' collective fears and hopes. In addition, many lengthy and unbroken sets of correspondence survive published or unpublished, as do many personal diaries and notes. "Perfect" archival materials, in the sense of unmediated representations of truth, do not exist for French soldiers of the Great War. But taken together, these sources do make it possible to arrive at meaningful conclusions as to how soldiers arrived at and communicated their understanding of their world.

To some extent, we make a convenient abstraction in speaking about a generic "French soldier." By so doing we collapse many important differences. Even within the metropolitan army, for example, soldiers came from all classes, from farms, factories, and offices, and from regions where Breton or Provençal rather than French were the predominant languages. Even so, the war of the trenches was long enough and general enough to act as something of an experiential crucible, melting together to some extent their identities and experiences. Soldiers came to use a common language, understood and accepted by all, that mixed standard French with slang from the barracks and the trenches. This *argot des tranchées* largely overcame regional dialects or *patois*, which became impractical as regiments had less and less of a regional recruitment.

This phenomenon of "nationalization" also showed itself in changes in the eating habits of the French, people who take their food quite seriously. Changes in food consumption in the French countryside after the war could be directly attributed to how rural soldiers had eaten in the army. It bears keeping in mind that fully 70 percent of French soldiers had rural origins. Consumption of wine, tobacco, camembert cheese, and coffee all increased in the countryside after 1918. Likewise, rural people generally ate *viande salée* (meat soaked in salt) before the war. At the front, soldiers ate meat butchered nearby, known as *viande douce* ("soft" or fresh meat). After 1918, fresh meat became the norm in the countryside. In these subtle but revealing ways, the war changed the French through the experiences of daily life in the army.

In similar ways, soldiers' opinions, at least as expressed in the public sphere, became more uniform. For example, postal censorship records confirm that the minority of soldiers who remained faithful to the international workers' movement as it had existed before 1914 took care to hide their views from even their closest comrades, and to express it only in letters to their families. Of course, letters from soldiers from different backgrounds and with different military records operated in different semantic fields. But underneath the particular forms of language used lies a clear structuring of combatants' discourse around a few key words and fundamental ideas. In this way, the primary documents created by French soldiers of the Great War testify to a soldiers' war culture, representing and represented through a common experience of warfare.

One such commonality among soldiers, though more so for soldiers from the cities than from the countryside, was a sense of having been cut off from the rest of the national community. Trench newspapers were filled with complaints of civilians living in luxury in the interior, impervious to the suffering only 100 kilometers away. "One thing strikes the soldier on leave," observed a June 1917 article in *Tacatacteufteuf* (an

onomatopoeic title referring to the sound of a machine-gun) "is the inertia of the public, its indifference, its lack of discipline . . . In the interior,
there is the most appalling waste, the most incorrigible confusion." A
famous joke had two soldiers talking in the front line of trenches. One
assured the other that France will win the war, "*Pourvu qu'ils tiennent.* (As
long as they [the civilians] hold out.)" The fanciful and mindless versions
of life at the front that continued to find their way into civilian newspapers drew particular contempt, as did the journalists who wrote them.
Soldiers invented a term for such propaganda, *bourrage de crâne* (literally
"skull torture," most often translated into English as "eye wash"). One
resilient myth held that every soldier called his bayonet "Rosalie." In April
1915, *Le Poilu* responded: "The bayonet is called Rosalie only in a song
by Théodore Botrel, which nobody sings, and in the *Bulletin des Armées
de la République* [an official publication], which nobody reads." Such
resentment became a staple of soldiers' accounts published after the war
as well. Soldiers expressed a conviction in the insularity of their world, as
cut off from the very nation they risked their lives every day to defend.

But upon closer inspection, soldiers' writing reveals great conflict-
ing emotions about the interior. Despite frequent expressions of scorn
for civilians, most particularly for the archetypal civilian, the shirker or
embusqué, soldiers continued to hold a deep fascination with everything
that happened in the interior. It remained, after all, the world to which
they fought to return. Unsurprisingly, given the wholly masculine character of the world of the trenches, much of soldiers' fascination revolved
around women. Soldiers represented women in various and often contradictory ways – as unfaithful wives, as mothers and saviors, as licit and
illicit objects of desire. Various propaganda efforts, pointedly unsuccessful, were made to channel this desire into a higher birthrate (see Plate 5).
In each of their guises women had great symbolic power. Simply meeting
a woman in a rest camp could draw strong reactions. One soldier wrote
in *L'Horizon* in July 1917: "We had the exquisite impression of being free
men again, that the war was over, and the land cleansed of all the blood
spilled. There were only carefree hearts, brave young people dreaming
of peace and love." Beneath the surface of disdain for civilians lay a desperate need for recognition. "I assure you that we are at once very proud
and very humble," wrote a soldier in *Le Filon* (The Cushy Sector) in
August 1917, "and that these sentiments are not contradictory. We do
not ask that they [civilians] kiss our feet. But we would be content if,
when we return on leave for a few days of contact with civilian life, we
would encounter civility."

Moreover, we need to put the separation between soldiers and civilians in its proper perspective – and above all not to exaggerate it. To

Plate 5. Postcard: "The repeating rifle is good for repopulation." Reprinted with the permission of Marie-Monique Huss.

be sure, soldiers and civilians inhabited different worlds, unlike in 1870 when both shared in the defeat of France more or less simultaneously. But French soldiers fought in their own country, many less than a one-day train ride from the front. Significant contact remained between soldiers and their loved ones. The postal service delivered packages and above all letters to the front lines with remarkable speed and reliability. Leave, instituted after July 1915, became soldiers' most prized possession, and a crucial link in maintaining links with their lives beyond the war. A soldier writing in *Le Périscope* in 1917 described leave as "a link between the past and the future." A conversation both emotional and professional continued between the front and the interior. Soldiers passed on highly detailed instructions in professional, financial, and family matters, particularly soldiers in independent professions, such as farmers and shopkeepers. They did their best to manage their affairs from afar. They remained civilians in uniform, still tightly bound psychologically to civilian life. As we will show for 1917, and to the extent that we can measure it, "morale" evolved in parallel directions in the interior and at the front.

The very language used to represent the war joined the front and the interior. Soldiers avidly read civilian newspapers. In 1916, for example, postal censorship authorities identified seventeen events that led to extensive comment in soldiers' correspondence, with shifts in "morale" that closely paralleled those among civilians. Moreover, their exasperation at the *bourrage de crâne* notwithstanding, soldiers often used very recognizably journalistic language to describe a battle or the enemy, and to discuss the meaning of the war and their participation in it. Pacifist and bellicose sentiments expressed themselves in remarkably parallel ways. Less educated soldiers sometimes adhered to this rhetoric more closely than the more educated. The writings of the vast majority showed in one way or another the influence of a heroic ethic and a sense of duty assimilated over a long period of time. In part, this shared language between the interior and the front spoke to the massive project of primary and secondary education undertaken by the Third Republic. No one did more to create the preconditions of soldiers' and civilians' war culture than the schoolmasters of the Republic.

Soldiers' sense of duty to the *patrie*[7] was not entirely self-evident, much like their relationship to civilian society. On the surface, soldiers seemed only rarely to refer to mythical, eternal France. Most frequently, they

---

[7] *Patrie* is not an easy term to translate. It has less racist and exclusionary connotations than the German *Vaterland* or the English "Fatherland," though it has the same literal meaning. But it has more metaphysical and especially emotive connotations than most uses of "country" or "nation."

wrote about concerns of private life, both at the front and at home. They sometimes even expressed their willingness to continue the war in microscopic rather than macroscopic terms. As Louis-Jean Mairet put it in *Carnet d'un combattant* (A Combatant's Notebook, 1919) "the soldier of 1916 does not fight for Alsace, neither to ruin Germany, neither for the *patrie*. He fights out of honesty, out of habit, and because he has to." But upon closer inspection, such views, in their way, in fact speak to interiorized and deep patriotic sentiments. At the heart of how soldiers represented their commitment to the war lay a *defensive* patriotism, resulting in part simply from the geography of the war. To be sure, even the Germans spoke of the war in defensive terms, of the need to defend the *Vaterland* by conquering its enemies. But defending the country had a special meaning in France, where the Western Front ran across the national territory and left all or part of a number of departments (as well as Alsace and Lorraine) still in enemy hands.

The *patrie* existed in a highly material sense, in the physical territory of France. In 1914 and then again in 1918, German advances brought them to within fifty kilometers of Paris. But unlike in the motorized Blitzkrieg of 1940, the French army in the Great War had the time and the means to react decisively. Far from provoking a collapse in the morale of the French army, the German advances strengthened it. Soldiers felt shame and humiliation at the success of the invader – resulting in the exodus of civilian populations and the forced abandonment of cemeteries just behind the front line. In a fictional dialogue in *Le Sel de la terre* (The Salt of the Earth, 1924), Raymond Escholier has one soldier explain to another how he will come to interpret the war once peace comes: "Your brother lies there, you will say, your brothers, your friends, your dead sleep there coming from all of France. Your village cemetery has expanded. Now it occupies all of France, this France that from that moment on you could no longer dream of not defending. This land certainly is yours because those who belong to you lie there."

Indeed, we can speak without exaggeration of a sacralization of the national territory. Today, orders from the command structure to retake any ground lost even a highly localized attack seems irrational, and given the casualties certainly counterproductive. But French soldiers from generals to privates understood trench warfare as digging into the ground and defending the land centimeter by centimeter. Particularly for the more than two-thirds of the French infantry that had rural origins, the defense of the soil was never an abstraction. The defensive instinct likewise expressed itself far from metropolitan France – in the Dardanelles in 1915, in Salonika from 1916 on, and in Italy after late 1917. For French soldiers, the Great War was not strictly speaking a "world war" in the sense of the conflict of 1939–45. But they expressed themselves in terms of defending the *patrie* well beyond the national borders.

National and personal conceptions of duty met through the family. The sense of duty, so prominent in soldiers' vocabulary, spoke to this instinct to protect territory, women, and children. The importance of young men in the French army notwithstanding, many soldiers had families with children. Defending the home through holding the line in the trenches assumed paramount importance. Soldiers responded to highly dramatized stories of atrocities committed in occupied France with an acute awareness of the need to defend the interior against further enemy advance. The postal censorship authorities had no trouble identifying a particular combativeness in soldiers who came from the invaded regions, who the Germans had cut off from their families, and to whom the war had become a very specific war of liberation. Likewise, the theme of defending the home became prominent during the supreme defensive battle, the siege of Verdun in 1916. Children in particular assumed enormous significance, and became the ultimate justification of the war. The present generation sacrificed itself so that their children could live in a nation and a world freed from war. "I am a soldier but also father of a family," one soldier wrote to his children in 1916. "Verdun cannot make me forget all those who are dear to me. It is you who I was defending there, my dear ones."

Duty also had religious roots. For Catholic soldiers, that is to say, the vast majority, obligation to the nation merged easily with duty to God. The presence of many clergy at the front, both as chaplains and as comrades in the trenches, gave soldiers some measure of spiritual comfort. Christian soldiers also encouraged each other to see their ordeal as an imitation of Christ on the cross. The most militant believers saw themselves as the *miles Christi*, soldiers of Christ and active seekers of martyrdom. Catholics and Protestants read the war in scriptural terms, as "bountiful unto death," a sign of grace and election. In private writings published after the war, Lieutenant Etienne Derville expressed joy at getting wounded, because he believed it would serve God's own war aim, the re-Christianization of France.[8] Before entering the battle of the Somme in September 1916, he recorded a prayer in his journal in which he submerged his own identity into the divine plan: "I ask only, Dear Lord, that you give me the means of doing my duty, all of my duty. This matters not only for the good of my soul, but also that I may contribute my bit to your reign in the world."

---

[8] Etienne Derville, *Correspondance et notes (août 1914–juin 1918)* (Tourcoing: J. Duvivier, Éditeur, 1921), p. 63.

At least during the war, Germany and the Germans remained the "other," the enemy who invaded the *patrie* and who continued to fight for its ruin. Certainly, many veterans denied hostility toward the enemy after 1918 – particularly a strident and articulate elite of born-again pacifists. Some sought through pacifism a means of giving a higher meaning to the dreadful experience they had suffered, and also to renounce their own consent to the conflict between 1914 and 1918. Some even did so explicitly. In 1927, pacifist writer Paul Vaillant-Courturier was asked what he had learned from the war. He responded that he learned he could sleep soundly the night after his tank annihilated the better part of an entire German battalion.

Soldiers sometimes rejected violence explicitly, such as in tacit truces and, more rarely, in fraternizing across no man's land. The most famous incident occurred at Christmas 1914. At various locations throughout the French and British sectors, soldiers would sing Christmas carols across no man's land, then cross it to speak with the Germans, exchange small gifts with them, and even play football. On more frequent if less festive occasions, soldiers would refrain from firing across no man's land, or would fire only at certain times of the day, so that the enemy would know when to take cover. *La Saucisse* (The Sausage) reported an incident in June 1916 in which a German patrol with rifles slung over their shoulders and lost in the fog simply ran into a French outpost. The surprised French did nothing for a moment. A German noncommissioned officer simply said to them, in French. "*Triste guerre, messieurs! Triste guerre!* [Sad war, gentlemen! Sad war!] The French allowed the patrol simply to slip back, unharmed, into the fog. Such episodes were not uncommon in the Great War, as in most wars.

They do not, however, indicate that soldiers were at heart pacifists, or that hatred of the enemy was something imposed on them by their generals and politicians. Rather, such incidents show the fragility both of aggression and of amiability. The enemy conceived collectively and in the abstract could mean one thing, the specific fellow man in a German uniform less than a meter away quite another. Most racial hatred depends on seeing the "other" in aggregate. It is also crucial to keep in mind that combatants on both sides had much in common. Neither had much of an interest in violence for its own sake, particularly if that violence could have no practical impact even on a given tiny portion of the front. At some points, twenty meters or less of no man's land separated the two sides. Both Germans and Allies had an interest in restraining violence when there was nothing to be gained by it – and an interest in renewing violence when there was, as in pitched battle. French soldiers transformed easily enough the Germans who sang Christmas carols in 1914 into the enemy in the Artois a few months later, and perhaps more easily still at Verdun in 1916.

During the war, most French soldiers considered the Germans the "Boche," a term existing but little used before the war indicating a wooden head. "Boche" remains a racial epithet and indicates an aggressiveness not really there in the German term *Franzmann* or even in the British terms *Fritz* or *Jerry*. The Germans were barbarians, an enemy of unredeemable moral inferiority. French soldiers remembered not just the German atrocities committed in 1914, but the deliberate and systematic destruction carried out in the territory evacuated during the partial withdrawal to the Hindenburg Line in the spring of 1917. *L'Argonnaute* reported the reaction of soldiers from Normandy (a region famous for apples) marching forward into this territory to take up new positions: " 'Oh, the bastards! They cut down all the apple trees!' They will never forgive the Boche." The resilience of the French army, like the resilience of French society as a whole, cannot be separated from hatred of the enemy, a hatred constructed only in part by intellectuals and propagandists.

Likewise, if the war refined the barbarity of the Germans, it refined the civilized nature of the French. And like the image of the enemy as barbarians, the notion of the war as a terrible form of "civilizing" France and the world came from soldiers and civilians, from elites and common people. The more desperate the struggle became, the more important it became to see the war as something that would open the way to a higher civilization, a more just and fraternal world in which right triumphed over force – in short, a new Golden Age. Many soldiers believed in the Great War as the *Der des Der*, *(dernière des dernières*, or "last of the last"), as humanity's final conflict. Barbusse's *Le Feu* is perhaps the most famous expression of wartime millenarianism, described in remarkably ferocious language given how fervently he embraced pacifism after 1918. One character observed that "War must be killed, war must be killed in the belly of Germany!" Corporal Bertrand, the most admired (and most devoutly socialist) character in the novel, corrected him by arguing that the war is against capitalism rather than against a particular nation. Yet he recalled without regret that he personally killed three Germans, adding that "it was necessary, for the future's sake . . . The work of the future will be to wipe out the present, to wipe it out more than we can imagine, to wipe it out like something abominable and shameful."

As we will see, French soldiers by the thousands did resist the war, or at least appeared to, in the mutinies of 1917. But the intellectual challenge of the mutinies involves determining not why there was so much insubordination, but so little, and why it took so long to develop. Most soldiers simply wanted to win the war, showing for four years a deep and complex consent that historians have only begun to understand. Victory for the army that had thrown back the invader at the Marne had become an act of faith, based not in a rational analysis of the balance of power and the forces in the field, but rather in the certainty of the rightfulness of the French cause. Consequently, French soldiers concluded that they could not experience complete defeat. From this point of view, military setbacks raised no fundamental doubts of this certainty: they only delayed its realization and extended the suffering required to attain it. Jean Galtier-Boissière, war writer and editor of *Le Crapouillot*, called French soldiers "excellent war workers." The model of labor, as we will see, provides an imperfect model for understanding the mutinies of 1917. But it does speak to the notion of military service in the Great War as a task, as a responsibility inculcated into citizens as they became soldiers and that they accepted as such.

4   The crises of 1917

On November 20, 1917, George Clemenceau gave the customary speech of investiture in the Chamber of Deputies preceding the vote of confidence in his newly formed government. Never in more than three years of war had the prospects for victory seemed so dim. In March, the tsar's regime had fallen in Russia, inaugurating what would become Russia's year-long collapse into revolution and defeat by Germany. In April, the French would launch the last of their major "over-the-top" offensives against entrenched German positions this time along the Chemin des Dames. Following the dissipation of this offensive would come the most serious mutiny among troops on the Western Front. Also in the grim spring of 1917, strikes simmering since the winter came to a boil, some of them in key armaments factories. The autumn brought still more bad news – the slaughter of British and Dominion troops to no effect at Passchendaele, the defeat of the Italians at Caporetto in October, and the Bolshevik Revolution in Russia in November. Increasingly, signs of disunion appeared within French politics. Socialist Albert Thomas had resigned as minister of armaments in September 1917, thereby ending Socialist participation in wartime governments. The Left in France became more and more divided as to how and whether to go on.

To be sure, the United States had entered the war in April, as an "associated power" alongside France, Britain, Italy, and what remained of Russia. But the colossus across the Atlantic had a tiny army and no military industry to speak of. In the short run, the new ally would have to be supplied by Britain and France, and was as much a burden as a help for the time being. And in the long run, the entry of the United States into the war posed risks of its own. The term "associated power" implied a certain New World disdain for Europe, and a need for moral distance from Europe's Great War. For some time, President Woodrow Wilson had preached an end to the war without annexations or indemnities. The greater the American contribution to victory, the greater would be the American influence over the peace. France, after all, had not sacrificed so much in order to become a ward of the United States.

Clemenceau was seventy-six years old in 1917, and his political career had spanned the entire history of the Third Republic up to that time. A physician by training, he entered politics as mayor of the 18th Arrondissement of Paris (the Montmartre area) in the immediate aftermath of the German victory of 1870. He unsuccessfully attempted to mediate the tensions leading to the uprising of the Paris Commune, an experience that, he quipped many years later, prepared him for the absurdities of public life. Throughout his long career, Clemenceau carefully cultivated an image of ferocity, in word and deed. His journalistic tirades were legendary, whether against General Boulanger, against French imperialism, or in favor of Captain Dreyfus. Clemenceau took part in at least a dozen duels, the last in 1898 at the age of fifty-seven. He had been prime minister between 1906 and 1909, when his policy of repressing strikes through using the army earned him a title he coined for himself, *le premier flic de France* ("the first cop of France"). He reveled in his other sobriquet, "the Tiger." On personal grounds, President Poincaré loathed Clemenceau not much less than trade unionists, and called on him to form a government in 1917 because, as we will see, he had no other choice.

Winston Churchill, then Minister of Armaments in Britain, witnessed Clemenceau's speech from the gallery of the Chamber. Churchill described him as "a wild animal pacing to and fro behind bars, growling and glaring; and all around him was an assembly which would have done anything to avoid having him there, but having put him there, felt they must obey."[1] The speech deeply affected Churchill, and plainly influenced his own formidable rhetoric years later, when he led Britain during its darkest hours of World War II. Clemenceau called on his compatriots to wage "total war" (*une guerre intégrale*), the complete fusion of the military and home fronts. The French have "one duty," he proclaimed, "to stand by the soldier, live, suffer, fight with him. Forsake all that which is not of the country. The time has come for us to be entirely French, with the pride to tell ourselves that that is enough."

The rhetoric of national mobilization had shifted by 1917. Back in 1915, Clemenceau's friend Sarah Bernhardt in *Les Cathédrales* had appealed to the French in terms no less emotional than those of Clemenceau. But Bernhardt had relied on a brutal but abstract religious symbolism in order to assure a national community already magically united. She imagined that the spire of the Strasbourg cathedral would somehow skewer the German eagle, bringing victory. That victory seemed to amount to expelling the invader and reconquering Alsace and

---

[1] Winston S. Churchill, *Great Contemporaries* (New York: G. P. Putnam's Sons, 1937), p. 272.

Lorraine. To be sure, at least since the Enlightenment in the eighteenth century, the French had considered their culture in some sense universal, supreme for all of humanity. But in 1917, Clemenceau brought the ideological globalization of the conflict to center stage in remobilizing the French war effort. The just war forced on France back in August 1914 had become the cause of humanity itself. True to his anticlerical form, Clemenceau evoked a completely secular vision of the crusade to defeat Germany. But he provided a far more sweeping vision than that of Sarah Bernhardt, and one quite intentionally appropriated by Churchill in 1940. The cause of the nation and the cause of the world had become one.

Bastion of ideals, our France has suffered for all that is human. Firm in the hopes borrowed from the most pure springs of humanity, she accepts that she must suffer still more, for the defense of the soil of our great ancestors, with the hope to open, always wider, all the doors of life, to individuals as to whole peoples. The force of the French soul is there.

Paradoxically, this "second mobilization," in which France sought to renew the nation and save the world, ultimately destroyed the Union sacrée. As a whole, the national community remained deeply committed to winning the war, and in stages reaffirmed that commitment over the course of 1917. The decision for a second mobilization rested with millions of soldiers and workers, without whose support Clemenceau's words would have gone the way of those of Alexander Kerensky, another formidable orator, who led a provisional and hapless democratic regime prior to the Bolshevik Revolution in Russia. Sovereignty in France in 1917 lay with the people, the men and women who decided to continue the fight. France showed itself a republic in 1917, accountable even to those to whom it did not accord full rights of citizenship. But as the nation rearticulated its commitment to winning the war, it turned to leaders to whom remobilization meant exclusion.

As we saw, the Union sacrée had relied upon inclusion – most notably of the Catholic Church and the Socialists. As the nation remobilized in 1917, the French would become either part of the solution or part of the problem. At times, political exclusion would turn brutal. The most famous portion of Clemenceau's speech would have sounded familiar to the Jacobins, who likewise had sought to save humanity through purifying France and its Revolution back in 1793.

Alas, there have also been crimes, crimes against France, which call for swift punishment. We undertake before you, before the country which demands justice, the responsibility that justice will prevail to the full extent of the law . . . Weakness will be considered complicity . . . The soldiers first, ourselves in solidarity with the combat soldier. No more pacifist campaigns, no more German intrigue. Neither treason, nor half-treason: war. Nothing but war. Our armies will not be captured between two fires. The country will know that it is being defended.

Particularly in the English-speaking world, historians have often described Clemenceau as having flogged his compatriots to victory – the great man who stood taller than the nation he led. However, Clemenceau's rise to power constituted not so much a new beginning as a culmination. The Chamber of Deputies ratified the decision to continue when it accepted the formation of the Clemenceau government. But that decision had already been made in French society writ large in several stages over the course of 1917. Clemenceau articulated, and drove in a specific, exclusionary direction, the desire of the national community to prevail in the conflict.

Indeed, it is precisely because the decision to continue came from the French people as a whole that it had such grave consequences. For 1917 proved, in Jean-Jacques Becker's words, the "impossible year," the year in which ends and means in the French war effort became irreconcilable.[2] Clemenceau's speech of investiture sent the message to the French and to the world that the nation would win the war or die in the attempt. Churchill phrased his own calls to arms in 1940 in just these terms. But like imperial Britain after 1940, by deciding to win at any cost, Third Republic France in time evoked its own destruction. In France after 1917, as in Britain after 1940, "total" mobilization might have staved off defeat, but it could never in itself have brought total victory.

For as we will see in Chapter 5, "total" victory was probably not achievable at all, and certainly not by the French acting on their own one way or another. A short parliamentary debate followed Clemenceau's speech citing victory as his sole war aim. Jean Parvy, a Socialist deputy, responded aptly enough that "the Germans have the same goal as you." The stalemate of force that had characterized the Western Front since 1914 would not be broken through Clemenceau's words, nor entirely through his policies. The second mobilization deepened long-standing divisions within French society, between classes, between various political factions, and between the genders. It raised seemingly new issues of race. No realistic form of victory could satisfy all these constituencies, or convincingly justify the cumulative sacrifices in blood and treasure. The decision to continue in 1917 put in place a structural disparity between the price of victory and its practical results. This disparity ate away at the Third Republic until it died following the German invasion of 1940.

---

[2] Jean-Jacques Becker, *1917 en Europe: l'année impossible* (Brussels: Éditions Complexe, 1997).

The disillusionment with the peace so soon after 1918 proceeded from the gravity of the decision to achieve "victory" at any price in 1917.

The Chemin des Dames offensive and the mutinies

The decision to continue was made first and most fundamentally at the front, by thousands of citizen-soldiers of France. The mutinies of 1917 began in the wake of the failed offensive along the Chemin des Dames, the last great attempt of the French to achieve a *percée* of the German lines. But the mutinies quickly became about much more than an unsuccessful offensive, or even about the strategy, tactics, and leadership behind that offensive. As the external means of controlling soldiers' discontent evaporated, at stake became nothing less than soldiers' whole relation to the war and to the national community fighting it. In the end, the mutinies proved an anguished affirmation of the nation and the regime, as French soldiers began to rebuild the war effort from within.

Military historians still disagree about many of the great battles of World War I, whether their outcome was inevitable, and whether the generals plotting them were fools, rogues, or heroes. Not so for the Chemin des Dames offensive, which military historians condemn unanimously as employing the wrong tactics in the wrong place at the wrong time. The plan for the offensive was born amid the military and political confusion that beset France in the second half of 1916. As we saw, the French role in assisting the British along the Somme achieved little but attrition, as usual more at the expense of the attackers than the defenders. The siege of Verdun ground on through the summer and fall, with huge casualties and little movement. Joffre managed to push aside General Ferdinand Foch for the lack of success along the Somme, but many were beginning to wonder whether the blame lay elsewhere. As Joffre began his third year in supreme command of the army at war, his reputation for military genius earned along the Marne at last began to fade.

In October 1916, France finally had something that could pass for good news along the front at Verdun. General Robert Nivelle and his principal subordinate, General Charles Mangin, made unprecedented gains. They retook the ferociously contested forts at Vaux and Douaumont, with relatively few casualties. Nivelle, an artillery man by training, had hit upon a genuine tactical innovation. He concentrated French heavy artillery along a narrow front, and had launched the sort of barrage that normally preceded an infantry assault. The German artillery immediately launched a counterbarrage, thereby revealing their positions. But the expected infantry assault was delayed until a second French barrage attacked the exposed artillery. Known as the *barrage roulant* or "rolling barrage," it lay at the heart of the new tactics. The artillery and the infantry would simply move forward at the same predetermined speed, thereby guaranteeing cover for the men advancing on foot. Nivelle, like most of his colleagues not afflicted with undue modesty, proclaimed that he had found the key to obtaining the *percée* of the German lines.

At a critical time, Nivelle could represent himself as everything Joffre was not. At sixty-one years old, Nivelle was only four years younger than Joffre. But he conveyed an image of youth and vitality, not least because of his comparatively slender build. Nivelle was also a Protestant, a characteristic not unnoticed both among the British and among those who sought to blame the high command's lack of success on its stereotypical image as a bastion of Catholic reaction. Best of all, given the increasing reliance of France on Britain, Nivelle had an English mother and spoke excellent, idiomatic English. With such an attractive candidate waiting in the wings, the government of Aristide Briand summoned up the courage to rid itself of Joffre. It lured him into relinquishing day-to-day command of the French armies by offering him a vaguely defined post that Joffre imagined would give him great influence over the entire war effort. In fact, Briand envisaged the empty title of "technical adviser" to the government. The disillusioned Joffre resigned this post in December 1916. One month later, he was made a Marshal of France, and eventually was sent on a harmless morale-boosting mission to the United States.

Nivelle had formed an elaborate plan to win the war based on applying the tactical innovation of Verdun on a vast scale. The center of the German front comprised a salient of some 150 kilometers running from Arras to Craonne. This constituted the area of the deepest German advance into France. Nivelle envisaged a British offensive south of Arras, complemented by a French attack to the east of the Chemin des Dames, a ridge near the Aisne River. With the Germans distracted to their left and right, a third Allied force would smash through the middle of the salient, creating a huge hole in the middle of the Western Front and, theoretically, end the war. To be sure, there were problems with the scheme from the outset. Any pretense of surprise was forsaken. It was generally known on both sides of the Western Front well before April 1917 that the French were planning a major offensive along the Aisne. There were even reasons to doubt the tactical innovation in the artillery. It had never been tried on such a large front. To some extent, the *barrage roulant* was also a one-time trick. The Germans quickly learned to recognize an artillery feint when they saw one, and could simply withhold their counterbarrage until the creeping barrage began. And no barrage could creep forward indefinitely, at least not unless the defending artillery had been silenced.

Worst of all, beginning in February 1917, the Germans deprived the Allies of the salient itself. Over the course of the next six weeks, they withdrew some forty kilometers to the east, to deep and elaborately constructed defensive positions known as the Siegfried Line. The Germans gave up more French territory than had been gained by any of the Allied armies on the Western Front since September 1914. Any Allied offensive that conquered this much ground would have been deemed a resounding success. And the ground relinquished had been pillaged, aptly earning its name of Operation Alberich, after a malign dwarf from the Nieblung story. With thousands of buildings destroyed, bridges and railways blown up, wells poisoned, and civilians displaced and robbed, the Germans handed themselves yet another propaganda disaster. But it proved one of the shrewdest defensive maneuvers of the war. With there now being no salient to rupture and charge through, Nivelle's plan seemed to lose its very reason for being. Yet Nivelle refused to scale down the ambitions of his plan. The British would simply attack further north, near Cambrai. The French would attack along the Chemin des Dames rather than east of it (and thus uphill). The definitive rupture of the enemy position would just occur a bit further south than previously planned. As for the shorter German defensive line and the likelihood of German reinforcements delivered from the Eastern Front, Nivelle is alleged to have responded perkily, "I do not fear numbers. The greater the numbers, the greater the victory."

But if the Chemin des Dames offensive was such a bad idea from the outset, why was it allowed to proceed? The British government backed the plan, in part and paradoxically because it gave Nivelle some small measure of authority over the British forces during the battle itself. David Lloyd George, the wily prime minister, hoped thereby to begin reigning in his own high command. Since his first meeting with Nivelle in January 1917, Lloyd George had also been completely seduced by Nivelle's charm and optimism, all masterfully conveyed to him in his own language.

But most of the answer lies in the political vacuum emerging at the top of French politics. As the Union sacrée weakened, the Third Republic reverted to form. Governments were cobbled together one by one, so as to divide the National Assembly the least. The Briand government (in office since October 1915) had handled the ouster of Joffre carefully, with a subtle maneuver to reassert civilian control over the military. The government installed General Hubert Lyautey, best known as the conqueror of Morocco, as Minister of War. Easily Nivelle's equal in national reputation and superior to him in seniority, Lyautey would not be bullied as Joffre had his predecessors. Lyautey was frankly hostile to Nivelle's plan, at one point calling it worthy of a light opera of the day, *The Grand Duchy of*

Gerolstein. Yet Lyautey, long a monarchist in his personal politics, had his own difficulties with civilian rule. He resigned after a stormy encounter with the Chamber of Deputies on March 14, in which he refused to reveal certain military information even to a secret parliamentary committee. The Briand government fell two days later. Paul Painlevé, war minister in a new government led by conservative (and octogenarian) Alexandre Ribot, likewise took a dim view of Nivelle's plan. But in a meeting with senior French commanders on April 6 (in which only Philippe Pétain frankly expressed reservations about the offensive), Nivelle threatened to resign unless the government allowed him to proceed. Painlevé believed the country could not stand a crisis in its military leadership so shortly after the fall of Joffre and Lyautey. Moreover, no other general (least of all Pétain) promised victory any time soon.

Nivelle's Order of the Day for April 16, a cold day with rain mixed with sleet and snow, read simply: "The hour has come. Courage and confidence." The results have certainly been no surprise to military historians. Soldiers slogged through near-frozen mud uphill to battered but strong and very deep German positions. Nivelle's optimism kept the attacking barrage moving forward at a brisk pace, at times faster than the infantry. In some parts of the front, the barrage moved so fast that it stopped before the attackers reached the other side of no man's land. This presented them with one of the worst horrors of the World War I battlefield – having to attack with no artillery support at all. Nearly 130 tanks were used, the first time the French used them on a large scale in battle. But unlike the Renault light tanks used toward the end of the war, the Schneider and Saint-Chamond tanks used at the Chemin des Dames could only travel three kilometers per hour on an incline, and, remarkably, were especially vulnerable to enemy fire because their fuel tanks were located in the front of the tank! Nearly sixty percent were destroyed or had simply broken down by the end of the day.

General Mangin, commander of the 6th Army, had boasted that he would have his afternoon apéritif near Laon, some ten kilometers inside the German first line. In fact, his army advanced only about 500 meters. The Senegalese soldiers leading the attack suffered particularly heavy losses. Ill-accustomed to such a disagreeable climate, frostbitten, and trapped in semi-frozen mud up to their knees, some 6,300 of 10,000 Senegalais troops became casualties on the first day. Somewhat unfairly, given that he used the white troops no differently, Mangin soon acquired the sobriquet "*broyer du noir*" (crusher of the black).[3] In a secret parliamentary investigation of the Chemin des Dames offensive that took place in the summer of 1917, Blaise Diagne, a black African elected from

---

[3] This is an untranslatable pun. *Broyer de noir* means to brood or to become depressed.

Senegal, heaped scorn on the metropolitans for the way they used black troops. With a dubious sympathy toward his compatriots, Diagne told his colleagues that he found it humiliating that France should hope that its "salvation will come from the blacks out of the depths of Africa, from the primitive simplicity of a barely emergent mentality."

In all, the French made small and irregular gains along the Chemin des Dames. The British attack near Arras, which had begun on April 9, advanced about ten kilometers. Thanks particularly to Canadian units, this attack did at least conquer an important piece of high ground, the Vimy Ridge. But it resulted neither in a rupture of the German position nor even drew significant German forces away from the Chemin des Dames. From the beginning of the Chemin des Dames offensive to the end of April, the French suffered some 147,000 men killed, wounded, or missing. As early as April 22, Nivelle scaled down his objectives, now limiting themselves to taking the Chemin des Dames plateau – precisely the sort of "tactical gains" at high casualties that had eventually led to the downfall of Joffre. Nivelle shabbily attempted to shift blame for the lack of success of the operation to his subordinates. He dismissed several of them, including Mangin. Nivelle himself was shown the door on May 15, and replaced by Pétain, the hero of Verdun and the apostle of the defensive.

But by then, the situation on the ground could not be resolved simply. In the short run, Pétain could not handle affairs much differently from Nivelle. The irregular gains of the offensive had either to be consolidated or abandoned. Abandoning the partial gains would have amounted to a resounding admission of failure, a risky choice given the rising discontent both at the front and in the interior. But consolidating the gains meant, in effect, continuing the offensive in its scaled-down form. Blood would continue to be shed for tactical rather than strategic gains. However many of them perished, French soldiers knew that the continuing engagement would not in itself win the war. Once again, the hoped-for *percée* had yielded to the grim and indecisive business of *grignotage*. The point in connecting the Chemin des Dames offensive to the 1917 mutinies is not so much that this particular effort was any more militarily disastrous than the French offensives that preceded it, but that the pattern of expectations falling from *percée* to *grignotage* had become unacceptable to many French soldiers.

Some disagreement still persists over just what to call the French army mutinies of 1917. Contemporaries rarely used the term "mutiny" in the rivers of paper flowing up and down the chain of command. Soldiers never brought serious violence to bear against officers, a striking contrast to the 1917 mutinies in the Russian Imperial army. Sometimes, officers emphasized the "political" character of the events, in order to distinguish them from more conventional conceptions of military mutiny. "Acts of collective indiscipline," "pacifist demonstrations," the "movement of disorder," or simply "the movement," were evoked most commonly at the time. Historians have often compared the mutinies to a strike, the military equivalent of an industrial labor action. This term has some advantages, given that soldiers' demands actually proved limited in critical ways. Moreover, the soldiers themselves made the decision to return to the trenches and to accept formal command authority. Yet "mutiny" remains the operative term. The discontented soldiers openly and collectively defied the army, the most foundational institution of the French state. Soldiers are supposed to operate under a system of authority far more absolute than even the most watched and constricted miner or factory worker. Workers also strike according to a more or less predefined script. They down tools, they negotiate, and eventually they return to work. Not so when soldiers refuse to obey their commanders. Defying so central an institution of state must by definition cancel all bets as to the outcome.

The most common form of mutiny involved soldiers' collective refusal to take up positions in the front lines when ordered to do so. They would then depart to open areas and hold demonstrations airing their myriad demands. No demonstrations took place in the front lines themselves. Acts of collective indiscipline began virtually from the day the Chemin des Dames offensive began on April 16. They became most serious *after* Pétain replaced Nivelle because, as argued above, there was little Pétain could do differently right away. By the beginning of June, the threat of violence seemed to increase, as well as the alarming prospect of soldiers marching on Paris to air their demands. In the second half of June, the number of incidents began to decline. Pétain himself considered the crisis definitively over only in October 1917, when he finished consolidating the gains of the Chemin des Dames offensive.

Incidents of collective indiscipline occurred in nearly one half of all of the divisions in the French army. The total number of "mutineers" is most reliably estimated at 25,000–30,000. But such estimates are intrinsically misleading and perhaps a bit beside the point, since the French army mutinies comprised hundreds of thousands of individual decisions made and remade over a period of several weeks. An essential fluidity characterized events. Any estimate of the number of soldiers involved in a particular demonstration is necessarily a mental snapshot, representing a guess as to how many soldiers passed into open defiance at a specific moment in time. Moreover, if a given regiment or battalion could not take up positions in the front lines because of a demonstration, each individual in the unit had the same chance to reflect on his relationship to the war, whether he took part in the demonstration or not. Postal censorship records, a crucial source for determining soldiers' demands, did not attempt to distinguish between "mutineers" and the non-demonstrating majority – because there was no meaningful way to do so. The mutinies must be considered a crisis of the French army as a whole.

Senior commanders more or less literally retreated to their tents until something resembling order returned to the troubled units. They appear to have spent most of their time struggling to understand the turmoil beneath them. Generals sometimes hesitated to put much in writing, lest the documents fall into wrong hands. But senior commanders are above all administrators, and the bureaucratic impulse itself generated a tremendous amount of paper. General Louis Franchet d'Esperey, commander of the Army Group North, met virtually every day with Pétain during the worst part of the crisis, yet his memos to his superior are so prolific as to seem compulsive. Generals spent a good bit of time trying to get their subordinates to take a more active role in heading off and ending demonstrations. Pétain lauded the case of one army corps, in which the commander surrounded the would-be demonstrators with cavalry and gendarmes, whereupon he gave them a certain amount of time to rejoin their units. For good measure, he had each company commander identify five "leaders" from each company. The incident fizzled, and the discontented soldiers returned to their duties. "Here is how a leader," Pétain wrote, "worthy of the name, who knows how to join firm words and energetic action, can bring back together a group of men led astray and terrorized by a few leaders." Such observations would play a critical role in putting a certain "spin" on the mutinies once they were over.

But the matter on the ground was much more complicated, and the stakes far higher. A brigade commander from the 41st Infantry Division tried to intervene directly in a demonstration, only to find himself surrounded by some 2,000 discontented soldiers, some of whom roughed him up and tore away his regimental lanyard. The division commander diffused a situation that could quickly have gotten out of control by promising that the two regiments involved in the demonstrations would not have to take up positions in the front lines for the time being, and that he would transmit their concerns to his superiors. A company commander from the 109th Regiment, a lawyer in civilian life, put the matter frankly to his superiors:

If the command structure take care to look deeply into the soul of the French soldier, it will see that the best of our men will never consent to fight against their fellow citizens . . . Many officers will never, never, never agree to order their men to attack French soldiers. And our soldiers would refuse to execute such an order if it were given to them.

The command structure simply lacked the means to resolve the matter in its favor if words passed to deeds. Only the cavalry (particularly from colonial units) were deemed certain to fire on French soldiers if ordered to do so. Particularly by this point in the war, cavalry were not nearly numerous enough to prevail over infantry who, after all, were heavily armed themselves.

The key role in mediating between discontented soldiers and their commanders fell to junior officers and non-commissioned officers, who themselves shared the physical deprivations and perils of the demonstrators. Typically, division and regimental commanders expressly ordered their subordinates not to do anything that would provoke violence. This combination of reticence from the highest levels of command and conciliation at the lowest levels is crucial in understanding the outcome of the mutinies. To a great extent, the mutinies displaced the formal authority structure in the French army, from the moment soldiers openly disobeyed orders to go into the front lines. Consequently, understanding the mutinies must focus on the discontented soldiers themselves. For a brief moment in time, they were essentially free to decide what to do next.

Letters continued to flow between the front and the interior throughout the mutinies. An increasingly complex postal censorship apparatus existed, but the authorities rarely seized letters unless they contained overtly subversive opinions, such as advocacy of a socialist uprising. More often, the authorities simply sampled sentiments expressed in letters, resealed them, and sent them on. Postal censorship reports thus provide a precious source for discovering what soldiers wanted out of the mutinies. Soldiers often wrote with remarkable candor, as in a very typical letter from a soldier from the 36th Infantry Regiment to his uncle in the interior:

> When the time came to advance to the front lines, an incident happened in the army corps in which we demanded our rights in the following things:
> 1. Peace and the right to leaves, which are in arrears.
> 2. No more butchery; we want liberty.
> 3. On food, which is shameful.
> 4. No more injustice.
> 5. We don't want the blacks in Paris and in other regions mistreating our wives.
> 6. We need peace to feed our wives and children and to be able to give bread to the women and orphans.
>
> We demand peace, peace.

Nothing is more surprising about the demands of the discontented soldiers of the spring of 1917 than their diversity. With external authority so suddenly and so completely pushed to the margins, soldiers could contemplate their entire relationship to the war, all at once. They moved effortlessly from relatively mundane matters such as the quality of their food (a complaint of soldiers at least since antiquity), to great concern for their families behind the lines, to issues as abstract as "injustice." The worry that "blacks" were mistreating soldiers' wives referred to widespread (but apparently untrue) reports that colonial troops had been used to suppress women's strikes. Soldiers sought very traditional male roles as protectors of and providers for their families. Above all, soldiers wanted "peace." But as we will see, when pressed they plainly did not mean peace on any terms, or even on terms inconsistent with the war aims of the national community for the preceding three years. They sought *both* immediate peace and a reformed leave policy, though the former presumably would render the latter irrelevant.

Beneath this initially baffling array of demands, and at the heart of the drama of the mutinies of 1917, lies the negotiation of the political identity of the French citizen-soldier. The mutinies brought to the surface a tension as old as French democracy itself between direct democracy and representative government. In their open defiance of military authority, the mutinies became an exercise in direct democracy. Soldiers took matters into their own hands, much like the people of Paris at various times during every French revolution since 1789. Commentators from the political Left such as Joseph Jolinon, who defended mutineers before courts martial, seized on this image. He wrote, a bit romantically, of the mutinuous soldiers as formulating "a democratic republic on a war footing."[4]

Yet in difficult but essential partnership with direct democracy existed representative government, the centerpiece of modern republicanism in France. The state and its army drew their power from representative government. The citizen-soldier served the army as a representation of the state, and the state as a representation of the sovereign people. Discontented soldiers returned again and again to the necessity of transmitting their concerns to their elected representatives in the Chamber of Deputies. A soldier from the 274th Infantry Regiment wrote to his deputy: "Do not forget that we hold in our hands the destiny of the country. If by this winter you have not shown your willingness to negotiate [with the Germans], we will give way." A soldier from the 36th Infantry Regiment writing home likewise saw the mutinies as an anguished appeal by citizen-soldiers to their government, though he had a less focused outcome in mind. "We refused to march not to bring about a revolution," he wrote, "rather to attract the attention of the government in making them understand that we are men, and not beasts to be led to the *abattoir*

---

[4] Joseph Jolinon, "La Mutinerie de Coeuvres," *Mercure de France*, August 15, 1920, p. 82.

to be slaughtered, that we want is what is due to us and that we demand peace."

Both aspects of French republicanism had been linked since the Enlightenment through Jean-Jacques Rousseau's logic of the Social Contract. Both direct democracy and representative government drew their legitimacy from the same source, the General Will of the sovereign people. Consequently, the soldier obeyed a source of authority originating in himself and his compatriots. Whether in obeying his commanders as the instrument of representative government or disobeying in claiming his right as a citizen to agitate against the war, the soldier remained bound to an authority ultimately emanating from himself and his compatriots. The representation of the General Will in the form of the Third Republic and its institutions of state demarcated the boundaries of soldiers' political imagination during the mutinies.

The grassroots politics of the mutinies kept soldiers closely bound to the national community. The longer the demonstrations continued, the clearer became the military dilemma underpinning them. Nothing about the exercise of direct democracy in the spring of 1917 could win the war for France. The soldiers did not have the secret to victory that had hitherto escaped Joffre, Nivelle, Pétain, or anyone else before 1918. Failing a *vox populi* solution, soldiers would have to decide whether to lose the war or to endorse conventional command authority and, consequently, their commanders' solutions for winning the war.

Through working out this choice, the discontented soldiers made the mutinies an anguished affirmation of the war effort and the Third Republic that governed it. Paradoxically, the French army mutinies of 1917 became one of the Great War's most extraordinary exercises in patriotism. The command structure sent a policy spy into one brigade of the 5th Infantry Division, to try to understand precisely what the soldiers wanted and what they expected to happen next. He reported the same confusing combination of Wilsonian idealism and French nationalism that would inform much of the debate on French war aims through the end of the war: "They demand Alsace, Lorraine, and the maintenance of the status quo (no indemnity, no annexations)." Once more, the lost territories emerged as the supreme symbol of the French war effort, the essence of French war aims. Presumably they did not qualify as annexations because the soldiers never (or no longer) considered them to be anything but French. What many of the French in and out of uniform came to see as a "negotiated" or "compromise" peace looked a lot like a French victory. Asked further what they would do if the Germans chose this moment to attack, the soldiers responded using the words of Verdun, "*les Boches ne passeront pas* (the Boches shall not pass)." Even the soldier cited above from the 274th Infantry Regiment added that if the Germans refused a peace in accordance with French honor, "we will push them out ourselves."[5] The soldier from the 36th Infantry Regiment added that eventually the soldiers would agree to march again, because otherwise "we will be obliged to sign shameful treaties, which will bring us misery and ruin, of which we have already seen too much in France." Through this difficult rethinking of what it meant to be a citizen-soldier of the Republic of France, the mutinies ended. The repression took place only after soldiers made the essential decision to continue.

Gradually, the French command structure remobilized as well. Pétain made important reforms in food distribution and in leave policy. Above all, he made certain that there would be no more foredoomed offensives like the Chemin des Dames. "We will wait for the tanks and the Americans," went his famous expression. But there was more to Pétain's military policy than simple *attentisme*, or waiting. Pétain pursued the evolving policy of *défense en profondeur*, or "defense in depth." This involved thinning out troops in the first lines of trenches and the construction, in some sectors, of a fifth or sixth position. This gradually made possible the formation of a strategic reserve, which the French would put to good use in 1918. Nor was Pétain's program entirely defensive. He sought to consolidate the gains from the Chemin des Dames offensive, in relatively small, limited attacks, well supported by artillery. Pétain completed this protracted and difficult process with the French victory at Malmaison in October 1917.

Military command also remobilized at the lower levels, in a very clever way that made its own contribution to ending the mutinies. Knowing that it did not have enough force at its disposal to suppress the mutinies through violence, the command structure used the threat of force symbolically, in order to make soldiers choose between submission and armed revolution. For example, the command structure ordered the exceptionally restive 129th Infantry Regiment to be evacuated by truck at 4 AM on the night of May 29–30. Some cavalry were posted at the transit point, though it is hard to see how they could have prevailed if the infantry had been determined to resist. The soldiers certainly knew that they were to be transported to some form of repression. One company commander described the scene poignantly:

[5] It is not true, as was long believed, that the Germans had no information at all about the mutinies. At least one German newspaper reported them on June 30, an account of which made its way back to French intelligence. The Germans had been badly battered themselves along the Chemin des Dames, and from their deep defensive positions were in no position to counterattack. Moreover, given the dynamic of the mutinies and the fact that no protests took place in the front lines, there is no reason to believe that a German attack would have been met with anything but ferocious opposition.

During the night of the 29th–30th, the order arrived to prepare for the embarkation by truck. We sounded the reveille at 4h. Getting the men up was painful. For the first time, I made my men face reality. I said to them that there was still time for them to regain control of themselves, and if they did not obey, they would cause the shedding of French blood. My efforts and those of my officers were finally crowned with success. My men decided to take up their packs and get into the trucks.

The symbolism of the occasion was lost on no one, as the men were moved from trucks to trains to take them further into the interior. The infantry division commander wrote poignantly of the way the departing soldiers "rendered the honors with dignity and by the way the men saluted me from the cars as I watched the trains leave." He added that the officers of the regiment, who had done so much to prevent the mutinies from exploding into violence, "are absolutely heartbroken ... Many had trouble hiding their tears when the time came to bid farewell." Only in such an environment, in which the discontented soldiers agreed to accept military authority when no external coercion could have compelled them to do so, could the repression of the mutinies begin.

One significant mutiny in a colonial unit highlighted the difficulties of remobilizing conventional military discipline. In August 1917 (by which time incidents in the metropolitan army had died down), some 200 men from the 61e Bataillon de Tirailleurs Sénégalais (Senegal infantry) refused to take up positions in the trenches along the Chemin des Dames. The command structure found itself more than usually unable to identify "leaders," because of the need to use Senegalese interpreters, who took great care to emphasize the collective nature of their complaints, and not to name names. The battalion (also referred to as Bataillon Malafosse, after its commander) had already been used three times in the Chemin des Dames sector, on April 16, in early May, and in late July. It had suffered heavy casualties. "Bataillon Malafosse has no good," complained one soldier, "no rest, always make war, always kill blacks." The practical complaints of the Senegalese, in fact, did not differ much from those of metropolitan soldiers, except that in the record that survives they made no appeal to rights as citizens, either of France or of their homelands. The reason for this was not primitive stupidity, as Deputy Blaise Diagne had suggested. Rather, the discontented Senegalese had no reason to invoke a political community that had never treated them as anything but indentured servants.

But from the command structure's point of view, how to respond to a challenge from troops of color? The idea had been floated of surrounding the Senegalese with European troops, machine-guns, and artillery, and if they refused to surrender, simply executing them *en masse*. The division commander rejected this option, not, it would seem, out of humane concern for the soldiers, but "because it would produce a disastrous effect in other colonial units, and even the Madagascar soldiers, Tonkinois, and other colonials who would not neglect saying that the whites massacre them." France would mobilize over 600,000 soldiers from its empire in the Great War, enough to make a good bit of trouble if the colonial relationship turned sour. In the event, several Senegalese soldiers were court martialed and four condemned to death, though none was actually executed. Several others were sent to a disciplinary battalion. But by late September, the Senegalese battalion had taken up its position along the Chemin des Dames, without further incident. The command structure, it would seem, tried to call as little attention to the matter as possible.

As the remobilized command structure began to organize the repression of the mutinies once they had ended, it found itself in something of a quandary. The mutinies, after all, had effected a major change in French military strategy, as well as a number of particular reforms aimed at ameliorating the conditions of daily life. "Rightly or wrongly," fretted 2nd Army commander General Louis Guillaumat, "the good soldier as well as the bad is not far from thinking that the regrettable mutinies were not without usefulness and that because of them soldiers have received certain concessions, or at least certain promises." Even assuming the low-end estimate of 25,000 "mutineers" (men who took an active role in the antiwar demonstrations), there were simply too many of them for them all to be shot. Increasingly volatile public opinion would never have stood for such a massacre. In any event, with the manpower situation so dire, the army could scarcely have afforded simply to rid itself of the equivalent of nearly two whole divisions. Consequently, the repression of the mutinies relied on two elements – courts martial to identify and punish symbolic "leaders" of the mutinies, and a remarkably successful effort on the part of the generals to command the narrative of the mutinies, to cast it in terms favorable to itself.

Military justice had long been held to be exceptionally severe in France, particularly by enemies of the army. This image is exaggerated, even though the German army executed soldiers far more sparingly than the French or the British. Nevertheless, the court martial provided the perfect institutional instrument for the ritual display of reasserted command authority. Far more explicitly than civilian courts, courts martial seek to control a subject population. Military justice articulates the meeting place of the modern state and the Old Regime right of the officer to take the lives of his own men if necessary in order to enforce obedience. This being said, the raw numbers suggest considerable prudence on the part of the French high command. French historian Guy Pedroncini arrived at numbers of 3,427 soldiers tried as a result of the mutinies, with 554 death sentences, and 49 soldiers actually shot.[6] Pétain, Pedroncini argued convincingly, knew where to stop.

Yet the numbers tell only part of the story. Remobilizing the national community in 1917, in the trenches as in parliament, seemed to require victims. The courts martial were as much about identifying a group of "leaders" as punishing them. This relatively small population could accept blame for the disturbances, and in a very real sense pay the symbolic price for the reassertion of command authority. Soldiers' acceptance of this solution constituted the ugliest aspect of their decision to continue the war. Probably "leaders" did exist in the sense that particular individuals did no doubt initially called upon soldiers to demonstrate against the war. But these "leaders" were no more responsible for the mutinies than matches for forest fires. Dubious and vague criteria were applied capriciously. For example, a company commander from the 74th Infantry Regiment simply identified four privates who "by their poor spirit and their usual manner of service must be considered among the leaders." Two other privates were named simply because they were "intelligent and well instructed."

Considerable suspicion persists as to the criteria for deciding whose death sentences would be commuted and whose would be carried out. Jolinon, writing of the mutiny at Coeuvres, suspected that the only soldier among thirty-two soldiers condemned to death who was actually executed was chosen because he had no family to mourn him (or to investigate what Jolinon clearly considered a case of judicial murder).[7] But the polemic throughout the interwar years about the application of the death penalty during the war certainly suggests that, on the contrary, plenty of executed soldiers left friends and family behind who would pursue the matter after their deaths. Of those whose death sentences were commuted, a series of amnesties would result in the release from prison of nearly all of them by 1922. With the war won, the group selected to take responsibility for the mutinies soon lost its reason for being.[8]

The command structure's broader efforts to control the narrative of the mutinies began virtually from the moment of the first demonstrations, and persisted long after the repression proper concluded. The matter particularly for senior commanders was a delicate one. Conventional military

---

[6] Guy Pedroncini, *Les Mutineries de 1917* (Paris: Presses Universitaires de France, 1967), pp. 194, 215.

[7] Jolinon, "La Mutinerie de Coeuvres," p. 88.

[8] Perhaps not by coincidence, those purged from politics through the rise of Clemenceau had likewise begun their comeback by the early 1920s.

discipline holds officers at all levels responsible for the conduct of their men. The likes of Nivelle and Mangin could take the blame for the lack of military success along the Chemin des Dames. But the mutinies required a deeper explanation, preferably one that found a cause outside the army, so as to exculpate the command structure. The high command blamed the mutinies on a massive defeatist conspiracy in the interior. "The situation is clear," wrote Army Group North General Franchet d'Esperey, "it is a general organization coming from Paris at the instigation of the Germans in order to deliver France to the enemy." Pétain, though less obsessed with outside subversion than most of his colleagues, likewise cited in a 1926 report "the launching and exploitation of a pacifist propaganda campaign" as the first cause of the mutinies. Generals, after all, could not be held responsible if the civilian leadership failed to protect the army and its soldiers from "political" issues, as though this were possible in a mass conscript army of citizen-soldiers. But this explanation perfectly suited Clemenceau's campaign against "defeatism" once he came to power in November.

No substantial links have ever been established between the mutinies and pacifist movements in the interior. But by assigning such a large role to internal subversion, the command structure made the mutinies yet another battle in the war between the army and the Republic – a war both sides knew how to fight very well. Unsurprisingly, an antimilitarist interpretation of the mutinies soon emerged. Enemies of the army labeled the soldiers tragic but essentially helpless victims of command hubris, and the events as harshly repressed and then hushed up by a conspiracy of silence after the war. Some estimates ran to over 2,500 soldiers shot, in addition to those alleged to have been summarily executed. The French have continued sporadically to argue about the mutinies in largely the same terms ever since, as we will see, as recently as November 1998. Sadly lacking on both sides of such debates has been an appreciation of the soldiers as complex, reflective human beings in themselves, and of their agonized decision to continue the war. For in the end, the mutinies of 1917 were more about consenting to the war than about rejecting it.

Labor and the troubles of 1917 in the interior

Of course, it is impossible and ultimately misleading to try to disentangle the strains of war on the military front from those in the interior. Yet the concerns of the interior and the dynamic of the decision to continue the war in 1917 remained distinct from the situation in the trenches. The "total" mobilization of French society had confused hierarchies of class, gender, and race. The crisis of war weariness in 1917 both conflated and aggravated conflict along these fault lines. Discontented workers agitated for higher wages in a situation of exploding inflation, as well as better working conditions and a more fair sharing of sacrifices. Many of these workers were women, trying to cope with unprecedented responsibilities as wage earners and heads of families. The class politics of 1917 separated women from men, and native French from thousands of foreign workers brought in to support the war effort.

Yet despite these serious and deepening divisions, the French in the interior made their own decision not to lose the war. The decision to continue in the interior lacked much of the immediate drama of the decision to continue at the front. But the resolution of the crises of 1917 in the interior would have even more far-reaching consequences. By definition, after all, the military world created by the war was relatively transitory. Soldiers would one day become civilians again, indeed far sooner than most of the French expected as 1918 dawned. They would return to an interwar France shaped and ultimately embittered by the decision of the civilians to continue in 1917.

The unhappy results of the Chemin des Dames offensive certainly disappointed the civilian population. Nivelle's command, never famous for its ability to keep a secret, wanted to shore up civilian morale by letting it be known that a major effort could be expected in the spring of 1917. As a postal censorship report from Bordeaux observed cheerfully:

The dominant note is thus of absolute confidence, as much among the population in the rear as among the soldiers at the front. "We are getting ready," writes one soldier [to people in Bordeaux], "for the march forward." Here is what everyone wishes for ardently, because "we must finish this." This phrase neatly summarizes general opinion on the eve of the offensive.

Civilians had two sources of information on the battle itself: official communiqués and letters from soldiers. After nearly three years of war, people in the interior had become adept at reading between the lines of news coming from the high command. They knew that a phrase like "desperate battle" and praise for the valor of French soldiers against "the energetic resistance of the enemy" meant that the German position had not been broken, and probably not even seriously undermined. The family in Nantes receiving a letter dated April 24 from a soldier of the 118th Infantry Regiment could scarcely have missed the point: "What butchery, for only the tiny advance that we have made and the few prisoners. How many men will be left alive?" Such news could only have deepened the dismay of the huge civilian population already in mourning. For most of the 1.3 million Frenchmen killed in the Great War were already dead by the end of May 1917.

The dashed hopes for an early end to the war converged with deteriorating material conditions in the interior. The winter of 1916–17 had been exceptionally cold, with freezing temperatures well into April. Some eighty people had died of exposure in Paris in 1917, compared to only six in 1916. France had always been a country rich in agriculture, and the food situation there never became as serious as in Germany or Austria-Hungary, or even Britain at the height of unrestricted submarine warfare. For this reason, plans to ration food in France took shape very slowly, and did not become general before the last summer of the war. In the meantime, rationing took place by price, through accelerating inflation. An index of thirteen food items set at 100 in July 1914 had increased to 139 by January 1917. By July 1917, this index had reached 183. Between April and July 1917, inflation was running at an annualized rate of 100 percent. Proportionally, the middle classes probably lost more than the working classes through stagnant salaries and savings inflated away. Peasants did well, provided they could keep the farms going with so many men in uniform. But serious and chronic working-class deprivations, coupled with gathering doubt as to whether the war would ever end, made for volatile labor relations in the factories.

Gender and race divided working-class politics in France in 1917. Male workers remained relatively quiescent. Essentially, two varieties of Frenchmen remained in the factories by 1917 – men either too young or too old to serve in the army (in other words, teenagers and men in their late-forties and above); and skilled workers released from active duty for essential war work. The latter group remained under military discipline, and theoretically could be sent to the front at any time by order of the army. For the duration of the war, controversy swirled around mobilized men in the factories. Ever more desperate for men to send to the trenches, the army focused especially on younger workers who reached prime military age (early twenties) during the war. Not coincidentally, men this age were also considered highly susceptible to labor activism. The legislature had passed two laws, the Loi Dalbiez in August 1915 and the Loi Mournier in August 1917, setting up boards that would cull genuinely needed workers from the ranks and send flagrant shirkers (*embusqués*) to the trenches. With the army quite literally looking over their shoulders, most men trod carefully in asserting demands as workers.

Men's labor militancy was also restrained by union leadership. From its origins, organized labor in France has always been far weaker than in Germany, Britain, or Italy. Membership in the largest union organization, Conféderation Général du Travail (CGT), expanded rapidly during the war – from 100,000 in 1916 to 300,000 in 1917 to 600,000 in 1918. But Secretary General Léon Jouhaux had staunchly supported the Union sacrée ever since his fiery speech against the enemies of France at Jaurès's funeral back in August 1914. "Continue your confidence in us," Jouhaux wrote to Interior Minister Louis Malvy at one point during the labor unrest in 1917, "and we will take responsibility, in the name of the working class, for preventing all disorder in the streets." Clemenceau would echo the contention of the high command that pacifist and defeatist "leaders" in the interior had stirred up labor unrest. But he carefully avoided applying this charge to labor leaders, who consistently strove to keep workers at their jobs.

Some of the frustrations of 1917 vented themselves on non-European foreign workers, over 220,000 people (mostly men) from the French Empire and China brought into France to work for the war effort. Working conditions seem to have been more harsh for people of color than for either native French or European foreign workers. "I work like a condemned man in coal mines and limestone quarries," wrote a North African worker in December 1917, "I work from morning to night with infidels who have no pity on us; they are the enemies of religion." Theoretically, non-white workers were strictly segregated and kept under close surveillance both at work and in their living quarters. But sealing off such a large population proved simply impractical, particularly in the big cities. As shown in postal censorship reports, the authorities were especially anxious about prospective sexual liaisons between non-whites and native French. Perhaps this anxiety resulted in part from a theme running through countless cartoons in French newspapers and magazines of frankly expressed sexual attraction to colonials on the part of native Frenchwomen, particularly from the middle classes.

But plenty of men and women viewed foreign and particularly non-white labor as a threat to native workers, a tool of the government and the employers to send more men to the front and to reduce the wages of the women left behind. Race plainly trumped class during the labor unrest of 1917. In June, a North African street sweeper named Chaouch Ali discharging his duties along the Boulevard Saint Michel in Paris found himself surrounded and taunted as a shirker who did "woman's work." A riot took place in a gunpowder plant in Saint Medard when Indochinese workers were brought in to break a strike. In Dijon, French workers threatened to tear down a camp housing Moroccan workers and to kill those living inside, following an incident in a cafe between a metropolitan French soldier and a Moroccan playing his mandolin. Many individual foreign workers who left their camps at night were beaten up by native French.

The racial politics of the interior in 1917 seemed to unify the French in their desire to rid themselves of non-white workers after the war. Thousands of European workers immigrated to and remained in France

Plate 6. Cartoon from *Le Rire Rouge*. Reprinted with the permission of the BDIC.

between the wars; indeed France had roughly the same percentage of foreign-born population in the 1930s as it had in the 1980s. But workers of color were repatriated after 1918 by any means necessary, including police round-ups in Paris and Marseilles. Only about 25,000 workers from

China and the colonies remained in France by 1921, most of them illegally. In the short run, the French assured themselves of their perceived racial homogeneity. But traditions of labor and migration had been established. The Great War proved an important first step in rendering France a multiracial country.

Women led conventionally construed labor activism in France in 1917. Many male labor leaders had at best ambivalent views of female labor. As women filled the factories of Europe in the Great War, men saw quite conservative work practices threatened by "dilution," the breaking up of skilled work most often done by a well-paid and unionized man into a variety of more rudimentary tasks done by several poorly paid and often non-unionized women. Moreover, women represented a far larger potential labor pool to replace men in the factories than foreign workers. This point was lost neither on the army nor on the unions. "The intensification of women's work," commented Alphonse Merrheim, head of the relatively militant Féderation des Métaux in 1916, "leads only to men being sent to butchery."

Interior Minister Malvy estimated that 80,000 of the 100,000 workers striking in Paris in May and June 1917 were women. Like other women in Europe for centuries, women in France took advantage of their unequal political status to take part in forms of resistance too risky for men. No woman, after all, stood any risk of being sent to the front. Women in the factories began to become more restive in the second half of 1916, beginning with an eleven-day strike at the Dion works beginning on June 29. Strikes continued to break out in armaments factories, such as at the Schneider works in Harfleur in Normandy in January 1917 and at a cartridge factory in Vincennes just outside of Paris the following March. "Have you thought of the enemy," said reformist Socialist and Minister of Armaments Albert Thomas as he scolded the Schneider workers, "who never ceases his labors, of your brothers, your husbands who impatiently await the means of defense that you provide them? . . . Be here on the job tomorrow, each and every one of you." Yet the discontented workers got much of what they wanted, including a narrowing of the gap in piece rates between women's and men's work. In January 1917, Thomas ordered mandatory government arbitration of labor disputes, which many employers and some labor leaders saw as weakening their hand.

The most significant wave of strikes in 1917 took place, by all evidence coincidentally, during the army mutinies. Strikes began in the fashion industry, among workers called the *midinettes*. In the end, some 10,000 women in the textile industry would march, waving the tricolor flag and calling for a cost-of-living raise and the *semaine anglaise* (Saturday afternoons off) with no loss of pay. The matter became more serious when strikes spread to the metalworking and munitions factories throughout the Paris region. Probably in conscious contrast to the *midinettes*, the metalworkers carried the revolutionary red flag. Some women encouraged their colleagues to down tools by arguing that the war would end when they stopped building the means for it. Over 42,000 workers in these industries went on strike in all, nearly 75 percent of them women. Given that only about 30 percent of all metalworkers were women, this meant the strikers were disproportionately female.

Strikes, unlike mutinies, do have a largely predetermined script, and generally have as their cause specific conditions of work and compensation. First and foremost, the women striking in France in the spring of 1917 wanted higher wages and shorter hours, so as to be able to meet the new responsibilities the war imposed on them at home. By striking, they asserted themselves at the meeting place between the private and public spheres. Until recently, even most labor historians concluded that this rendered them "nonpolitical," much like the mutinies. To be sure, the strikers' demands were quite silent on issues such as woman's suffrage, though the fact that no national elections were held during the war made the point a bit moot for the duration. Police investigators were unlikely to interrogate women's political views, choosing most often to conclude that they had none of consequence and focusing instead on their private morality. Of one striker in the Renault works, a police spy wrote: "She has no known connections in syndicalist or revolutionary circles; we know only that she receives many men at her home, apparently workers, whom she takes as lovers."

But like another subject population – the discontented soldiers in the trenches – women striking in the factories sought to make themselves heard before a regime ruling in their name. Certainly, the striking women wanted "peace." Who in France by June 1917 did not? "Down the war!" striking women would cry, but in virtually the same breath "Long live our *poilus!*" Apart from higher wages, women most fervently sought the equalization of sacrifice in carrying forward the war effort. At least as fervently as anyone in the army, women wanted the *embusqués* sent to the front, to replace their loved ones. They applied this epithet liberally to harsh foremen, arrogant skilled workers, and incompetent male colleagues. But only a tiny percentage of the French wanted peace at any price. According to a study of letters from civilians in Bordeaux in June 1917, only 5.3 percent of all letters mentioning "peace" advocated peace at any price. Some 34.5 percent advocated a victorious peace, while 60.2 percent either mentioned "peace" vaguely or sought some sort of truce. When pushed, this sort of peace advocacy usually amounted to France regaining Alsace and Lorraine, and the Germans accepting financial responsibility for the material damage they had done. Such a peace could (and eventually did) pass for a French victory. Like discontented soldiers at the front, discontented women in the factories declined to abandon the war effort. Women returned to their duties with relatively minor concessions (wage increases, rapidly inflated away) and relatively mild repression (lost wages from the strike, and a few women sacked and/or arrested). The claims and expectations of labor were largely deferred to the day of victory.

No one in France knew in 1917 when or how victory would come. Nor did anyone know quite how the brave new France, to which workers and soldiers quite justly felt themselves entitled, would emerge from it. In the meantime, the French in the interior as well as at the front had decided to continue the war. But until the day the Armistice was signed, doubts lingered about the durability of the renewed national consensus. In August 1917, French postal inspection officials opened and read a letter written in English by Slater Brown to Dr. Gerhardt Lomer, of the Columbia University School of Journalism. The part of the letter copied by the officials before they sent it on perfectly reflected these doubts:

Here everyone is disgusted with the war, and I foresee a revolution in France soon. The French soldiers are discouraged, and no one among them believes that Germany will be beaten. They continue the war just like they continue to go to church or to a wedding or to any other old institution.

The rise of Clemenceau and the brutalization of French politics

"High politics," the realm of representatives, ministers, and the head of state, was the last sector of the French public sphere to embark upon a second mobilization in 1917. Yet from this sector came the loudest and perhaps the most explicit decision not to lose the war. The rise of Georges Clemenceau and his ministry epitomized the remobilization of high politics, and the message that France would stay in the war for the duration. Once in power, Clemenceau turned on his political rivals with a ferocity seemingly at odds with the social consensus underpinning the second mobilization. Indeed, to the surprise of many, Clemenceau treated his rivals more roughly than he did trade unions and their leaders.

Yet the brutal symbolism of Clemenceau's attacks on his enemies became the point. He consciously appealed to the Jacobin tradition and the great mobilization of the national community during the Revolution. According to that tradition, internal enemies had to be pursued as vigorously as external enemies. As one contemporary put it, Clemenceau found enemies because he needed them. Pétain found it necessary to allow the execution of "only" forty-nine men as a result of the mutinies out of tens of thousands of men involved. Those executions nevertheless had immense symbolic significance, in order to demonstrate the reestablishment of something that could pass for conventional military discipline. Likewise, Clemenceau needed symbolic heads to show to the nation. All of this worked well enough at the time, as France found its most dynamic leader at least since Léon Gambetta in 1870. But inclusion under the Union sacrée yielded to exclusion under Clemenceau's neo-Jacobin dictatorship. The country would remember the brutalization of French politics long after 1917.

Antiwar opinion did emerge from the shadows in the months preceding the rise of Clemenceau. As we will explore further below, more than one French newspaper had taken laundered German money to disseminate views opposing the war. In a novel published late in 1916, Henri Barbusse's *Le Feu* (Under Fire), to this day the best-selling French novel of the Great War, openly praised German Socialist Karl Liebkneckt and advocated peace based on socialist internationalism.[9] On the initiative of the Mensheviks in Russia, socialists in Europe tried to revive their prewar unity through organizing a conference in Stockholm to discuss a peace without victory or annexations. President Poincaré asked Pétain the somewhat loaded question of whether he could guarantee the morale of the French army if French Socialists attended the conference, to which Pétain dutifully replied in the negative. The government refused to grant the Socialists passports, and their estrangement from the Union sacrée deepened. One outraged young Socialist deputy named Pierre Laval declared: "The way to give hope to the troops and confidence to the workers – whether you like it or not, is Stockholm!"

Exactly what the emergence of antiwar sentiment in the public sphere amounted to is hard to say. Discontented soldiers and workers did not need German agents to tell them that the war was not going well, and that peace would be a fine idea. But as we have seen, very few of the French in or out of uniform wanted peace at any price, or indeed any peace that could not pass for a French victory. There is no reason to believe that even German Socialists would have agreed to a peace that denied Germany all the fruits of its military success in 1914, let alone 1870. The problem with a "negotiated peace" remained essentially the same from 1914 to 1918. France had nothing it could negotiate, and Germany had gained far more than it could consider giving up.

[9] Barbusse cleverly structured the book in such a way as to connect the victory of socialism with the victory of France.

Paradoxically, civil–military relations improved in this otherwise poisoned period in French political history. As we have seen, War Minister Painlevé failed to stop Nivelle's offensive, even though in theory he had the power to do so. But having rid himself belatedly of Nivelle, he got on much better with Pétain. He supported Pétain's cautious policy of waiting for the tanks and American reinforcements, with limited but well-supported attacks until that time. Painlevé defended Pétain against other generals and politicians (particularly on the Right) who advocated a more "vigorous" military policy, meaning renewed offensives. Pétain, in turn, recognized Painlevé as his political master. The days when generals such as Joffre or Nivelle could impose military policy on the civilian leaders had ended. Clemenceau would preserve this *modus vivendi* with his generals in the dark military days of 1918.

By the summer of 1917, the mutinies were essentially over and the wave of labor unrest was in remission. But as the "home front" gradually calmed, parliamentary politics descended into a series of scandals so ridiculous that even their collective gravity cannot wholly erase their humor. Clemenceau could not have hoped for (let alone planned) such an implosion of the forces against him, though he exploited it with great skill. He had long nursed a personal grudge against the government of the day, particularly against Interior Minister Malvy. He had neither forgotten nor forgiven Malvy's refusal back in 1914 to arrest those listed in Carnet B, even though doing so would have pointlessly undermined the Union sacrée at its inception. Despite Malvy's indulgence toward people Clemenceau had considered *a priori* traitors, Clemenceau's newspaper *L'Homme libre* (The Free Man) had gotten into so many disputes with Interior Ministry censors that he changed its name to *L'Homme enchaîné* (The Enchained Man). In parliament, the practice of questioning the government by deputies had largely ceased, as a concession to wartime unity. Supervision of the government took place largely through secret committees, of which Clemenceau's army committee in the Senate was one of the most prominent. Clemenceau advocated a full investigation of the mutinies, but was hampered by Malvy's refusal to turn over what Clemenceau saw as essential dossiers.

The affair of the Left-wing newspaper *Le Bonnet Rouge* (The Red Bonnet, a reference to the headgear of radical revolutionaries during the French Revolution) began in July 1917, when the newspaper's business manager, Emile-Joseph Duval, was arrested at the Swiss border with a check for 150,857 francs signed by a German. Duval was questioned and set free, and even had the check returned to him when he presented himself at the Ministry of the Interior a few days later. It turned out that the funds had come from a German agent in Switzerland. The scandal quickly deepened. *Le Bonnet Rouge* had been subsidized by the French Interior Ministry back in 1914, in order to ensure its support for the war. This subsidy ended in 1916 as the paper began to take a more pacifist stance, only to have its dicey financial position shored up by funds from Germany. Perhaps to help cover up the earlier domestic subsidy, officials in the ministry quietly returned the check.

Clemenceau issued a blistering attack on Malvy in a widely publicized speech on July 22, which in retrospect marked the beginning of his rise to power. Clemenceau received considerable assistance from an old enemy, the Right-wing nationalist and virulently anti-Dreyfus *Action française*, which published numerous lurid articles on the Malvy affair. Politics made for strange bedfellows in 1917. Attention came to focus on the director of *Le Bonnet Rouge*, an exceptionally shady character named Eugène Vigo, who preferred his pen name of Miguel Almereyda (an anagram of "*y a la merde*," or "there is shit"). He was arrested in early August, though hopes for a boisterous trial were dashed on August 18, when Almereyda allegedly strangled himself with his own shoelaces in his jail cell. Clemenceau and his new friends in the Action française did not accept the official verdict of suicide, and assumed that Almereyda had been deemed to know too much to have his day in court. They redoubled their attacks on the government. Malvy's fortunes were not enhanced by repeated allegations that he numbered among the lovers of stripper, courtesan, and alleged German spy Mata Hari. That Mata Hari probably was not a German spy and Malvy probably had never been her lover seemed not to matter. He resigned on August 31, and Ribot's government fell in early September. Mata Hari was executed in October.

War Minister Painlevé became the new premier, as President Poincaré and Clemenceau's many enemies sought to avoid a Clemenceau ministry at almost any cost. Painlevé had been a mathematician of great distinction, so much so that his work still commands attention among mathematicians today. But politics did not always lend itself to his accompanying sense of logic. Painlevé tried to rule from a vague Center-Left. The Chamber of Deputies, it will be recalled, was the same Left-leaning body elected back in April 1914. Yet Painlevé retained Ribot (who had helped make sure the French Socialists would not go to Stockholm) as foreign minister. This led Albert Thomas and his colleagues to end participation by Socialists in wartime governments. In his miserable two months in office, Painlevé could expect no more than toleration from this key player of the Left. Paradoxically, Painlevé was also weakened by his efforts to create a unitary command of the Allied armies. French politicians clamored for such a solution, not least because any supreme commander would have to be French. The fighting, after all, was in France, and the French army still held most of the Western Front. Yet Painlevé had to obfuscate his behind-the-scenes efforts so as not to inflame opinion in Britain. This made him look ineffectual in France.

Most importantly, Painlevé could not stem the tide of further scandal. He had to order the arrest of one supporter, the deputy Victor Turmel, after he proved unable to explain the 25,000 Swiss francs found in his locker in the Chamber of Deputies. Senator Charles Humbert, who with uncomfortable accuracy had been criticizing the insufficiency of the French army's artillery since before the war broke out, had been a colleague of Clemenceau on the Senate army committee. Humbert's newspaper, *Le Journal*, had encountered financial problems remedied through purchase by a former dentist and champagne importer named Paul Bolo, better known as "Bolo Pasha," once he granted himself an Egyptian title. It turned out that the funds to rescue *Le Journal* had come from the Deutsche Bank, laundered through New York. Clemenceau saw to the removal of Humbert from the Senate army committee, and he eventually was tried (though acquitted) for treason.

With Malvy gone and Painlevé sinking, the most charismatic politician of the Center-Left, Joseph Caillaux, began to reemerge from the shadow that had covered him and his wife ever since her surprising acquittal of murder back in August 1914. After a short and stormy time in the army, Caillaux had been sent on a mission to South America, supposedly to help procure food supplies for the French army. Caillaux told anyone there who would listen, particularly spies for both France and Germany, of his contempt for Poincaré in particular and the government in general. He claimed war would never have happened had he been at the helm. Caillaux returned to France in 1915, where he made a new friend in Bolo Pasha, and maintained various levels of contact in France and Italy with dubious characters in touch with the Germans. Anticipating a return to power if the war dragged on enough, Caillaux wrote a long tirade called "Les Responsables" (Those Responsible), in which he blamed Poincaré for not calling upon him to avert war back in August 1914.

Yet even as he imagined himself approaching power, Caillaux inadvertently prepared his own destruction. He publicly defended the *Bonnet Rouge*, as well as Bolo Pasha. Still a member of the Senate, Caillaux made various speeches advocating a "compromise" or "negotiated" peace, though even he agreed that France could not end the war unless it regained Alsace and Lorraine. The lost territories remained the one war aim upon which the French sincerely could agree. In advocating a peace without victory that looked a lot like peace with victory, Caillaux represented a substantial body of opinion in France. But, like that point of view, Caillaux collapsed through his own internal contradictions. Painlevé's moribund ministry fell on November 13, over the remarkably trivial matter of when to debate whether a Socialist deputy was guilty of cowardice in the face of the enemy, as had been alleged by a colleague on the political Right. But by that time, Caillaux looked too compromised and perhaps even too silly to come under serious consideration as premier.

Reluctantly, though by now unavoidably, Poincaré asked Clemenceau to form a government. Clemenceau, as many have remarked, had avoided having shady friends by not having any friends at all. Even the opportunistic cohabitation with the Action française did not make anyone forget the Dreyfus Affair. But Poincaré knew he could count on Clemenceau to end the ambiguities about what constituted the national interest in the grim days of late 1917. As Poincaré remembered his meeting with Clemenceau after the war:

The Tiger arrives; he is fatter, and his deafness has increased. His intelligence is intact. But what about his health, and his will-power? I fear that one or the other may have changed for the worse, and I feel more and more the risk of this adventure. But this *diable d'homme* [devil of a man] has all patriots on his side, and if I do not call on him his legendary strength would make any alternative cabinet weak.

The Chamber of Deputies accepted Poincaré's choice, and approved Clemenceau's government by a thumping margin of 418 votes to 65 (mostly Socialists). But even the Socialists calmed with time, and quietly allowed two party members to take office as "commissioners." There seemed little left to argue about, as Clemenceau's self-consciously Jacobin cry of *la patrie en danger* (the fatherland in danger) fell on receptive ears. He rallied the national community by calling a spade a spade – the situation was such that France could not contemplate peace without victory that called itself victory, whatever the cost. Clemenceau assembled a government of politicians of secondary or even tertiary rank, men who would serve quite clearly as his lieutenants. He reserved the War Ministry for himself.

Like any talented politician, Clemenceau stole the best-looking clothes of his predecessors and rivals. He continued the working arrangement between Painlevé and Pétain, meaning that he would give his generals political protection in exchange for explicit deference to civilian authority. In December 1917, he bluntly told a Senate committee dissatisfied with Pétain's caution: "I alone am responsible here. I am not for the offensive, because we do not have the means . . . General Pétain is under my orders; I cover him fully." Clemenceau also adopted for himself Pétain's policy of regular visits to troops in the front lines. The image of him striding briskly in his raincoat and floppy hat is immortalized in the statue of Clemenceau still standing near the Petit Palais in Paris. He did not push the issue of unified command until the British found themselves near defeat in the spring of 1918, though, ironically, the establishment of such a command would give rise to his conflict with General Foch later on.

Clemenceau's bark proved much worse than his bite on labor unrest. Essentially, he continued the policy of selective repression of strikes and concessions in the form of wage increases. (Rather parallel, in fact, to Pétain's approach to the mutinies.) Historians have noted that whereas previous ministries had conciliated loudly and repressed softly, Clemenceau did the reverse. Raising wages without increasing supply, of course, fed inflation in the short run and increased the cost of the war in the long run. But this backhanded concession to what remained of the Union sacrée kept the factories of France producing down to the end of the war. Even Clemenceau remarked that President Poincaré and General Foch caused him more grief than people he referred to as "anarchists."

French politics brutalized in 1917 through the various trials of people deemed "traitors" or simply "defeatists." Yet while Clemenceau had certainly been among the most vocal politicians calling for a war on people he saw as internal enemies of the war, it would be a mistake to call the juridical blood-letting of 1917 and 1918 his doing alone. All of the major investigations had begun before he came to power in November 1917. Some of the cases were quite straightforward, given the dire political situation. The evidence plainly marked Almereyda for the firing squad. Clemenceau and others lamented his passing only because he had not been given the opportunity to incriminate his associates. Clemenceau certainly did not go out of his way to save Bolo Pasha (shot in April 1918), Duval (shot in July 1918), and a handful of others executed for their work in undermining the French war effort. But their fate would probably have been sealed no matter who had been premier, save Caillaux, who had been a serious contender principally in his own mind anyway.

Malvy and Caillaux, Clemenceau's main enemies, enjoyed immunity from criminal prosecution as members of parliament. Malvy had been accused of passing the plan for the Chemin des Dames offensive on to the Germans. Whether out of hubris or simple indignation, Malvy requested that the Chamber lift his immunity just a few days after Clemenceau came to power. The Senate acting as a High Court, acquitted Malvy of treason but convicted him of the more amorphous (and more patently political) charge of failing to oppose enemy propaganda. The Senate sentenced Malvy to five years' exile from France, and duly had him escorted to the Spanish border. In December 1917, the government asked the Chamber to lift Caillaux's immunity, and ordered him arrested one morning in January 1918. Caillaux was still in his dressing gown and Mme. Caillaux was still in the bathtub. Clemenceau kept him in jail without trial for two years. Indeed, the Senate heard his case only after Clemenceau himself had fallen from power, in February 1920. Still stridently nationalist, the Senate convicted Caillaux of a vague and frankly political charge, as it had Malvy. It found Caillaux guilty of "damage to the external security of the state." He was fined, sentenced to time already served, and, most oddly, banished for five years from cities in France with over 50,000 people, except Toulouse.

Clemenceau, like Pétain, knew not to push the symbolism of power too far. He never moved against Painlevé, who in any event had never directly compromised himself. But Painlevé was pushed aside politically until after the war. Aristide Briand, it turned out, had his own set of friends who had friends among the Germans. Yet Clemenceau contented himself with frightening Briand into silence until Clemenceau himself left politics, after he lost the presidential election of 1920.

Wartime politics in 1917 showed itself a tough game in the country that, after all, had given the world the guillotine. But although Clemenceau personified the brutalization of politics in France in 1917, he did not effect that brutalization all by himself. The nation decided to continue the war, and accepted and even embraced Clemenceau's method of doing so. But the second mobilization meant polarizing of the national community. Previously, and periods like the Dreyfus Affair aside, the Third Republic had functioned as a collection of more or less amiable middle-class men ruling from a broadly defined republican center. After 1917, this broad consensus came to an end bit by bit. Clemenceau's enemies, unlike those of Robespierre or even Robespierre himself, would live to fight another day. Indeed, they would reenter the arena far sooner than the Tiger might have anticipated. Disillusion with the peace made by Clemenceau spread quickly, and was exploited by his enemies. Painlevé and Briand would both help engineer Clemenceau's defeat in 1920. Malvy and even Caillaux would return to office by 1924. None of these men had forgotten how ugly politics had become after 1917. Chronic economic turmoil, continuing into the 1920s as the full costs of the war hit home, and deepening with the Great Depression of the 1930s, further polarized French politics. The politics of exclusion in 1917 set the stage for the self-inflicted crippling of the Third Republic in the 1930s.

5 The ambiguous victory and its aftermath

The last year of the Great War proved the most paradoxical, and remains even today the year least understood by historians. Germany finalized its victory over Russia in March 1918, by concluding a harsh peace with the Bolshevik successors to the tsar's regime with the Treaty of Brest Litovsk. That same month, the Germans began a drive for total victory along the Western Front that again brought them within a two-day march of Paris. Yet at no time in the war would success prove so deceptive, or so perilous. By November, the Germans had to request an armistice, and it seemed as though the Allies had won. But to the end, the Great War remained a war of attrition. To the end, attrition weakened both sides. The Allies, and particularly France, had good reasons to stop the war when they did. No one could be sure just how long support for the war would hold up anywhere, and leaders through Europe feared that the communist revolution preached by the new regime in Russia might overwhelm them all. As hard as the French tried to make it look like one, the Armistice signed in November 1918 was not quite a German surrender. The German army returned home in good order, greeted by an explanation of what had happened that would come to haunt all of Europe – that the German army had not been defeated, but had been "stabbed in the back" on the home front, by socialists and by Jews.

The French believed fervently that they had won the war after the signing of the Armistice. In many respects, they had done so. But having fought a total war, the French wanted a "total" peace in the absence of a total military victory. The British and the Americans would remind the French often that the Germans had been driven out by an international coalition that would speak from divergent interests in cobbling together a peace. The Treaty of Versailles, signed in July 1919, would not resolve the disparity between what France had sacrificed and what it had gained out of the war. The end of the war, the expulsion of the invader from occupied France, and even the reintegration of Alsace and Lorraine into the national territory, did not seem adequately to explain why the war

146

had been worthwhile. In this sense, the war continued long after the Armistice, as the French struggled in mass mourning to understand the meaning of the war and of the national community that had fought it and had survived it. Commemoration sought, at times desperately, to provide what the bare facts of the end of the war did not. Clemenceau had good reason to title his 1934 memoirs *Grandeurs et misères d'une victoire* (Grandeurs and miseries of a victory).

From the *Kaiserschlacht* to the clearing at Rethondes

In his first order of the day for what turned out to be the last year of the war, General Pétain, never a man known for undue optimism, struck a somber note: "1918 begins. The struggle must continue, the fate of France requires it. Be patient, be persistent... You have shown the firm will to fight as long as it takes to assure peace to your sons, because you know that if the most hard-pressed call for peace, the most resilient fix its conditions." He promised his troops only more hardship and death, and never in the document used any form of the word *victoire*, or victory. And not without reason. The cathartic experience of the crises of 1917 and the rededication of the national community to the struggle might have prevented the French from losing the war. But nothing about the second mobilization could in itself guarantee that the French would win it. Pétain had essentially lost faith in a complete Allied victory by 1918. His strategic plan called for a major offensive in Alsace and Lorraine in 1919, in order to guarantee that France would have something to show for the war should peace break out.

Not least among the paradoxes of 1918 is that the Allied victory came largely at the hands of the Germans. The massive German gamble that began with the declaration of unrestricted submarine warfare at the end of January 1917 (and that drew the United States into the war) culminated in the last great German offensive on the Western Front. This offensive is known variously as the *Kaiserschlacht* (or the Emperor's Battle), the Ludendorff offensive (after its mastermind General Erich Ludendorff), or as Operation Siegfried (meaning the victory to bring peace). Its objective was to take advantage of the temporary superiority Germany enjoyed as a result of the defeat of Russia to win a definitive victory in the West before the Americans arrived in large numbers.

Though Allied commanders on the Western Front had not wholly appreciated it at the time, the Germans had revolutionized tactics in the victory over the Italians at Caporetto in October 1917. They created gaps in the enemy positions by a short but fierce artillery barrage, then used specially trained units called *Sturmtruppen* (stormtrooopers) to infiltrate

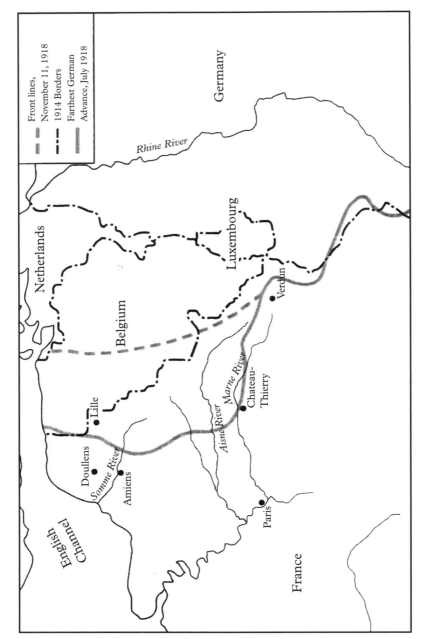

Map 2. The end of the war: March–November 1918.

these positions and create chaos through destroying communications. The regular infantry would then destroy remaining islands of resistance. In themselves, these tactics were neither entirely new nor unique to the Germans. But in March 1918 they would be employed on a larger scale and to a greater effect than ever before, in hopes of ending the war in a German victory. Indeed, tactical innovation and the resulting *percée* came to be seen as ends in themselves. As at Caporetto, the Germans did not have a specific strategy for turning a tremendous tactical success into a strategic victory. Ludendorff himself in planning for the March offensive pointedly avoided the terms "strategy" or even "operation." He sought to rupture the enemy position. "For the rest," he concluded, "we shall see." This lack of strategic focus proved critical as the offensive proceeded.

In retrospect, and from the point of view of the Allies, the first phase of the Ludendorff offensive posed the greatest danger. On March 21, 1918, the Germans attacked the British 5th Army at a quiet sector of the front where the British and the French armies met. Within forty-eight hours, the British had been driven back nearly forty miles, with horrendous casualties. But the possible separation of the two Allied armies posed the greatest danger. If the British retreated north to the ports along the English Channel and the French retreated south and east to protect Paris, the Germans would find a war-winning open corridor into the rest of France.

The prospect of just such a scenario was far more real than many cared to admit after the Armistice. In a spirit of gathering disaster, Allied military and political leaders met on March 26 in Doullens, fewer than thirty kilometers from the front lines. Lloyd George and War Minister Lord Milner were there for the British, and President Poincaré and Clemenceau for the French. Poincaré claimed later that Pétain had confided in him that British commander Field Marshal Sir Douglas Haig would shortly have to surrender to the Germans in open field, and himself not long thereafter. After years of dithering, the time had come to unify Allied military command. Because the fighting took place in France, because the French still held most of the front, and because Lloyd George had little confidence in his own generals, the job of directing the Allied response had to go to a Frenchman.

The Doullens conference completed the ascendancy of General Ferdinand Foch. Known before the war as an apostle of the doctrine of the offensive at the École de Guerre, Foch's star had risen and fallen with that of Joffre. After Joffre's removal at the end of 1916, Foch had been given the humiliating task of studying the unlikely prospect of a German invasion of France through Switzerland. But after the 1917 mutinies, Foch had been made Chief of General Staff, a post redefined as senior military adviser to the government. At Doullens, Foch carefully set himself up as everything Pétain was not – full of confidence and as someone who saw the opportunities presented by the return of the war of movement, provided the Allied armies remained together. The key, as he saw it, involved holding on to the railway and road junction of Amiens. "My plan is not complicated," he exclaimed to the company. "I want to fight! I would fight to the north, I would fight along the Somme River, I would fight along the Aisne River, in Lorraine, in Alsace! I would always fight! I would strike at the Boche until we bring him down!" Such extravagant talk may have seemed at best peculiar at the time. But Clemenceau knew how to make use of it:

Pétain said we were beaten, while Foch behaved like a madman and wanted to fight. I said to myself, "Let's try Foch. At least we'll die with the rifle in our hand." I dropped the sensible man, full of reason, Pétain, and adopted the madman, Foch. The madman saved us.

Clearly, of course, Foch was not so mad as all that. The most famous expression attached to him was "*De quoi s'agit-il?*" (What is at stake here?). At least by 1918, and better late than never, Foch had acquired an exceptional understanding of what the essential strategic questions were. He had learned how to play to his strengths and his enemy's weaknesses. In the short run, he understood that the Allied armies had to remain joined and that they could surrender neither Amiens, nor the Channel ports, nor least of all Paris. But he understood that the German offensive would dissipate sooner or later, provided the Allied lines held. In the meantime, the Allies could trade a considerable amount of space for time, so that the unlimited resources of the United States could be brought to bear.

The Allies gave Foch the authority to effect a genuinely unified Allied strategic plan, for the first time in the war. He became first "coordinator" and in April 1918 "commander-in-chief" of the Allied armies. He had responsibility for strategic direction of the British, French, and (most reluctantly) the American armies, though the commanders of each national army retained tactical direction. Each commander also retained the right to appeal to his political leaders if he felt his army was in grave danger because of decisions made by Foch. Most importantly, these arrangements gave Foch the authority to build up a large body of reserves and to deploy them when he believed they could be used to determine the outcome of the war. In August, Clemenceau made Foch a Marshal of France, the highest honor in the French army. Joffre had been made a marshal at the end of 1916, but as a means of softening the blow of his dismissal. Foch became the only marshal of France in the twentieth century actually to lead troops in battle as a Marshal.

In the meantime, Germany played into the hands of the Allies. German misfortune in the propaganda war continued. On Good Friday, March 29, 1918, a shell landed on the Saint-Gervais Church in central Paris, killing eighty-eight people and providing fresh evidence of German "barbarism," as if any artillery piece in the world was accurate enough to hit that specific church by aiming at it. The Germans also played into the emerging Allied strategy. Thwarted in his effort to split the British and French armies, Ludendorff attacked the British army in Flanders on April 9. He sought to threaten the Channel ports directly, and thus force the British to withdraw there to defend them. Paris came within shell range from the "Big Bertha" artillery piece. When after substantial gains the Flanders offensive bogged down, Ludendorff attacked the French along the Chemin des Dames on May 27. In so doing, he hoped again to threaten Paris, and to draw French reserves away from the British front. Once more, the Germans enjoyed considerable success, as parts of the French army again found themselves south of the Marne River. The Germans had gained considerably more ground than any army on the Western since 1914. But they had paid a huge price – by official figures 915,000 casualties between March and the end of June. They had broken through the Allied lines in a number of places, but proved unable to exploit any of these *percée* strategically. Once the Allied position stabilized, the Germans found themselves exposed in several dangerous salients. They had staked everything on routing an enemy alliance that grew stronger every day in numbers and in materiel. By July, Foch and the Allies were ready to respond.

The series of Allied counteroffensives between July and November 1918 that finally ended the Great War can only be understood as a common Allied effort – not that one would be able to tell this from what remains a stunningly nationalist historiography. The British had their own "crisis of morale," to some extent analogous to the French army mutinies of 1917, in their initial response to the Ludendorff offensive. But the British army, together with its imperial counterparts, recovered remarkably, first in wearing down the German offensives and then in being able to resume offensive warfare. The Americans fought with the enthusiasm (and the casualties) of the armies of August 1914. But they had made time the friend of the Allies. Their presence and the knowledge on both sides that millions more "doughboys" were en route to Europe convinced Germany that its cause was lost. The French rose to the challenge of the final liberation of their homeland. A truly international history of the battles of 1918 remains to be written.

Clemenceau once quipped that war had become too important to be left to generals. This may have been true, but Foch and his colleagues in the national armies in 1918 at last put together a coherent strategy that overwhelmed the Germans. Beginning on July 15, 1918, a series of Allied counteroffensives began that essentially did not let up until the Armistice on November 11. In August 1918, Colonel Mott, liaison officer from American commander General John Pershing to the Allied High Command, met Marshal Foch returning from mass in a small village. As Mott recalled:

I ventured the remark that the Germans seemed to be getting more than they could stand. He came up close to me, took a firm hold on my belt with his left hand, and with his right fist delivered a punch at my chin, a hook under my ribs, and another drive at my ear; he then shouldered his stick and without a single word marched to the chateau.

Since late-1914, strategists had dreamed of a single grand *percée*, in which the cavalry followed by infantry would flood into the gap and end the war. Instead, Foch coordinated a succession of smaller-scale Allied counteroffensives up and down the front – from the Marne in August, to Picardy and Flanders in August, along the Aisne River and toward Lorraine in September.[1] In a sense, his strategy mirrored what Ludendorff had done since March. But unlike his German counterpart, Foch had the resources to pursue major attacks in several sectors of the Western Front simultaneously.

Through the fall of 1918, the Allied pressure on the Central Powers expanded to various other theatres, many of which had laid dormant for some time. In the Middle East, British and some French troops moved toward the Ottoman Empire through Palestine and Mesopotamia (present-day Iraq), bringing pressure on Germany's most remote ally and setting the stage for interwar Allied imperial expansion in a part of the world even then important for its oil reserves. The Allies also advanced on the Salonika front, which hitherto had served mostly as a de facto internment camp for French, British, and Imperial forces. Somewhat reluctantly, the Allied political leaders permitted the French commander, General Louis Franchet d'Esperey, who had been sent there partly as a punishment for reverses on his sector of the Western Front in the spring of 1918, to dust off a scheme formulated by General Sarrail to attack Germany's tiny and feeble ally Bulgaria and to advance on Austria-Hungary through the Balkans. On September 18, French and Serbian troops broke through the Bulgarian lines at Dubropolje, and by the end of October the Allies

[1] It was with this sort of counteroffensive strategy, and not strictly speaking a Verdun-style defensive strategy, that the French and British used against the Germans with disastrous results in the spring of 1940. For their part, the Germans learned the lessons of the spring of 1918, and made their first goal driving apart the French and British armies.

had reached the border of Hungary. Certainly, this often-forgotten Allied military success helped hasten the disintegration of the Habsburg Monarchy. Italian, French, and British troops attacked on the Italian front on October 24, regaining the ground lost at Caporetto in 1917 and helping seal the fate of Austria-Hungary. Even the peace imposed on the newborn Soviet Union at Brest Litovsk in January 1918 came back to haunt the Germans, for it kept on occupation duty a German army of one million men badly needed in the West and elsewhere. The Allies could fight on all of these fronts; Germany and its faltering allies could not. The Central Powers called for an armistice when the Allies overwhelmed them inside Europe and beyond.

In the end, the dirty little secret of the Great War was that although it took more than four years, the Allied strategy of attrition ultimately worked. The Allied naval blockade had a gradual but serious impact on German supplies of food and raw materials. By 1918 even the German army, which had highest priority in food distribution, experienced real hunger. To some extent, hunger proved a factor in driving the Germans forward, so that they could fall on enemy food supplies. But Ludendorff complained that soldiers slowed their advance and sometimes stopped completely once they encountered the opportunity to eat. In the next war, Hitler would see to it that Germany remained well fed, if occupied Europe starved.

To be sure, a more coherent Allied command under Foch proved adept at taking advantage of the opportunities presented by the Germans. Technological innovations helped, particularly in the last six months of the war. Allied tanks outnumbered German tanks by about 800 to 10. The French light tank made by Renault proved the most effective tank made in the Great War. The Allies used some 4,500 airplanes for reconnaissance and early forms of bombing, the Germans 3,800. Indeed, tanks broke down frequently, and airplanes were small and fragile. But careful coordination between the two new kinds of forces supported the step-by-step, methodical advance managed by Foch that kept the front from recongealing, as it had after every German or Allied advance up to that time.

Fundamentally, the Allies simply proved better at waging total war, not least because they had more resources to wage it with. The Germans suffered 1.76 million men killed, wounded, missing, or captured between March and November 1918 and could not replace them. The French army was able to expend 280,000 of the 75mm shells per day at the beginning of its counteroffensive, in addition to an emerging formidable heavy artillery. In an attack by the French 5th Infantry Division on July 25–7, the division artillery fired one heavy shell per 1.16 meters of front, and three 75mm shells per meter of front. Plainly, the victory of 1918 was not the sort preached by Foch at the École de Guerre back in 1903, in which he maintained that war was the domain of moral force. The battles of 1918 showed that the spirit rested on material foundations.

But as had been the case throughout the war, attrition wore down both sides. The Allies suffered fully as many casualties as the Germans, and could not have prevailed without essentially unlimited reserves of American manpower. The French army suffered 306,000 men killed, missing, or taken prisoner between March and November 1918 – the most lethal phase of the war since its first battles. For French soldiers in the field, hope for victory combined with a particular form of anguish – the prospect of death or mutilation in the last quarter hour of the war. One soldier from the 224th Regiment wrote of a volatile state of mind:

It is impossible to describe to you the weariness, the discouragement (happily ephemeral) that was on the face of all these men, bowing under the same discipline, under a single will. There are moments when you are tempted to throw everything to the ground, but against yourself, in seeing all your comrades march, personal dignity rises up again, and self-respect once more takes hold of you. It is at this moment that the memory of those dear to you brings back the strength and the energy that had escaped.

This soldiers' division, the 5th Infantry Division, saw its last action in the war marching into Belgium alongside the Belgian army. The Germans never fought more than a rearguard action, with machine-guns and artillery. Nevertheless, casualties between October 13 and November 11 were surprisingly high – 210 men killed, 1,068 men wounded, and 210 men missing. The number missing seems suspiciously high, given that there had been virtually no contact with German infantry that could have taken them prisoner.

Even the Allied superiority in artillery proved a diminishing resource. No one had done more than General Pétain to put into practice his adage that artillery conquers and infantry occupies. But as early as July 19 (a mere four days after the beginning of the French counteroffensive) he expressed concern about the French expenditure of shells: "The habit has been established of firing daily five or six times the number of projectiles fired by the Germans, and no one dares claim that the results are worth the expenditure of shells . . . This bad habit must not continue." The supply of 75mm shells stood at 28 million in March 1918 and at 8.5 million in October. And new doubts arose as to how long French workers would be willing to toil all-out to replace them.

A new wave of labor unrest broke out in France in the spring of 1918, when German victory seemed like a real possibility. The authorities noted a disquietingly "political" tone to these demonstrations, often more so than with the strikes of 1917. The prefect of the department of the Isère wrote to the Ministry of the Interior of a strike in Grenoble in April 1918: "The workers have but one idea anymore that haunts them – the social revolution." The strikes shortly spread to the metallurgy industry, particularly in the critical arms production areas of Paris and the department of the Loire. Some strikers employed rhetoric remarkably reminiscent of the army mutinies. "What we want," proclaimed a delegate from a Hotchkiss machine-gun factory in May 1918, "is first of all that the government tell us what are its war aims and its conditions for making peace. We want to know why and for whom our fellows fight, because we say that enough blood has been shed and that it is time to seek, by any means possible, an end to the carnage."

But perhaps it is precisely the similarity between these strikes and the mutinies that explains why most strikes dissipated within a few days. Clovis Andrieu, a labor militant before the war and a soldier released for factory work, demanded in the name of the working class during a strike in the Loire in May 1918 that the government open negotiations with the Germans. Yet the previous December he had told Clemenceau directly that "he would always be a pacifist, but never a defeatist." He told a police commissioner during the May strike that if the conversations he demanded with the Germans did not produce results, "we will come back to offer our very hides to the country." In the end, fears that the working classes of Western Europe would abandon the struggle were probably exaggerated. Distrust of working-class patriotism persisted because workers gave clear notice that patriotism by no means excluded class struggle. No trade union leader had worked more closely with Albert Thomas and the Ministry of Armaments than Alphonse Merrheim, head of the Fédération des Métaux. Yet that same Merrheim told a meeting on October 13, 1918, less than one month before the Armistice:

For us, the real war will begin the day after the signing of the peace. At that moment, we will stand up to our exploiters. We must not be vanquished as we were in August 1914.

Ideological remobilization in 1917 and 1918 had reopened the whole question of what the war was about, and had raised the ideological stakes in ways European politicians on both sides found unsettling. In 1959, Arno Mayer provided an intriguing explanation of the ideological configuration of forces in 1918. Mayer wrote against the backdrop of the Cold War, a time when Europeans had largely lost control over geopolitics in Europe. He posited a new and bi-polar ideological configuration as early as 1918, with the forces of movement (Wilson and Lenin, the unlikely pair of utopians), opposing the forces of order (less visionary leaders such as Clemenceau and Lloyd George).[2] V. I. Lenin, leader of the new Bolshevik regime in Russia, called for a general European revolution to stop the war and overthrow capitalism itself. Throughout Europe and particularly in Germany, workers listened to Lenin and his followers with considerable sympathy. President Wilson had made his utopian statement in a speech to Congress in January 1918, in which he outlined his "Fourteen Points". He put forward a vision of a nineteenth-century liberal paradise, in which the market and the ballot box would, as if by magic, end conflict among nations and classes. Diplomacy would henceforth be conducted openly, without secret agreements. Germany, of course, would have to withdraw from its ill-gotten conquests of 1870 and 1914. But, chastened and presumably democratized, it could thereafter resume its traditional role among the Great Powers of Europe. Wilson, whose constituency comprised millions of German-Americans, proclaimed himself no enemy of German "greatness" as such.

In different ways, Lenin and Wilson both horrified Clemenceau and Lloyd George. The war leaders of France and Britain had seen regime after regime to their east topple since 1917, and no one could be entirely sure where the tide of revolution would stop. And both Clemenceau and Lloyd George were very much opposed to German "greatness" as such. But European politicians and Foch all realized that each day the war continued increased American power, and thus American influence over the peace. Clemenceau, Lloyd George, Kaiser Wilhelm II, along with German, French, and British High Command all came to have a common interest in ending the war when they did. Politics never made stranger bedfellows than in 1918.

The German call for an armistice came amidst the military and political disintegration of Germany's allies, and ultimately, of the kaiser's regime itself. The Germans appealed, quite publicly, to President Wilson on October 4 (more than a month before the war actually ended) for an end to the war based on the Fourteen Points. The appeal held out the prospect of an idealistic peace before the peoples of Europe. Millions on both sides came to hope that the war might actually end. They would not suffer these hopes being dashed lightly. Civilian war weariness increased further through the effects of the coincidental global pandemic of the (misnamed) Spanish Influenza, which killed some 20 million people worldwide, among them Guillaume Apollinaire.

In France, Right-wing newspapers particularly made the case that the Allied advance should continue into Germany, and not stop short

---

[2] Arno Mayer, *Political Origins of the New Diplomacy* (New Haven: Yale University Press, 1959).

of an unconditional surrender. Many on the American side supported this view, perhaps not surprisingly given that American troops had only been engaged in large numbers since the summer of 1918. After the war, recriminations emerged that France, and particularly Clemenceau and Foch, had agreed to an armistice precipitously. But foremost in the thoughts of those who bore responsibility for the war effort was ending the fighting as soon as possible, consistent with conditions that would make it impossible for Germany to resume the war once the shooting stopped.

On November 8, German emissaries met Marshal Foch in the office car of his personal train. Major General von Winterfeldt wore the medal of the Légion d'Honneur, a prestigious French decoration given to him before the war. Foch set the tone by snapping at him, as if he were Foch's subordinate, "I authorize you not to wear that." The verbal taunting continued. When Foch asked the purpose of their visit, they told him that they had come to hear Allied proposals for an armistice. Foch responded that he had no proposals to make. Count Oberndorff, another member of the German delegation, asked how they should express themselves, and what were the conditions of the armistice. Foch replied that he had no conditions to offer. Exasperated, Mathias Erzberger read a note from President Wilson stating that the Allies had authorized Foch to make known the conditions for an armistice. Foch responded that he was authorized to make these conditions known if the Germans asked for an armistice, and inquired whether they now did so. Only when Erzberger and Oberndorff replied in the affirmative did Foch actually read the conditions for the armistice. During the encounter in his railroad car, Foch played a delicate game that would foreshadow the French approach to peacemaking. The term "armistice" implies a cessation of hostilities, not a surrender. He did everything he could to make these terms synonymous, and to give France the total victory it had not quite won in the field.

On November 11, 1918, after the German delegates consulted with what remained of the German government and after a few minor changes in the armistice agreement, the German delegates again presented themselves in Foch's railway car, then parked in a clearing at Rethondes in the Compiègne Forest. The agreement required a German withdrawal from occupied France, Belgium, Luxembourg, and Alsace and Lorraine within fifteen days. The Germans had to hand over to the Allies 5,000 artillery pieces, 25,000 machine-guns, 3,000 trench mortars, 1,700 airplanes, and all of their submarines. The Allies had agreed to 5,000 fewer machine-guns than they had originally demanded, so that the government could guarantee internal order in Germany. The Germans had to withdraw all military forces from the right and left banks of the Rhine, which would become an Allied zone of occupation pending the signature of a final peace treaty. The French made sure to send black African colonial troops into the Rhineland, as a clearly racist gesture to humiliate the Germans as much as possible. In addition to the strictly military equipment demanded by the Allies, the Germans had to turn over 5,000 locomotives, 150,000 train cars, and 5,000 trucks, despite German protests that this could lead to famine among the civilian population. German troops in Austria-Hungary, Rumania, and the Ottoman Empire had to return to Germany immediately. Significantly, German troops in Revolutionary Russia had to return "as soon as the Allies shall think suitable, having regard to the internal situation of these territories." This provision clearly indicated continuing Allied concern about containing the threat of a general European revolution. The German delegates signed the agreement at 5:00 AM, and it came into effect at 11:00 AM. After signing the Armistice, Erzberger read a statement that concluded:

> The German nation, which for fifty months has defied a world of enemies, will persevere, in spite of every kind of violence, its liberty and unity.
> A nation of seventy million suffers but does not die.

Nearly 1,600 days after the declaration of war, the shooting finally stopped, on the eleventh hour of the eleventh day of the eleventh month of the fifth year of the war. Throughout France, people poured into the streets to celebrate, in one of the three greatest outpourings of national joy in France in the twentieth century.[3] People ran through the streets, crying, shouting, and singing the national anthem, *La Marseilleise*. Strangers kissed each other passionately. It was said that 50,000 Parisians filled the Place de l'Opéra. One observer wrote: "Even the parents of the dead got caught up in it, in spite of themselves. For one brief moment, they forgot their pain." A bit before 4:00 PM, Clemenceau appeared before the Chamber of Deputies. He read the terms of the Armistice, and added simply: "At this terrible hour, great and magnificent, my duty is done ... In the name of the French people, in the name of the Republic of France, I send the salute of France, one and indivisible, to reclaimed Alsace and Lorraine!" Clemenceau received a tumultuous and well-deserved standing ovation.

Yet just what it all had been for proved much less clear than perhaps it seemed to the revelers of the night of November 11, 1918. Indeed, the invader had finally been expelled. But had the war really made France safe once and for all from the enemy across the Rhine? France had not

---

[3] The other two were the liberation of France from the Germans in 1944, and the unexpected victory of France in the World Cup soccer competition of 1998.

suffered 1.3 million dead for 25,000 German machine-guns, still less to give Marshal Foch the pleasure of bullying a German general. Eventually, the country would need an even better explanation than regaining occupied France and Alsace and Lorraine. Against a backdrop of popular frenzy and relief, what became the failed quest for peace began.

Commemoration: memory and the struggle for meaning

No one in France after the Great War better understood the cultural ordeal of mourning and memory than Marcel Proust, perhaps the greatest French novelist of the twentieth century. The introverted Proust wrote in dense and elliptical prose that does not translate easily. Too old to have been mobilized in the war, he had only begun to achieve celebrity in the last years before his death in 1922. In a private letter written in 1918, he compared the soldiers of the Great War to the cathedrals north of Paris that he had visited before the war: "Today I weep, and I admire the soldiers even more than the cathedrals. For the cathedrals are but the setting in stone of a heroic gesture, which the soldiers today renew at every moment."[4] In these few words, Proust posed the problem faced by those who had lived through the Great War in France and elsewhere. After the war, the living could rebuild the cathedrals destroyed by the war, and thus set again their various meanings in stone. But what meaning could one fix on the dead, apart from a double injunction repeated endlessly in France after 1918 – never forget and never allow such a catastrophe to happen again? The absurd, abstract questions posed in *Parade* in 1917 now seemed immediate and unmistakably real.

A few years after the war, Maurice Halbwachs became the first professor of sociology at a French university. Not by coincidence, this position was created at the University of Strasbourg in Alsace. By this kind of innovation, the French included an intellectual component in their reconquest of the lost territories.[5] Halbwachs had worked for Albert Thomas in the Ministry for Armaments during the war. Upon resuming his academic career, Halbwachs pioneered the concept of collective memory.[6] Taking the ideas of Henri Bergson and Sigmund Freud on dreams as his

---

[4] Marcel Proust, *Correspondance générale*, 6 vols. (Paris: Plon, 1930), vol. VI, p. 193. For purposes of clarity, we have provided a somewhat liberal translation. The original French reads: "Je pleure et j'admire plus les soldats que les églises qui ne furent que la fixation d'un geste héroïque, aujourd'hui à chaque instant recommencé."

[5] Many of the most important university teachers of their day taught at Strasbourg, including historians Marc Bloch, Lucien Febvre, Etienne Gilson, and Charles Blondel.

[6] Maurice Halbwachs, *On Collective Memory*, Lewis Coser, ed. and trans. (Chicago: University of Chicago Press, 1992 [originally published in French in 1925]).

À MON ÉPOUX CHÉRI

TERRIBLE GUERRE, toi qui m'a enlevé mon bien-aimé où tu n'as mis à la place plus que des pleurs et n'a pas voulu notre bonheur.

Tu m'as fait quitter ma robe d'épouse pour prendre le grand voile de la veuve éplorée. Pourquoi! Étais-tu jalouse de notre bonheur?

À trente-huit ans, mon mari bien-aimé, tu as quitté ta femme chérie pour venger ta Patrie me laissant peu d'espoir et à trente-neuf ans, après un an de souffrances endurées, tu m'as quitté, hélas pour toujours, me laissant le cœur brisé.

Maintenant pour me consoler, il ne me reste plus qu'à aller m'agenouiller sur cette pierre glacée.

Adieu mon mari chéri Je te pleurerai toute ma vie.

C. IMBERT - 7 RUE HOCHE   TOULON

Plate 7. Enameled metal plaque. Translation: "To my dear husband: TERRIBLE WAR, you who have taken away my beloved, to leave in his place only tears, you who did not want us to be happy. You made me leave behind my wife's dress to take up the great veil of the widow in tears. Why? Were you jealous of our happiness? At the age of thirty-eight, my beloved husband, you left your dear wife to go avenge your *Patrie*, leaving me little hope, and at the age of thirty-nine years, after a

points of departure, Halbwachs argued that memories are both individual and private. But if individuals remembered, in a literal sense, groups established what was "memorable." Memory is thus complete only in a social setting. There would be as many "memories" as there are groups and institutions in a given society. Because of the social character of memory, public events heavily imprint themselves on the people, particularly among the young still in the process of forming their adult identities. Such a conception of memory helps us understand veterans of the Great War, who it is easy to forget were often young men in 1918. Collective memory also helps understand how the war profoundly shaped the lives of their children, particularly those born during and above all just after the war, who grew up encased in its heroic or tragic memory.

Halbwachs further argued that personal memory retains traces unique to each individual, traces which mix in various ways with shared and collective memories. But as Freud argued with desires, memories also take shape in a context of resistance, whether through forgetting or through repression. While much about everyday life can simply be forgotten, trauma can be repressed. Although he pointedly avoided the phenomenon of repression, Halbwachs believed that memory and the pain of mourning had to be understood at both their individual and collective levels, and in their creative as well as negative aspects. For Halbwachs, what societies and individuals remember thus involves subtle, complex, and often subconscious choices, whether we think of interior and interiorised memory or of publicly demonstrated historic memory. Each operates both according to a continuity with the past and to a selection from it. Memories create new memories. From this process is constructed a new continuity.

Taken together, the ideas of Proust and Halbwachs seem a good way to begin to understand how the French in public and private tried to come to terms with loss after the Great War. As might people anywhere who had been through such a traumatic experience, the French tried to fix the meaning of the war, like the stones in a cathedral. And they constructed that meaning through constructing memory, a process that took place individually and collectively through remembering, repressing, and forgetting. In very different ways, Proust and Halbwachs illustrate tensions in the ways the French came to terms with the Great War. They help illuminate why memory of the war cast such a long shadow over the history of France in the twentieth century.

> Plate 7. (*cont.*) year of living in suffering, you left me, alas forever, leaving me broken-hearted. Now, in order to console myself, I can only kneel before this frozen stone. *Adieu*, my poor dear husband. I will weep for you all of my life." Reprinted with the permission of the Historial de la Grande Guerre.

Certainly, as the quote from Proust suggests, the end of war did not diminish the inclinations of the French and others to view the war and its end in religious terms, indeed to set nations and their struggles at the heart of an intense cosmological mystery. The French continued to combine the secular struggle between civilization and barbarism to the religious struggle between good and evil. Soldiers had suffered, died, or even survived in imitation of Christ. France, always personified as female, imitated the Virgin Mary. The living had a religious duty to honor the dead. Abbé Lemerle, inverting the call in Jacques Péricard's war story "Debout les Morts!" discussed in Chapter 2, told believers: "So then, arise the living! Yes, arise to honor the valiant defenders of the country!" Most crucially in the weeks and months after the Armistice, the French retained a sort of religious certainty that the "Just Peace" concluding the Just War by definition would avenge the evil caused by the war. Faith, grief, and revenge could meet in making the peace and commemorating the war.

Faced with the catastrophe of the Great War, many found meaning in the death of their loved ones as martyrs in the cause of God's own war. Catholics in particular proved adept at blurring the contentious line drawn in 1905 separating Church and State by combining religious and political commemoration of the dead. In churches as well as in "secular" public spaces, countless stained-glass windows, monuments, sermons, and speeches testified to the compatibility of political liturgy, religious sentiment, and private mourning. Simply adding a prayer for a fallen soldier to the Mass on a given saint's day could create a particular kind of religious memory. Catholics evoked these new and unofficial saints more discretely than saints already recognized on the liturgical calendar. But in various ways into the 1920s and 1930s, the French created religious and political memory through mourning.

Thousands of individual communes, not just in traditionally devout regions but throughout France, memorialized the dead in Christian idioms. Representations of Joan of Arc on monuments mixed together her patriotism and her Catholicism. Perhaps it was not a coincidence that the Pope canonized her in 1920. Catholic commemoration privileged the suffering of Jesus in the Passion. In memorials and stained-glass windows, churches represented the war as a vast Good Friday, the day Jesus was crucified. The front line became Golgotha, the site of the Crucifixion. The soldiers became so many Christs, and Christ became a soldier. The Christian soldier emulated the sacrifice of Christ. When the soldier's mother, the new version of Virgin Mary, found her son and held him in her arms, the memorial became a wartime *pietà*, a representation of the Catholic prayer *Stabat mater dolorosa*, the holy mother of sorrows. Artists sometimes portrayed these weeping mothers in regional dress, occasion-ally even accompanied by an inscription in Basque or Breton, regional languages completely distinct from French. National mourning mingled with local identity.

Immediately after the war, the French created what historian Pierre Nora called *lieux de mémoire* or "sites of memory," both on the former battlefields and behind the lines.[7] The national community consecrated places where soldiers suffered and died, transforming them into places where the living, both individually and collectively, could remember them – cemeteries, ossuaries, and monuments. Everywhere French sol-diers fought – most importantly the Western Front, but also the Balkans and the Dardanelles, even prison camps – cemeteries, stelae, or com-memorative monuments recall the sacrifice. French monuments outside of France also served to nationalize territories permanently marked by the death of Frenchmen. In military cemeteries as remote from France as Istanbul and Sed ul Bar, in the Gallipoli peninsula, the authorities engraved the famous, haunting words of Charles Péguy's *Eve* (1913):

> Happy are those who die in a just war.
> Happy the ripened grain, the harvest wheat.

Monuments of memory and mourning extended the Great War through-out the country, to the places where the soldiers had worked, loved, stud-ied, and prayed. Through commemoration, civilians brought the front back to the interior – sometimes literally. Local authorities would bring in soil taken from Verdun and place it in urns in front of war memorials or in the town halls. Commemorative space could be created through bringing sacralized soil into rituals of mourning.

Commemoration sought to restate the Union sacrée in ceremony, as well as cast it in stone and bronze, at precisely the moment when the French could begin to calculate its full cost. Some expressed a virulent anti-commemorative pacifism, such as veteran and barrelmaker Louis Barthas, who wrote in February 1919:

In the villages, people are already talking about putting up monuments to glory, to the apotheosis of the victims of the great killing, to those, as the flag-wavers put it, who "voluntarily made the sacrifice of their life," as if the poor men could have chosen, or done otherwise . . . Oh! If the dead of this war could climb out of their graves, how they would break down these monuments to hypocritical pity, for the people who set them up sacrificed them without pity.

---

[7] Pierre Nora, ed., *Realms of Memory: Rethinking the French Past* (New York: Columbia University Press, 1996 [originally published in French, 1984–92]).

But the vast majority of French people, like people throughout the victorious and vanquished countries of Europe, shared a remarkably similar commemorative frenzy, a general homogenization of public space, devoted to memory of the war.

In paradoxical ways, the dead lived on in the war culture of France, even as that culture began to demobilize after 1918. The collective presence of the dead, or their constant "return" found many forms of private and public representation. In Abel Gance's silent film *J'accuse* (1919), the dead rose in a dream of the main protagonist, Jean Diaz, not to return to their graves until the civilians assured them that they would construct a more virtuous France after the war.[8] In daily life, each war dead was remembered in his family, his village, his parish, his place of work. The French state itself took care to remember him by sending representatives to ceremonies of national or local commemoration. In large cities the state might send the prefect, members of the National Assembly, military officers from the area, or any combination of the above. Even in the tiniest French village, duty required the mayor and the local president of the veterans' association to attend ceremonies honoring the dead. Any elected or functionary position turned its office-holder into a state representative of mourning during the 1920s and 1930s, whether that office holder had himself served in the war or not. Public officials stood at the head of bereaved public communities.

The dead met the living in the commemorative ceremonies of November 11, when the entire national community that fought the war met at the same time and in set locations, at monuments to the dead throughout France. Each French man, woman, and child would be called upon to remember that at the eleventh hour of the eleventh day of the eleventh month, in the fifth year of the war, the guns fell silent and transformed the battlefields into sites of mourning. Although November 11 did not become a public holiday until 1922, by 1919 it had already become a day of remembrance and one of the few fully achieved expressions of civil religion.

At these ceremonies, the tricolor flags, the black crêpe, the wreaths of flowers, and the speeches, created a moral and civic pedagogical space in which, at least during the ceremony, the dead would take their place alongside the living. Dead and living veterans, husbands and widows, fathers and orphans seemed to find each other again in the symbolism of the cortège and the silence. To this was added the drama of publicly reading in loud and clear voice the list of the dead, usually by a war orphan.

---

[8] Gance made a sound version of the film in 1937, in which Diaz became something of a mad scientist, who raises the dead to stop, at the last minute, another general European war.

The community would respond in unison "*Mort pour la France* (died for France)." In the villages where this ritual endures even today, this secular "amen" remains even today one of the most poignant moments of the ceremony.[9] Prewar traditions from other holidays like as Bastille Day (July 14), such as fireworks, illuminations, banquets, and sporting events, would sometimes be drawn into this civic liturgy of mourning. But this did not undermine the essentially religious character of the occasion.

It would be a mistake in considering commemorative practice to draw too severe a distinction between civil and religious forms of the sacred. Memorials in villages were often scarcely less overtly religious than monuments in parish churches, as shown in so many *pietà* figures in front of village town halls. Through civic rituals of mourning, an agnostic or an atheist could become adept at sacralization. This spoke to the continued appropriation of elements of Jewish and Christian belief by the national community. At the same time, taking part in civic rituals of mourning could help individuals come to terms with their own grief – in public spaces as large as the Arc du Triomphe in Paris or as small as the individual grave in a military or church cemetery. The French, as individuals and as a nation, sought through commemorative practice both to mourn and to make up for the deficit in meaning left at the signing of the Armistice.

The *Monuments aux morts*

What English speakers call "war memorials" the French call "monuments to the dead." The French term insists on death, the English term the war in its entirety, not just those who lost their lives in it. The French carved only the names of the dead in the official stonework, which forever sought to proclaim their heroism. Perhaps this proceeded from the logic of conscription, a recognition of the debt owed by the political community. Having so closely linked citizenship and military service, the Republic had given its soldiers little choice in the matter. On the other hand, the French have largely ignored the sort of "practical" memorials so familiar to Americans, such as named scholarships, stadiums, or libraries. The French remember their dead of the Great War primarily through a statue at the center of an open public space, as though this were the only true place capable of creating sacredness. In part, mourning became memory by means of sculptors, and then through ceremonies centered around the physical objects they produced.

---

[9] In contrast, commemorative ceremonies in Great Britain in the 1920s would culminate in two minutes of total silence, when all movement ceased. See Adrian Gregory, *The Silence of Memory, Armistice Day, 1919–1946* (Oxford: Berg, 1994).

Certainly, the French had erected monuments to previous wars, and far more than is generally realized to the Franco-Prussian war of 1870–1. But only with the Great War did memorials become universal, reminders throughout the country of the universality of the tragedy of 1914–18. France, like other nations that had fought the war, sought in a profound cultural sense to remake the national community through monuments. As Ken Inglis rightly observed, the creators of war memorials try to forget and to invent as much as to remember.[10] Each of the 36,000 communes into which France was divided had its monument. But to fully understand the intensity of commemoration after the war, we must multiply that number by four or five to include other public or private memorials. The dead might have their names inscribed in any number of places, their businesses, their schools, their parish churches. Millions of French families turned their living rooms into family altars displaying photographs and souvenirs from the deceased.

Monuments to the war dead in communes linked not just the military front and the home front, but Paris and the provinces, the political center of France and its periphery. The circles of mourning extended outwards from individuals and their families, to villages, towns, and cities. As had so often been the case in the history of France, the center could instruct the periphery, here on how to connect local mourning to the survival of the nation. In August 1920, a group of citizens from the village of Mons in the department of the Var protested the location of the proposed monument in a public square, where markets and holiday celebrations might trivialize its meaning. The prefect (the senior official of the central government in the department) responded:

The monument to be built is thus not solely a funerary monument; it is above the passions and sentiments and belongs to posterity . . . The committee should be praised for having chosen a site in a busy spot where the entire population will have forever in view the names of those who, through their sacrifice, contributed mightily to saving the world from barbarism.

War memorials both expressed collective mourning and sought to fix a universal meaning of the war. As such, they held a specific place in the rural or urban landscape as sites of power, where the politics of the individual, the locality, and the nation all came together.

Many communes chose a stela, often an obelisk, similar to the type used to embellish tombs. Inexpensive because of their uniformity, these memorials could transform any public square into a national cemetery, a point not lost on the concerned citizens of Mons. Architects, stone cutters, and

[10] Ken Inglis, "War Memorials: Ten Questions for Historians," *Guerres mondiales et conflits contemporains*, No. 167 (July 1992): pp. 5–21.

funeral directors found in these monuments the marketing opportunity of a lifetime. Shrewd dealers offered catalogues, where localities could customize commemoration by choosing decorations to set on the central stone, such as palms, a laurel-wreath, the military decoration the *Croix de guerre* (war cross), or the image of a soldier. The monument would rest on a plinth resembling a grave, and would carry selected inscriptions. The inscription would begin with some sort of general statement. The words *children, dead, heroes, war, 1914–1918, duty, nation, gratitude, sacrifice, martyrs, memory* appeared most frequently. Words matter in monuments, and the particular words chosen indicated nuances of meaning: "To our heroes" does not mean the same thing as "To our martyrs." The majority of inscriptions indicate gratitude to the dead for their ultimate sacrifice.

Like other aspects of French war culture, the passion for constructing monuments in the 1920s spoke not so much to state direction as to the need of millions of French soldiers and their families to mourn those who died and locate and even fix a meaning of the war. Most inscriptions maintained some degree of political neutrality, which in a particular way expressed the resilience of the Union sacrée. Only about ten monuments in the whole of France carried the inscription "*Que maudite soit la guerre*" ("Cursed be war"). This might seem surprising in a society heavily imbued with pacifist sentiment immediately after 1918. But at least in the 1920s, loss rather than specific lessons for the future seems to have mattered most in the construction of war monuments. In some cases, localities quietly (and harmlessly) defied the state. The Law of Separation of 1905 banned religious decoration from public structures and buildings. But public monuments in the most devoutly Catholic regions of France almost always included a crucifix.

The list of the dead constituted the second component of the inscription. The names usually appeared in alphabetical order, as they did in the military cemeteries. Naming the dead served an important function, both for the community and for each mourner. Naming the dead recalled each individual as such, and thus returned to him an individuated existence that in some symbolic way overcame death, which had despatched the deceased into nothingness. For the living, inscribing the names of the dead, reading them, and then touching the inscription (as was seen in some photographs from the 1920s) served to bring the dead out of the anonymous unreality of loss and emptiness.[11]

---

[11] Maya Lin, designer of the Vietnam Memorial in Washington, DC, understood well this aspect of naming the dead. She acknowledged the influence of memorials from the Great War. "Building a Memorial," *The New York Review of Books*, November 2, 2000.

Some monuments sought to represent the Union sacrée itself, in its combination of struggle, belief, and persistence. At the top of the monument, a rooster represented France, phonetically rather than etymologically – Gallus (the rooster) representing Galia (Gaul). In the center of the monument is a soldier, rifle in hand or throwing a grenade, described as a "worthy son of Vercingétorix" (who had defended Gaul against Julius Caesar). At the foot of the memorial are civilians, old people, women, or children. They either observe the heroic example of the soldier or go about their daily tasks – working in the fields or in the factories. Such memorials praised the courage of the survivors and sought to bind them together in the new ordeal of rebuilding the nation.

Statues of soldiers often sought to present courage and martyrdom in unproblematic ways, and so to put art in the service of a specific construction of memory. A community might choose a monument portraying a *poilu* to establish some sort of immediate connection to the dead from their particular part of France. In *Vieille France* (1933), novelist Roger Martin du Gard described *poilu* monuments with a certain tenderness: "In the midst of the graves, always cheerful, the granite *poilu* on the monument to the dead attacks with his bayonet. It is an old comrade, a kind of barometer. On rainy days he is entirely black; . . . but, in bright sunlight, he becomes blue, the 'horizon-blue' creature he should be. His helmet gleams, sprinkled with powdered glass." Upright on his pedestal, his uniform and weapons presented with great precision, he vows forever to fight for the noble cause for which he gave his life. This *poilu*, quite unlike his flesh-and-blood counterpart, fought an aseptic war, without mud, lice, or injury. He emerges from the war as clean and fresh as the lead soldiers manufactured as children's toys. Veteran and war writer Roger Vercel wrote in *Capitaine Conan* (1934) of "the monument to the dead . . . in which the soldier dies upright, without spoiling a fold of his cape, without releasing the flag which he holds on his heart."

And yet monuments, whether abstract or representational, remain tombs without bodies in them. The reality of death intrudes. Since death, whatever its cause, is always in some sense unthinkable, monuments could neither truly glorify death nor exalt it. Consequently, in the culture of mourning that engulfed France during and after the war, monuments sought at some level to deny death by representing the dead as eternally living, resurrected metonymically in stone and bronze. Only occasionally did creators of monuments lift the taboo on representing death itself. Among these cases, most portrayed a brave knight in his tomb, though a few portrayed a recumbent corpse invaded by rats, and so gave way to an unbearable realism.

Plate 8. Monument to the Dead, Péronne (Somme). Reprinted with the permission of the Historial de la Grande Guerre.

The bodies of the dead

As we saw in Chapter 2, the bodies of the dead of the Great War played an important role in structuring the grief of the survivors. Some of the most important sites involved places where soldiers had actually died, military cemeteries, memorial landscape parks and great battlefield memorials. Throughout the war, the authorities made graves as visible as possible, no doubt to restore an element of humanity to individuals, whose physical remains sometimes amounted to little more than scattered fragments. First in temporary graves and then in official military cemeteries, wooden crosses became the symbol of death in the Great War. Eventually, and in part through Roland Dorgelès's novel *Les Croix de bois* (1919), made into a film by Raymond Bernard in 1932, the "wooden crosses" became the symbol of the war itself.[12]

---

[12] The film has continued to be shown often on November 11 on French television, acquainting successive generations with its version of the Great War.

Through extending the articles of the Treaty of Frankfurt that set up the first European military cemeteries in 1871, Article 225 of the Treaty of Versailles stipulated that: "Allied and associated Governments and the German Government will ensure that the graves of soldiers and sailors buried in their respective territory are respected and maintained." For the French, this involved some 500,000 German dead on French soil. The former enemies did indeed transform grave sites into so many "reliquaries" of sacrifice, or what the Germans called *Heldenhaine*, or "heroes' gardens." But the superficial uniformity of French and German military cemeteries in France does not obscure how the French took revenge on their foes, even after death. French graves are marked by translucent stones that reflect a warm, bright light that obviously symbolizes purity. But the Germans had to mark graves by dark stelae or crosses, an unsubtle reference to the darkness of their cause. The Germans also often had to bury their dead in mass graves designated by the French, no doubt in order to "contaminate" as little French soil as possible.

Western theology and philosophy have generally closely linked the human body with human identity. Grief, as we have argued, requires a particular physical locus, preferably centered on the physical remains of the dead. The French, like the peoples of other belligerent nations, were obsessed with identifying the graves of their dead of the Great War. The legislation of 1920 discussed in Chapter 2, which enabled families to exhume and take home the bodies of their loved ones at state expense, resulted from a protracted political struggle. That struggle had pitted the personal grief of families against those who wanted to concentrate the symbolic importance of soldiers' graves. Yet not quite one-third of those eligible to repatriate the remains of their loved ones did so. More than 1 million French dead remained on or near the battlefields. This transformed battlefields into cemeteries on a scale that matched that of the conflict itself. Ossuaries, literally collection sites for bones, were built to house fragmentary remains. The French tried hard to identify the nationality of such remains, for example by scraps of uniform. But given the well-known effects of high explosives on the human body, these efforts often proved illusory, a fact only recognized much later. Absurdly, French officials maintained for years that the most famous French ossuary, at Douaumont near Verdun, contained the bones only of French dead, as though it were possible to distinguish French bones from German.

The French built three other battlefield ossuaries, Notre-Dame de Lorette (Pas de Calais), Dormans (Marne), and Hartmanwillerkopf (Alsace), renamed Le Veil Armand. They also built a commemorative chapel in Rancourt in the Somme, next to a military cemetery containing a large collective tomb. Each ossuary was located on the site of a terrible battle, and sought overtly to render the battlefield a *campo santo*, or holy field, where the cemetery, the ossuary, the lantern of the dead, and the chapel all met in a union of bones, stone, prayer, and spirituality. In pointed contrast to the *monuments aux morts*, by definition empty tombs, these sites preserved the remains and, in some sense, the identities of thousands of men. Any mourner whose loved one had never been found could imagine him resting in peace there.

Certainly, the bodies of the 1.3 million French dead figured prominently in the two greatest public spectacles in France commemorating the Great War – the victory parade of July 14, 1919 and the procession of the Unknown Soldier on November 11, 1920. Whether missing or present, metaphorical or physical, the bodies of the dead proved the cultural crucible for a nation struggling to reinvent itself in a state of mass mourning. In these two enormous ceremonies in Paris, the national community experienced what remained of the Union sacrée, in a volatile mixture of intensity and disorder often reactivated in national commemoration between the two world wars. In their unending struggle to fix the meaning of the war, the French found themselves caught between their respect for the sacrifice of their heroes and, increasingly, their horror at what many came to see as its uselessness.

The official celebration of the victory took place on the national holiday, July 14, 1919. In the tradition of Bastille Day parades, much of the occasion served to glorify the military, most prominently its hardware and its generals. The focal point was the Arc de Triomphe, a landmark dedicated to the notion that loving one's country requires an unending willingness to die for it. Marshal Joffre, the savior of France in 1914, rode alongside Marshal Foch, its savior in 1918. Underpinning the parade were Victo Hugo's words: "He who dies in piety for his country has the right that the crowd should come and pray at his grave." Yet there was much more to this day than the flags, the cheering, and the conspicuous display of what at least on July 14, 1919 stood by good measure as the most powerful army in Europe.

The military celebration, to some extent, was overshadowed by a complex and powerful set of gestures honoring the bodies of those the war had killed and maimed. The space under the Arc du Triomphe had been turned into an immense chapel, with a monumental cenotaph of gilded plaster at its center, bearing the inscription "*Aux Morts pour la Patrie* (To those who Died for the Country)." Throughout the night of July 13–14, mourners as individuals and in groups prayed and laid flowers at the base of the cenotaph. Crowds hovered around the base of the empty coffin, symbol of the emptiness left behind by the dead, whether their bodies had been located or not. Clemenceau himself made a dramatic appearance at 10:00 PM, though considering the cenotaph appallingly "Germanic" in scale and style, he saw to its removal as quickly as possible after the parade. The military procession itself was led by four "*grands mutilés*," horribly wounded men wheeled through the parade by nurses. One thousand *mutilés de guerre* followed them, some wheeled or led by comrades or nurses, others walking on their own. The French began the parade by representing their victory as the result of horrendous national sacrifice, with the bodies of its soldiers at its center.

Fifteen months later, on November 11, 1920, the French placed the remains of an Unknown Soldier under the Arc de Triomphe. This in some sense complemented the cenotaph placed in the same location before the victory parade. An unknown body replaced an empty tomb. The French thus helped inaugurate what became an international commemorative custom, by using anonymity to recognize general heroism and to facilitate general and individual mourning. The tomb of the Unknown Soldier became the altar of the nation, from Paris, to London, to Washington, DC, even to Baghdad following the Gulf War of 1991.

In France, the principle of burying an unknown soldier on the first anniversary of the Armistice evoked virtually no dissent. But the site proved extremely controversial, for 1920 also marked the fiftieth anniversary of the founding of the Third Republic. Ardent republicans argued that the obvious site for the ceremonies and burial of the Unknown was the Pantheon. The Pantheon was where the Republic had buried the heart of Léon Gambetta, the hero of French resistance in the Franco-Prussian War of 1870–1 and one of the founders of the regime. The heart of the great patriot of 1870 would lie next to the remains of the anonymous patriot who had sacrificed himself for the nation and for the Republic, that very Republic which had finally fulfilled Gambetta's promise one day to win back Alsace and Lorraine. Moreover, some argued, did not the eighteenth-century Pantheon, to this day one of the great landmarks of Paris, bear the inscription: "*Aux grands hommes la patrie reconnaissante* (to the great men, from a grateful nation)"?

For others, such a gesture overlooked the fact that the nation had prevailed as a whole community. Moreover, the veterans and their families, that is to say most of French society, contended that the dead required a fundamentally different form of national recognition. The Third Republic had well-established practices of granting apotheosis to its "star pupils," men whose scientific, literary, political, or military achievements now seemed almost banal in comparison. In the face of widespread popular opposition, the Ministry of Public Education, charged with organizing the ceremonies, decided on a compromise. The body of the Unknown would be honored at the Pantheon, and then buried under the Arc de Triomphe.

The ceremonies surrounding the procession of the Unknown Soldier proved the last great public performance of the Union sacrée. Socialists, who in December 1920 at the Congress of Tours would bitterly divide into Socialists and Communists, joined hands with republican Catholics, and indeed with compatriots of all political and religious shades of opinion. In a great departure from the rigidly secular practices of civil ritual under the Third Republic, the Archbishop of Paris was invited to bless the coffin of the Unknown.

But although Catholics made up the vast majority of the nation, who could say that the Unknown Soldier was not a Protestant, an atheist, or a Jew? A Protestant pastor had foreseen in 1915 that "Jesus Christ will have the final word. He will pass beneath the Arc du Triomphe of the new time, with humanity now humanized." A French rabbi, Honnel Meiss, expressed messianic republican fervor in verse. Like their compatriots, the Jews of France rose to defend the Republic in 1914. Dreyfus Affair or no, the Republic had accepted Jews as citizen-soldiers in the crusade for civilization. That Republic continued to see itself as the embodiment of the values of the French Revolution, which had first accorded French Jews citizenship. Meiss's elegy to the Unknown Soldier brought together the patriotism and the symbolic significance of a grave, which each member of the national community could consider at once unique and collective.

> Tell me, passer-by, what is the name
> Of this old or young man
> Who in such triumph
> Goes now to sleep in peace?
> His name is "conqueror," his name is "symbol,"
> His name is repeated from pole to pole
> His name is "honor," the "unknown soldier,"
> "The anonymous hero," lost in the crowd!
> Partisan of a fruitful labor,
> He saved the world.
> He died for liberty,
> And for humanity. . . .
> Oh France, my beloved France!
> Forever be blessed,
> For eliminating the pain,
> Which broke our hearts!
> Each wife, today, each sister, each mother,
> Exalting the career of her dearly "departed,"
> Will tell herself proudly, without self-deception,
> Surely it is He who goes to the Pantheon!
> Oh *poilu*, take your place
> There in the glorious monument
> The soldiers of your race,
> Deserve the giant granite bed!

On November 10, the coffin of the Unknown reached Paris in a special train from Verdun. It had been chosen from among eight coffins brought there from different military cemeteries, by a young corporal volunteer from the Class of 1919, whose own father figured among the unidentified dead of the war. Born on a gun carriage and draped in the tricolor flag, the coffin rested for one night under a funeral watch at the Place Denfert-Rochereau, named after a heroic colonel of 1871. The next day, the cortège proceeded first to the Pantheon and then to the Arc de Triomphe, carefully linking the reversal of the defeat in the Franco-Prussian War to the victory of the Republican regime, while paying due tribute to the price paid by the French people. As in the victory parade, *mutilés de guerre* accompanied the cortège. A symbolic family followed the coffin, to suggest that commemoration could resurrect and reassemble not just the nation, but each broken family. These "unknown" mourners comprised a woman who had lost her husband, a mother and father who had lost their son, and a child who had lost a father. As we saw in Chapter 2, the war reversed the logical order of generational succession. Commemoration would help to restore some form of symbolic normality. Each member of the national community adopted the Unknown as a husband, son, or father. Likewise, some village war memorials portray schoolchildren admiring a "son of the commune," who all are expected to recognize as their father. The war gave rise to curious genealogies.

The ceremonies of November 11, 1920 brought hundreds of thousands of weeping people out onto the streets of Paris, many encouraged to believe that the coffin that passed before them contained the body of the man they had lost. While the Republic sought in a sense to celebrate itself and its triumph, the intensity of emotion belonged to the anonymous mass of political opinion, which had united at such great cost to save the nation. The correspondent of the Socialist newspaper *L'Humanité*, himself a veteran of the Great War, claimed that he had followed the cortège only out of professional obligation. But this reluctant believer in the *patrie* provided his own poignant description of the Unknown: "Perhaps he fell near me in Artois, in Champagne or at Verdun. Perhaps he showed me photographs of his father and mother, his wife and children, during our long periods in the trenches."[13]

The coffin was finally buried under the Arc du Triomphe in January 1921. The grave bore an inscription that united the nation and the Third Republic: "Here lies a French soldier who died for the *patrie*, 1914–1918." On each side of that plaque lay two others that set in bronze the regime's interpretation of what the Great War meant for the French

---

[13] Gabriel Kreuillard, *L'Humanité*, November 12, 1920.

nation. One read: "4 September 1870, the proclamation of the Republic," the other "11 November 1918, the return of Alsace-Lorraine to France." Despite the horrible cost, the Third Republic had mended the nation by reconquering the lost territories. The triad of plaques, perhaps without great subtlety, sought to place beyond question the legitimacy of the regime. Throughout the interwar years and long thereafter, no visitor from the French provinces or from another country could come to Paris without visiting, usually as the first stop, the Tomb of the Unknown Soldier at the Arc du Triomphe. Between the two world wars, more and more French people came to reject the politicians and policies of Third Republic. In 1940, many would reject the Third Republic itself. Very few among the French ever rejected the veneration of the Unknown Soldier.

Commemorative practice created an explanation for France of the outcome of the Great War that sought to fill in the gaps in meaning left at the signing of the Armistice. Through an ongoing process of remembering, repression, and forgetting, French war culture created a narrative of national perseverance or even triumph based on the suffering of its people, particularly its soldiers. To be sure, this narrative proved as unstable as the victory itself. And it did not include everyone. It placed suffering in the trenches at the center of commemoration, and tended to exclude less spectacular forms of suffering, such as that of the occupied population or of prisoners. Most pointedly, it excluded the suffering of anyone whose situation proved in any way ambiguous, such as that of soldiers from reconquered Alsace-Moselle, who had fought in the German army.

Local choices and some nuances remained. No one seized more tightly a narrative of national triumph than the people of occupied France, where communities chose images of the fighting soldier and the triumphant *coq gallois*, to insist on the continuity between their experience and that of their compatriots. Paradoxically, this served further to marginalize that experience. In stark contrast, soldiers carved into memorials in Alsace often appear nude – for how could one discern between a German and a Frenchman without a uniform? Likewise, the statue of the weeping mother in Strasbourg holding the bodies of her two lifeless sons carried the inscription "To our dead," carefully omitting the customary "for the country." The national community as a whole, likewise, would have to make choices coming to terms with the enemy.

The Treaty of Versailles

Clemenceau, Lloyd George, Wilson, and Italian premier Vittorio Orlando met in Paris in January 1919 to begin negotiating a final peace treaty. Not surprisingly, they excluded from these discussions their former enemies – Germany, Austria-Hungary, and the Ottoman Empire. They also excluded Revolutionary Russia, a former friend. On June 28, 1919, the apparent victors and the apparent vanquished signed what became known as the Treaty of Versailles. The French made sure the signing took place in the Hall of Mirrors at the palace of Versailles, the site of the proclamation of the German Empire in 1871. Few documents of the twentieth century have attracted more scorn than the Versailles treaty, for creating a vengeful but not vanquished Germany, which under Adolph Hitler would rise again and twenty years later plunge Europe, and ultimately the world, into a conflict far worse even than the Great War. In the English-speaking world, a good bit of the blame for the failure of the treaty has been attached to the French, for demanding a vindictive peace that by the 1930s they lacked the means or even the will to enforce.

Whatever the justice of these claims, the provisions of the Versailles treaty cannot be understood apart from the ongoing struggle within French war culture to figure out what the war had been about and how the national struggle and the attending sacrifices could be justified. Peace-making for the French played a role in the effort to transform a narrative of national survival into a narrative of national triumph. In this sense, the Armistice, commemorative practice, and the French influence over the Versailles treaty reflect different aspects of the same cultural process – the gradual evolution of French war culture into a culture of mass mourning.

Central to the way the French understood the war were the *Kriegshuld* or "war guilt" provisions of the treaty, although these provisions could not wholly be blamed on the French. The Allies disagreed about a great deal, but not about who bore moral and financial responsibility for the war. German aggression alone explained what had happened, and consequently Germany had to pay for the harm it had caused.

Article 231: The Allied and Associated Governments affirm and Germany accepts the responsibility of Germany and her allies for causing all the loss and damage to which the Allied and Associated Governments and their nationals have been subjected as a consequence of the war imposed upon them by the aggression of Germany and her allies.

Article 232: . . . The Allied and Associated Governments, however, require, and Germany undertakes, that she will make compensation for all damage done to the civilian population of the Allied and Associated Powers and to their property during the period of the belligerency of each as an Allied or Associated Power against Germany by such aggression by land, by sea and from the air, and in general all damage as defined in Annex 1 hereto.

This Annex entered into details, effacing the barrier between civilian and military damage and in this way certifying the "total" nature of the conflict. Germany would have to pay for "damage to injured persons and to surviving dependents by personal injury to or death of civilians caused by acts of war," as well as "damage caused by Germany or her allies to civilian victims of acts of cruelty, violence or maltreatment (including injuries to life or health as a consequence of imprisonment, deportation, internment or evacuation, of exposure at sea or of being forced to labor)." German responsibility further extended to paying for the effects of the mistreatment of prisoners of war, and to paying for military pensions to those "mutilated, wounded, sick or invalided, and to the dependents of such victims."

Of course, on the face of it, and taken together, these provisions of the Versailles treaty were absurd. Probably, they were known to be so at the time. In the fraught atmosphere of 1919, Germany's financial responsibility for the war barely had imaginative boundaries, let alone any practical ones. The Allied leaders knew full well how much the war had impoverished Germany. Moreover, Germany would never be able to pay anything unless its economy revived, precisely what the Allies and particularly the French feared. So began the bitter history of the reparations question, which would do so much to poison international politics in Europe between the wars.

A variety of military and geopolitical provisions sought to keep Germany in a permanently weakened state. Germany could have an army of no more than 100,000 men, no military aircraft, and a navy suited only to coastal defense. It lost all of its prewar colonies, and some 13 percent of its prewar national territory. In addition to Alsace and Lorraine, Germany had to surrender territories with considerable ethnic German minorities to the new states of Poland and Czechoslovakia. But territorial concessions amounted to considerably less than the French had wanted. The French floated various schemes for annexing the rich industrial area of the Saar. Most importantly, military figures as prominent as Marshal Foch and General Charles Mangin believed that France could remain safe only through detaching the left bank of the Rhine from Germany, through an "independent" Rhineland which all understood would become a satellite state dependent on France. Clemenceau initially supported the idea, though he abandoned it when the other Allies opposed such a brazen attempt to dismember Germany. This led to a bitter falling out between Clemenceau and Foch. In the end, the French had to settle for a demilitarized Rhineland, enforced by a fifteen-year military occupation.

Some gestures were made in the treaty for collective security, through which a continuation of the wartime alliance would permanently guarantee European stability. Wilson's cherished scheme of the League of Nations seemed to provide the organizational means of doing so. Yet despite the popularity of the idea in the abstract, few had real faith in collective security. Clemenceau had wanted a permanent "victor's council," with the ability to enforce its will militarily. Britain still viewed itself as a global rather than a European power, and resisted any explicit, long-term commitment to security on the European continent. Wilson knew the American Senate would never agree to supporting an international organization that could command military forces, and also resisted Clemenceau's idea. In 1920, the Senate rejected American participation in the League of Nations entirely. Britain used the American rejection to invalidate any formal commitment to defend France.

The failure of collective security linked the safety of France to the weakness of Germany. Paradoxically, the apparently vindictive position of France in the peace negotiations showed the deterioration in the strategic position of France since 1914. France was still a nation of forty-five million people facing a Germany of over sixty million people. The French gladly accepted former German colonies in Africa and the Pacific, and new colonies in the Middle East, as thinly disguised League of Nations "mandates." But few deluded themselves that these would prove of any use against a resurgent Germany. In August 1914, French security based itself on an explicit alliance with Imperial Russia and a de facto alliance with Britain. By 1920, it had neither. The Bolshevik regime, in any event engaged in a desperate civil war to save itself, wished only ruin on capitalist regimes everywhere. With glee, the Bolsheviks defaulted on Russia's massive debt to France. As much as France, Britain pretended that the Great War had made it stronger, and focused on its empire. The successor states to the Habsburg Monarchy were small, weak, and embroiled in ethnic hatreds of their own, as they tried to create national states in the most multinational part of Europe. They made unpromising and, in the end, hopeless allies. France had not given up 1.3 million dead and ruined its economy to be less safe than before the war.

Throughout the peace negotiations and indeed throughout the interwar period, therefore, the French staked much on portraying Germany as the incarnation of evil. For they could justify a Germany permanently disarmed and economically hobbled by open-ended reparations only if Germany represented a permanent threat to the security of the world. Through perpetuating such an image of Germany and through sullenly refusing to make a real peace with the enemy, the French sought to reconcile the apparent disparity between what had been gained out of the war and its cost. France, the French told themselves and the world, had saved humanity in the Great War. Both could remain safe only if Germany was kept in a permanently inferior position – morally, politically, economically, and militarily. As we saw, France had sought security through military superiority over Germany ever since French diplomats began to seek an alliance with Russia in the late-1880s. For cultural as well as diplomatic and military reasons, France did the same after 1918.

This, of course, led to different conceptions of "justice" even among the Allies. Wilson, who always considered himself the "conscience of the Allies," had readily accepted the demonization of Germany in the last phases of the military conflict. But after the Armistice, he returned to the more nuanced position toward Germany he had put forward in his "Fourteen Points," speech of January 1918. "There is today in the entire world a passion for justice," he proclaimed to his colleagues at the Paris Peace conference in March 1919: "Some of the wrongs and even crimes which have been committed arose from a false view of what is just... This enthusiastic aspiration for just solutions will be changed into cynical skepticism if there is an impression that we fail to meet the rules of justice that we have pronounced..."[14] In other words, Wilson thus acknowledged in veiled terms that Germany ultimately should be accorded some form of moral understanding. Clemenceau, however, stridently disagreed: "Do not believe that the principles of justice that satisfy us will satisfy the Germans... I can tell you that their notion of justice is not the same as ours." He added: "You seek to render justice to the Germans. Do not think that they will ever forgive us; they will seek only an opportunity for revenge; nothing will destroy the rage of those who wished to establish their domination over the world, and who thought themselves so near to success..." The suffering of the French, living and dead, and in and out of uniform, demanded restitution: "Our ordeals have created in this nation a profound sense of the reparations which are due to us; and it is not only a matter of material reparations: the need for moral reparations is no less great."

In very different ways, Clemenceau and Wilson sought to restore "justice" to a world transformed by the violence of what both saw as the most just of wars. But paradoxically, peacemaking prolonged the justification of the war even while it attempted to locate the guarantees that would make war a permanent impossibility. It is easy today to scoff both at the preachy liberalism of Wilson and at the vindictive blindness of Clemenceau. But it asks a great deal of the French of 1918–19 to expect that they could set aside the passions, the suffering, and the hatreds that the war had called forth. No one in France had forgotten who had started the war, whatever the long-term threats to German security scholars concluded had been posed by French alliances. Today, we can see that a far more suitable peace might have resembled that of the Congress of Vienna

[14] For the exchange between Wilson and Clemenceau, see Paul Mantoux, *Les deliberations du Conseil des Quatre* (Paris: Éditions CNRS: 1955), vol. 1.

following the defeat of Napoleon in 1815. France had been shorn of ill-gotten territorial conquests, compelled to pay an indemnity, and quickly rehabilitated into the European family of nations. But the peacemakers of 1815 served monarchies, regimes that most of the time could ignore popular opinion. The peacemakers of 1919 had to conclude a "total" war that had engulfed the entire population. "Democracy" in this sense indeed did triumph in the Great War, in that peacemakers found themselves accountable in some way to public opinion at once weary of war and brutalized by years of bloodshed, hardship, and mourning. "The people" would demand a far more stern peace than the monarchs of 1815.

The apparent moral trump card held by France in the form of atrocities committed against civilians existed through a particular circumstance of asymmetry. While Germany had occupied French and Belgian territories, the reverse had not been the case. This point was not lost on German diplomat Count von Brockdorff-Rantzau, who observed upon delivery of the treaty in May 1919: "Public opinion in all the enemy countries complains of the atrocities that Germany committed during the war. We are ready to admit the wrong that we did. But Germany was not alone in committing mistakes, each nation committed them. The crimes committed during the war cannot be excused, but they were committed during a struggle for national existence, in the moments of passion which make the national conscience less sensitive." Today, we can take the count's point. What nation, after all, had resisted the slide into a culture of violence and total war? But not surprisingly, his argument fell on deaf ears at the time. From the beginning, the Germans castigated the Versailles treaty as a *Diktat*, an agreement forced on a party who could not dissent. Every German government between 1919 and 1945 saw undoing that treaty as its most important foreign policy goal.

In the end, the resilience of the French national community in the Great War cannot be completely separated from a burning hatred of the enemy that so fed the willingness of the French to continue the war. At the heart of the Versailles peace treaty lay a certain notion of the Germans as a race, a notion created during the war. Did not the Germans, *les Boches*, and not just their authoritarian rulers, bear responsibility for the war? And did not the Germans remain barbarians, beneath the superficial gloss of their technical skill and their sophisticated economy? Did not the victors, or at least those who were able to carry on the war a quarter hour longer than their enemies, need to punish the Germans for their intrinsic barbarity? To a France in mass mourning, the transformation of Germany into a democracy in 1918 marked only a superficial change. Essential and incommensurable difference confirmed Germany as the hereditary and permanent enemy. Since the racial and ethnic features of the German nation could not be altered, the Boche could be punished, he could be restrained, but he could not, in the end, be improved. A volatile mixture of remembering, forgetting, and repressing led to an intense struggle between the will to restore justice and the desire to punish, a struggle that did so much to shape the realities of the postwar world.

Captain Charles de Gaulle, a native of Lille in what had been occupied France, had been taken prisoner at Verdun in 1916. In the next war, de Gaulle would lead the Free French resistance movement from London. After he became president of France in 1958, no one would do more to effect Franco-German reconciliation. He did so largely through a personal friendship with West German Chancellor Konrad Adenauer, who as mayor of Cologne back in 1925 had tried unsuccessfully to persuade the Weimar Republic to build a monument to an unknown German soldier along the banks of the Rhine. Writing from a German prisoner-of-war camp in October 1918, Captain de Gaulle defined with admirable clarity what would be at stake in making peace, and in remembering, repressing, and forgetting:

Will France be quick to forget, if she ever can forget, her 1,500,000 dead, her 1,000,000 mutilated, Lille, Dunkerque, Cambrai, Douai, Arras, Saint-Quentin, Laon, Soissons, Reims, Verdun – destroyed from top to bottom? Will the weeping mothers suddenly dry their tears? Will the orphans stop being orphans, widows being widows? For generations to come, surely every family will inherit intense memories of the greatest of wars, sowing in the hearts of children those indestructible seeds of hatred? . . . Everyone knows, everyone feels that this peace is only a poor covering thrown over ambitions unsatisfied, hatreds more vigorous than ever, national anger still smoldering.[15]

[15] Charles de Gaulle, "La limitation des armaments," October 1918, *Lettres, notes et carnets, 1905–1918* (Paris: Plon, 1980), p. 536.

Conclusion

As France celebrated its triumph and continued to mourn its sacrifice in the victory parade of 1919 and the burial of the Unknown Soldier in 1920, it appeared as though the nation and the Third Republic had not only survived its supreme test, but had emerged from it stronger than ever. Alsace and Lorraine had again become wholly French. Through much of the interwar period, France had the most feared army in Europe. At least in terms of shaded areas on a map, the French Empire attained its zenith between the wars, through territories acquired with the breakup of the Ottoman Empire and the distribution of the German colonies in Africa and the Pacific. The German enemy lay disarmed and paying reparations to the victors.

Yet the limits of the bitter peace made at Versailles became clear within a few years. With the United States pointedly abstaining from postwar security arrangements in Europe, with Britain again holding affairs on the continent at arm's length, with the Soviet Union banned from the family of nations, and with Eastern Europe weak, embittered, and troubled, victorious France faced the future created at Versailles remarkably alone. The peace came to rest on a bluff – that Germany would accept defeat, disarmament, and reparations indefinitely, without an effective enforcement mechanism on the part of the Allies. The Versailles treaty had sought to delegitimize the enemy, as the party solely responsible for the war. But in the end, the Versailles treaty ultimately achieved precisely the opposite effect – the relegitimization of the war in the eyes of an enemy who felt fully justified in taking it up again.

That Germany had never been totally defeated became abundantly clear within a few years after 1919. A controversy over reparations in 1923 led to the French army occupying the German industrial region of the Ruhr. This proved a public relations disaster for France worthy of German mistakes such as burning of the library at Louvain in 1914 and the sinking of the *Lusitania* in 1915. Subtly revealing their underlying weakness, the French did not dare send black African troops to the Ruhr, as they had to the Rhineland after the Armistice. The Germans met the

French army with large-scale passive resistance. The French army had difficulty extracting reparations with bayonets. The famous Weimar inflation of the second half of 1923 was actually encouraged by the German central bank, as part of a self-immolating scheme to highlight the absurdity of the reparations regime. The American-led Dawes Commission finally worked out a comprehensive reparations agreement in 1929, the eve of the Great Depression, which in turn put an end to any payments at all. The economic crisis of the 1930s ultimately brought to power Adolph Hitler, who likewise ended the cautious *rapprochement* between France and Germany that began in the second half of the 1920s. Hitler called the bluff of the Versailles treaty, began German rearmament, and in September 1939, barely twenty years after the victory parade, plunged France, Europe, and ultimately much of the world back into war.

The Third Republic became more and more bitterly divided against itself over the course of the interwar period. Politics polarized, with the Left dividing between Socialists and Communists, and the emergence of a variety of extreme anti-republican groups on the Right. The Center remained an unstable mixture of personalities and policies, as had been the case for much of the Third Republic before 1914. But with the problems of the nation now so dire, muddle in the political center and poisoned opinion at the extremes led to inertia in foreign and internal affairs. France relied more and more on an alliance with Britain, which by the mid-1930s had espoused a policy of appeasement, of granting considerable concessions to Germany in hope of using it as a bulwark against Communism in the Soviet Union. At home, the French sank billions of francs into the Maginot Line, a collection of connected forts dwarfing those at Verdun, to stop the Germans at the French border. The Maginot Line rendered the citizen-soldier inert, encased in concrete. French strategists could not have chosen a more dramatic departure from the doctrine of the offensive in 1914.

Throughout the interwar period, the French tried to rebuild France in a context of deep and generalized mourning. Maurice Barrès had identified a sense of unredeemable sacrifice and unresolvable mourning back in 1914, when he wrote in an article for his newspaper *L'Écho de Paris*: "Why is it necessary for the old people to remain, and to send toward sacrifice their children, who could have brought to pass the most beautiful era in history of France?" The failed peace seemed to have proved Barrès right. By the 1930s, the French found occasion to mourn the victory itself, or at least to face the fact that it had never been a complete victory at all. In *Les Enfants humiliés* (The Humiliated Children, 1949), Great War veteran Georges Bernanos provided a harrowing metaphorical description drenched in gender symbolism of the victory as a sterile and doomed marriage. He adopted a common personification of Victory as female. "You did not know how to be proud of showing yourself in public with a beautiful woman on your arm, who took your name but refused to sleep with you." Although the marriage lasted twenty years, it had no love as well as no sex. Conversation ceased within the couple, and eventually Victory refused even her husband's name. Finally, on September 3, 1939 (the day war with Germany recommenced), the rejected husband returned home at 5:00 AM, to find the house empty. Victory had left without saying anything, taking the furniture with her.

Once war resumed in Europe, a succession of new traumas displaced the old. The crushing defeat of the Allies in June 1940 led to the occupation of northern France and the establishment of the collaborationist Vichy regime in the south. Marshal Pétain, the greatest living hero of the Great War, shook the hand of Hitler, both literally and in his policies. No sooner was France liberated (principally by its Allies, in stark contrast to the Great War), than it faced agonizing wars of decolonization in Vietnam and particularly in Algeria. The Algerian war destroyed the Fourth Republic amidst threats of a military coup. Political stability finally returned under the Fifth Republic, designed by Great War veteran and London resistance leader Charles de Gaulle. Prosperity began to return in the 1950s, in the long postwar economic boom which lasted until the mid-1970s. But by the 1960s, few among the dwindling number of veterans of the Great War and fewer still in the national community writ large had much patience for contemplating the legacy of the Great War. The French wanted to put the first half of the twentieth century behind them, repressing or simply forgetting the succession of tribulations in their recent past. The *mutilés de guerre* continued to enjoy the highest priority of seating on the Paris Metro, as they do to this day. But otherwise, the military and civilian victims of the Great War became subsumed into the rest of the national community, the tribulations of 1914–18 repressed and forgotten.

But at the very end of the twentieth century, a combination of factors returned discussion of the Great War to the public sphere in France, as elsewhere in Europe. With a handful of extremely elderly exceptions, the last of the veterans of the conflict had died. This made the Great War "the past" in ways simply not possible for decades after the war. Inevitably if brutally, death removed the veterans' claim over the memory of the living. In the meantime, the geopolitical landscape of Europe changed radically, calling into question the meaning of the nation itself in Europe. The Cold War ended following the destruction of the Berlin Wall in 1989. For the first time since 1945, Europeans became masters of their own affairs.

The longstanding if erratic project of European unification took on new life at the end of the century, with an expansion of the European

Union, a deepening of the single European market, and moves toward a single European currency. Power seemed to ebb from individual nation-states, with the consent of most Europeans. France and the now-unified Germany began to build a joint professional brigade of soldiers. France gradually phased out conscription, a school of national, republican, and conspicuously male citizenship since the days of the French Revolution. The government and the president quietly canceled the last call-up of conscripts in June 2001, with virtually no public reaction one way or another. But while the end of the Cold war seemed to stifle nationalism in some parts of Europe, it enflamed nationalism in others. The wars of nation building in ex-Yugoslavia provided grim reminders of the hatreds the nation-state had carried along with it – nowhere more so than in Sarajevo, where the assassination of Francis Ferdinand had ignited the Great War back in 1914. And their much-vaunted project of European unification notwithstanding, Europeans found they could do little to control ethnic conflict in Europe itself without American and other international help.

In short, Europeans across the continent faced a general rethinking of the nation, its powers, its limitations, its discontents, and the historical antecedents of the new Europe as it began the new millennium. Not surprisingly, a renaissance took place in the study of the Great War, which had done so much to set in motion the subsequent chain of disasters in Europe in the first half of the twentieth century. Europeans revisited the memory of the Great War, with creation working symmetrically alongside repression and forgetting.

For their own reasons, politicians also rediscovered an interest in the conflict of 1914–18. This interest peaked in 1998, the eightieth anniversary of the end of the war. Curiously central to the reemergence of the Great War in the public sphere became soldiers executed for desertion or cowardice. Certainly, soldiers who died before firing squads represented only a minuscule proportion of the millions of Europeans who died in the conflict. Yet they became the exemplary victims of this most tragic of Europe's wars. Prominent politicians suddenly discovered a need to comment on what generally had been a relatively obscure historical topic. The Italian minister of defense argued that honor needed to be paid to the 750 soldiers in his country executed for desertion. In Britain, the minister of defense expressed "regrets" for the 306 soldiers shot, while stopping short of granting a judicial pardon.[1]

---

[1] In Germany, which during the Great War had executed soldiers far more sparingly than Britain, France, or Italy, authorities in 1998 devoted their attention to commemorating the fiftieth anniversary of Kristallnacht, the beginning of the mass violent persecution of Jews in Nazi Germany. The Nazi era continued to define commemorative practice in twentieth-century Germany.

But it was in France in 1998 where the reconstruction of the memory of the Great War met with the greatest controversy.[2] On November 5, 1998, Socialist Prime Minister Lionel Jospin, serving under conservative President Jacques Chirac, gave a speech at Craonne, a site of the 1917 Chemin des Dames offensive. The place had been chosen carefully. Other great battlefields of the Great War had well-established commemorative connections with other nations. As we have seen, Verdun by the 1980s had become the symbolic center of Franco-German reconciliation. The Somme, of course, could not be commemorated without including the British. But the Chemin des Dames offensive was the last major attack of the Great War undertaken by the French alone. No site could better serve for making a political statement on the meaning of the Great War for the French people. Jospin praised the veterans of the Chemin des Dames, with a particular twist:

Some of these soldiers, exhausted by attacks condemned in advance, frozen in mud mixed with blood, plunged into bottomless despair, refused to be sacrificed. May these soldiers, "executed for example," in the name of a kind of military discipline whose harshness was equaled only by that of the battle itself, be *reintegrated, today, completely, in our national memory.*[3]

Jospin had chosen his words carefully, much as he had the site. Calling for the reintegration of those executed because of the mutinies certainly laid claim to interpreting not just the 1917 mutinies but the Great War itself, but in a remarkably amorphous manner. As we showed in Chapter 4, only 49 of some 147,000 French casualties at the Chemin des Dames had died before a firing squad. Moreover, soldiers executed in the Great War had never left "national memory," as evidenced by their sporadic but persistent appearance in books and films, as well as in scholarly works. Jospin thus pushed on a door that had long been at least part-way open. In addition, his call for "reintegration" rather than "rehabilitation" was clearly intentional. As had been the case in Britain, the term "rehabilitation" would have implied a change in judicial status.

Others, however, put the case more baldly. On the same platform as Jospin, the mayor of Craonne denounced the Chemin des Dames offensive as "the first crime against humanity [which] remains unpunished." An editorial in the Center-Left Paris newspaper *Le Monde* advocated "rehabilitation," which would constitute "the recognition that the fault

---

[2] It is difficult not to notice that 1998 was also the year of the unexpected victory of France in the World Cup soccer competition, an event that produced the greatest outpouring of nationalist enthusiasm in France since the end of World War II.

[3] Italics added. The phrase in French reads: "réintègrent aujourd'hui, pleinement, notre mémoire collective nationale."

did not lie with the mutineers, but with the officials, the generals, and the ministers, who did not want to know that in war men do not agree to die if they think they are dying for nothing." The author concurred that the mayor of Craonne had spoken a "terrible truth" in connecting the offensive to genocide. It seemed not to matter that the mayor had made an ahistorical claim. The expression "crime against humanity," today understood as a juridical term, did not exist as such until the Nuremburg trials following World War II.

The political Right took the bait provided by the Left. President Chirac played his cards as carefully as Jospin. His office issued a communiqué in which he declared "inopportune" any public statement that could be interpreted as calling for the "rehabilitation" of the mutineers (which Jospin had never explicitly advocated), and sought to refocus attention on "the more than one million French soldiers who gave their lives between 1914 and 1918 to defend their invaded country." But his lieutenants carried the counterargument forward, just as had happened on the Left. The head of a faction of the Rassemblement pour la République (RPR, Chirac's party in the National Assembly), Réné Galy-Dejean, accused the government of not understanding the needs of national defense as outlined in Article 21 of the French constitution, by seeking to honor those who disobeyed military authority. On November 9, RPR President Philippe Seguin made a speech in which he argued that those shot following the mutinies needed to be treated with "respect and compassion." But in a blistering attack on the Left, he argued that no sort of collective rehabilitation could be contemplated, "because if one so justifies disobedience in the army, we will open up ourselves to a field of consequences and quite considerable implications." Lest anyone miss the point, he asked: "Is it now a question of rehabilitating the Waffen-SS, those who joined Doriot and Déat, and perhaps in particular, some personalities of the Left?"[4] It seems clear that both Jospin and Seguin brought a certain amount of personal experience to the controversy. Jospin's father, Robert Jospin, a native of the region around the Chemin des Dames, had been a pacifist Socialist politician in the 1930s. In 1949, the six-and-a-half year-old Philippe Seguin had received decorations awarded posthumously to his father, who had been killed by the Germans in September 1944.

The polemic of 1998 reproduced two narratives of the meaning of the Great War for the French people, both justifying themselves, explicitly or implicitly, in the name of "duty to memory." Neither Left nor Right consulted historians until the battle lines were drawn, and reluctantly

---

[4] The Waffen-SS comprised non-German units serving alongside the German army in World War II. Doriot and Déat were French fascists.

even then. In their broad outlines, both narratives were wearily familiar to those who had followed polemics between Left and Right and between the army and the Republic for the preceding century. The Left-wing version sought to bring the pacifism of the 1930s into the unifying Europe at the dawn of the new millennium. The soldiers of the Great War, exemplified by those who died by French bullets from a firing squad, became complete victims, forced into a war they never accepted by brutal and mindless Right-wing nationalists. The mutineers of 1917 and most especially those executed, presumed to be pacifists, became the only true heroes of the war, and the precursors of European unity. The Right-wing version sought to invoke traditional notions of authority, and particularly of the army as the supreme protector of the French nation. The Left, by lionizing those who resisted military authority, showed themselves the destroyers of national unity. Their sniping at the army weakened respect for the Republic in 1998, just as it had in the 1930s. Lurking behind the Right-wing version of the story was the collapse of the Third Republic in 1940, and the rescue of democracy in France during World War II by Charles de Gaulle, who not by coincidence after the war was also the founder of the party that evolved into the RPR.[5]

We hope we have proved in this book that both narratives coming from the polemic of 1998 could only have been created with a substantial amount of repressing and forgetting. Both focused on soldiers, and largely left aside how sacrifice and mourning scarred the national community writ large. "Reintegrating" the mutineers of 1917 into national memory, at least as Jospin and his lieutenants seemed to suggest, meant repressing or forgetting that the French had rejected the war only in the years following the Armistice.[6]

Hatreds and the violence stemming from that hatred likewise had to disappear. It was easy to remember that grandfathers and great-grandfathers had sung Christmas carols across no man's land in December 1914 and had arranged tacit truces with the enemy. But this made it necessary not to remember that they had killed Germans by the hundreds of thousands, at the Chemin des Dames and elsewhere. Likewise, the Left-wing narrative had to leave aside the fact that the mutineers of 1917 had agreed to continue the war when no repressive mechanism existed that could have compelled them to do so. The mutinous soldiers who returned to the trenches consented to a power relationship that consigned a small number

---

[5] De Gaulle, of course, had himself defied French military and civilian authority back in June 1940 by fleeing to London and continuing the fight against the Germans from there.

[6] At the very least, the 1998 controversy did nothing to enhance the long-run popularity of Jospin and his government, as shown by the rout of the Left in the presidential and legislative elections of 2002.

of them to the firing squad, to pay the price for the rest of them. To the
extent that the Right-wing version provided its own explanation rather
than simply an attack on the Left-wing version, it reaffirmed a blind faith
in the French military and political leadership during the Great War. By
implication, it sought to reinscribe the myth of a French victory in 1918
and of a strong France thereafter. This was precisely the myth that fell
apart through its own internal contradictions by the 1930s. Sadly missing in the polemic of 1998 was what we have tried to capture here, the
complex and dynamic nature of the national community that fought the
war, and the multiform passions that drove French people in and out of
uniform to continue it to the end.

Predictably, the polemic of 1998 did not reach a definitive conclusion,
further suggesting that at its heart lay the complex, present-day political
dance of cohabitation between a president from the Right and a prime
minister from the Left. "Memory" on both sides trumped "history," if
history means furthering an intellectual understanding of the events of the
somber spring of 1917. But the polemic did show that the Great War had
again become a living past for the French, analogous in some respects to
the Civil War or the Holocaust for people in the United States, to the two
world wars for the British, and to the Nazi era for the Germans. A public
opinion poll taken in France in the middle of the polemic asked participants to rank the importance of certain events that shaped the twentieth
century. Among all of those polled, the Great War ranked fourth, behind
World War II, the student movement in France in 1968, and the fall
of the Soviet Union.[7] But the most striking finding of the poll was that
the younger the participants, the more highly they ranked the Great War.
Participants over fifty years old ranked the Great War sixth, those between
thirty-five and fifty ranked it fifth, and those under thirty-five ranked it
third. Participants aged between fifteen and nineteen, the youngest people surveyed, ranked it second. Those with the most at stake in the future
of France in the twenty-first century were also those most convinced of
the importance of the Great War in shaping the present.

What mattered most about the polemic of 1998 was the way it brought
to light the deep social and cultural currents at work among the French in
recreating the memory of the Great War. Both Left and Right had tried to
mobilize these currents, rather clumsily and without understanding them.
Even today, the Great War retains a remarkable ability to touch the lives
of people long after the fact. One of the authors received a letter in 1997
from a woman whose uncle had been killed at the front in December

---

[7] Oddly, the poll considered the Great War and the Russian Revolution in 1917 as separate
events, thus probably underestimating how participants actually ranked the Great War.

1914. Her father told her that his father (her grandfather) had forbidden anyone in the family to speak about his dead son, and had refused the repatriation of his body. No one in the family had been to his grave, and evidently no one even knew exactly where it was. After her own father's death in 1990, she embarked on the project of finding her uncle's grave. She did so in April 1993, in the cemetery at Esnes-en-Argonne, Tomb No. 280. By this time in poor health herself, she sent her sister to visit the grave that summer, and her daughter the summer after that. Despite the vast expanse of time since her uncle's death and the fact that she did not herself even visit the grave, her reaction was dramatic: "It was like an echo, a vibration found again across time, of this young life cut short in all its beauty and valor, and of the pain felt by my grandparents. I believe that I have truly lived this mourning, and that I can still feel it." Historians have barely begun to understand the myriad ways France experienced the Great War across generations.

Bibliography

Aldrich, Robert. *Greater France: A History of French Overseas Expansion* (New York: St. Martin's Press, 1996).

Ardant du Picq, Charles. *Battle Studies* (New York: MacMillan, 1921 [originally published in French in 1868]).

Asprey, Robert B. *The First Battle of the Marne* (Philadelphia: J. B. Lippincott Company, 1962).

Audoin-Rouzeau, Stéphane. *Men at War. National Sentiment and Trench Journalism in France during the First World War* (Providence: Berg, 1992 [originally published in French in 1986]).

"La Grande Guerre: le deuil interminable," *Le Débat*, no. 104 (mars-avril 1999): pp. 117–30.

Cinq Deuils de guerre, 1914–1918 (Paris: Édition Noêsis, 2001).

L'Enfant de l'ennemi, 1914–1918 (Paris: Aubier, 1995).

Audoin-Rouzeau, Stéphane, Annette Becker, Jean-Jacques Becker, Gerd Krumeich, and Jay Winter, *14–18: la très grande guerre* (Paris: Le Monde Éditions, 1994).

Audoin-Rouzeau, Stéphane, and Annette Becker, *14–18: Retrouver la guerre* (Paris: Gallimard, 2000).

Barbusse, Henri. *Under Fire: The Story of a Squad* (New York: E. P. Dutton & Co., 1960 [originally published in French in 1916]).

Barrès Philippe. *La Guerre à vingt ans* (Paris: Plon-Nourrit, 1924).

Barthas, Louis. *Les carnets de guerre de Louis Barthas, tonnelier, 1914–1918*, ed. Rémy Cazals (Paris: La découverte, 1997).

Becker, Annette. *War and Faith* (Oxford: Berg, 1998 [originally published in French in 1994]).

Oubliés de la grande guerre: Humanitaire et culture de guerre, populations occupées, déportés civils, prisonniers de guerre (Paris: Noêsis, 1998).

"Guerre totale et troubles mentaux," *Annales: Histoire, Sciences Sociales* 55e Année, no. 1 (2000): pp. 135–51.

Becker, Jean-Jacques. *1914: Comment les français sont entrés dans la guerre* (Paris: Presses de la fondation nationale des sciences politiques, 1977).

The Great War and the French People (New York: St. Martin's Press, 1986 [originally published in French in 1980]).

La France en guerre, 1914–1918: la grande mutation (Brussels: Éditions Complexe, 1988).

1917 en Europe: l'année impossible (Brussels: Éditions Complexe, 1997).

Bernanos, Georges. *Les Enfants humiliés* (Paris: Livres de Poche, 1968 [originally published in 1949]).

Bernier, Jean. *La Percée* (Paris: Albin Michel, 1920).

Bloch, Marc. *Memoirs of War, 1914–1915*, trans. Carole Fink (Ithaca: Cornell University Press, 1980).

Brissaud, André. *1918: Pourquoi la victoire* (Paris Plon, 1968).

Castex, Henri. *L'Affaire du Chemin de Dames: les comités secrets* (Paris: Éditions Imago, 1998).

Céline, Louis-Fernand. *Journey to the End of the Night*, trans. John H. P. Marks, (Hammondsworth: Penguin Books, 1966 [originally published in French in 1932]).

Cendrars, Blaise, *J'ai tué* (Paris: Georges Crès, 1919).

Lice, Rootes, Nina, trans. (London: Owen, 1973 [a truncated and poorly translated version of *La Main coupée* (1946)]).

Chaline, Nadine Josette. ed., *Chrétiens dans la Première Guerre mondiale*, (Paris: Cerf, 1993).

Challener, Richard. *The French Theory of the Nation in Arms, 1866–1939* (New York: Columbia University Press, 1955).

Chaumont, Jean-Michel. *La concurrence des victimes: génocide, identité et reconnaissance* (Paris: La Découverte, 1997).

Cobb, Richard. *French and Germans, Germans and French: A Personal Interpretation of France Under Two Occupations, 1914–1918/ 1939–1944* (Hanover: University Press of New England, 1983).

Cobban, Alfred. *A History of Modern France: Vol. III, 1871–1962* (New York: Penguin, 1965).

Cochet, Annick. "L'Opinion et le moral des soldats en 1916 d'après les archives du contrôle postal," (Doctoral Thesis, Paris X–Nanterre, 2 vols., 1986).

"Les paysans sur le front en 1916," *Bulletin du Centre d'Histoire de la France contemporaine*, no. 3 (1982): pp. 37–48.

Congar, L'Enfant Yves, *Journal de Guerre, 1914–1918*, ed. Stéphane Audoin-Rouzeau and Dominique Congar (Paris: Cerf, 1997).

Cork, Richard. *A Bitter Truth: Avant-Garde Art and the Great War* (New Haven: Yale University Press, 1994).

Craig, John. *Scholarship and Nation Building, the Universities of Strasbourg and Alsatian Society, 1870–1939* (University of Chicago Press, 1984).

Cross, Tim. ed., *The Lost Voices of the Great War* (Iowa City: University of Iowa Press, 1989).

Davis, Belinda. *Home Fires Burning: Food, Politics, and Everyday Life in World War I Berlin* (Chapel Hill: University of North Carolina Press, 2000).

Delaporte, Sophie. *Les Gueules cassées: les blessés de la face de la grande guerre* (Paris: Noêsis, 1996).

Delvert, Charles. *Histoire d'une compagnie* (Paris: Berger-Levrault, 1918).

Derville, Etienne, *Correspondances et notes (4 août 1914-juin 1918)* (Tourcoing: J. Duvivier, 1921).

Dorgelès Roland. *Wooden Crosses* (New York: G. P. Putnam's Sons, 1921 [originally published in French in 1919]).

Doughty, Robert. *Pyrrhic Victory: French Strategy and Operations in the Great War* (forthcoming).

Downs, Laura Lee. *Manufacturing Inequality: Gender Division in the French and British Metalworking Industries, 1914–1939* (Ithaca: Cornell University Press, 1995).

Ducasse, André. *Balkans 14–18: ou le chaudron du diable* (Paris: Laffont, 1964).

Ducasse, André, Jacques Meyer, and Gabriel Perreux. *Vie et mort des Français, 1914–1918* (Paris: Hachette, 1959).

Dupront, Alphonse. *Le Mythe de croisade*, 4 vols. (Paris: Gallimard, 1997).

Durkheim, Émile. *Lettres à Marcel Mauss* (Paris: Presses Universitaires de France, 1998).

Duroselle, Jean-Baptiste. *Clemenceau* (Paris: Fayard, 1988).

La Grande Guerre des Français, 1914–1918 (Paris: Perrin, 1994).

Essame, H. *The Battle for Europe, 1918* (London: B. T. Batsford, 1972).

Farcy, Jean-Claude. *Les camps de concentration français de la Première Guerre mondiale (1914–1920)* (Paris: Anthropos-Economica, 1995).

Faron, Oliver. *Les Enfants du deuil: orphelins et pupilles de la nation de la première guerre mondiale (1914–1941)* (Paris: Editions, de la Découverte, 2001).

Ferguson, Niall. *The Pity of War: Explaining World War I* (New York: Basic Books, 1999).

Foch, Marshal Ferdinand. *The Principles of War*, trans. Hilaire Belloc (London: Chapman and Hall, 1918 [originally published in French in 1904]).

Fridenson, Patrick. ed., *The French Home Front, 1914–1918* (Providence: Berg, 1992 [originally published in French in 1977])

Furet, François. *Passing of an Illusion: the Idea of Communism in the Twentieth Century*, trans. Deborah Furet (University of Chicago Press, 1999 [originally published in French in 1995]).

Galtier-Boissière, Jean. *En Rase Campagne, 1914; Un Hiver en Souchez 1915–1916* (Paris: Berger Levrault, 1917).

Garafola, Lynn. *Diaghilev's Ballets Russes* (New York: Oxford University Press, 1989).

Genevoix, Maurice. *Ceux de 14* (Paris: Flammarion, 1950).

Gerbod, Paul. "L'éthique héroïque en France 1870–1914," *Revue historique* no. 544 (October–December, 1982): pp. 409–29.

Giono, Jean. *Le grand Troupeau* (Paris: Gallimard, 1931).

Gold, Arthur, and Robert Fizdale. *The Divine Sarah: A Life of Sarah Bernhardt* (New York: Alfred A. Knopf, 1991).

Goldberg, Nancy Sloan. *Woman, Your Hour is Sounding: Continuity and Change in French Women's Great War Fiction, 1914–1919* (New York: St. Martin's Press, 1999).

Grayzel, Susan R. *Women's Identities at War: Gender, Motherhood, and Politics in Britain and France during the First World War* (Chapel Hill: University of North Carolina Press, 1999).

Gregory, Adrian. *The Silence of Memory, Armistice Day, 1919–1946* (Oxford: Berg, 1994).

Gsell, Paul. ed., *Le Carnet Sublime* (1921).

Hallé, Guy. *Là -bas avec ceux qui souffrent* (Paris: Garnier, 1917).

Hanna, Martha. *The Mobilization of Intellect: French Scholars and Writers during the Great War* (Cambridge, MA: Harvard University Press, 1996).

Hardach, Gerd. *The First World War* (Berkeley: University of California Press, 1981 [originally published in German in 1977]).

Hermann, David G. *The Arming of Europe and the Making of the First World War* (Princeton University Press, 1996).

Higonnet, Margaret R. ed., *Lines of Fire: Women Writers of World War I* (New York: Plume, 1999).

Horne, John N., *Labour at War: France and Britain, 1914–1918* (Oxford: Clarendon Press, 1991).

"Information, opinion publique et l'offensive Nivelle du 16 avril 1917," in Laurent Gervereau and Christophe Prochasson, eds., *Images de 1917* (Paris: BDIC, 1987).

Horne, John and Allan Kramer. *German Atrocities in 1914: A History of Denial* (London: Yale University Press, 2001).

Horne, John. "Corps, lieux et nation: la France et l'invasion de 1914," *Annales: Histoire, Sciences Sociales*, 55e Année, no. 1 (2000): pp. 73–109.

"German 'Atrocities' and Franco-German Opinion, 1914: The Evidence of German Soldiers' Diaries," *Journal of Modern History* 66 (March 1994): pp. 1–33.

Hunter, Lt. Col. T. M. *Marshal Foch: A Study in Leadership* (Ottawa: Directorate of Military Training, 1961).

Inglis, Ken. "War Memorials: Ten Questions for Historians," *Guerres mondiales et conflits contemporains*, no. 167 (July 1992): pp. 5–21.

"Entombing Unknown Soldiers: From London and Paris to Baghdad," *History and Memory*, vol. 5, no. 2, (Fall/Winter 1993): pp. 7–31.

Isselin, Henri. *La Ruée allemande: printemps 1918* (Paris: Arthaud, 1968).

Issilin, Henri. *The Battle of the Marne*, trans. Charles Connell (London: Elek Books, 1965 [originally published in French in 1964]).

Jacobzone, Alain. *Sang d'encre: letteres de normaliens à leur directeur pendant la guerre 1914–1918* (Vauchrétien: Ivan Davy éditeur, 1998).

Jauffret, Jean-Charles. "La question du transfert des corps, 1915–1934," in Sylvie Caucanas and Rémy Cazals, eds., *Traces de 14–18: Actes du colloque de Carcassonne* (Carcassonne: Éditions "Les Audois," 1997), pp. 133–46.

Johnson, Martin Philip. *The Dreyfus Affair: Honour and Politics in the Belle Époque* (New York: St. Martin's Press, 1999).

Keegan, John. *Opening Moves: August 1914* (New York: Ballentine Books, 1971).

The Face of Battle: A Study of Agincourt, Waterloo and the Somme (New York: The Viking Press, 1976).

Keiger, John F. V. *France and the Origins of the First World War* (New York: St. Martin's Press, 1983).

King, Jere Klemens. *Generals and Politicians: Conflict Between France's High Command, Parliament and Government, 1914–1918* (Berkeley: University of California Press, 1951).

Krumeich, Gerd. *Armaments and Politics in France on the Eve of the First World War* (Leamington Spa: Berg, 1984 [originally published in German in 1980]).

"L' Archéologie et la Grande Guerre," Dossier in *14–18: Aujourd'hui* 2 (1999): pp. 17–127.

La Chausée, Capitaine J. *De Charleroi à Verdun dans l'infanterie* (Paris: Éditions Eugène Figuier, 1934).

Laffargue, André. *Foch et la bataille de 1918* (Paris: Arthaud, 1967).

"Le Choc traumatique et l'histoire culturelle de la grande guerre," Dossier in *14–18: Aujourd'hui* 3 (2000): pp. 23–137.

Lepick, Olivier. *La Grande Guerre Chemique: 1914–1918* (Paris: Presses Universitaires de France, 1998).

Lintier, Paul. *Ma Pièce* (Paris: Plon, 1916).

Mairet, Louis-Jean. *Carnet d'un combattant* (Paris: Georges Crès, 1919).

Mangin, Charles. *La Force noire* (Paris: Hachette, 1911).

Mantoux, Paul. *The Deliberations of the Council of Four (March 24–June 28, 1919)*, ed. and trans. Arthur S. Link (Princeton University Press, 1992 [originally published in French in 1955]).

Martin du Gard, Roger. *Vieille France* (Paris: Gallimard, 1933).

L'Été 1914 (Paris: Gallimard, 1936).

Maurice Halbwachs, *On Collective Memory*, ed. and trans. Lewis Coser (University of Chicago Press, 1992 [originally published in French in 1925]).

Mayer, Arno. *Political Origins of the New Diplomacy* (New Haven: Yale University Press, 1959).

McPhail, Helen. *The Long Silence: Civilian Life under the German Occupation of Northern France, 1914–1918* (London: I. B. Tauris & Co., 1999).

Meyer, Jacques. *La Vie quotidienne des soldats pendant la grande guerre* (Paris: Hachette, 1967).

Michel, Marc. *L'Appel à l'Afrique: contributions et réactions à l'effort de guerre en A.O.F. (1914–1919)* (Paris: Publications de la Sorbonne, 1982).

Miquel, Pierre. *La Grande Guerre* (Paris: Fayard, 1983).

Offenstadt, Nicolas. *Les Fusillés de la grande guerre et la mémoire collective (1914–1999)* (Paris: Odile Jacob, 1999).

Offer, Avner. *The First World War: An Agrarian Interpretation* (Oxford: Clarendon Press, 1989).

Orledge, Robert. *Satie the Composer* (Cambridge University Press, 1990).

ed., *Satie Remembered*, trans. Roger Nichols, (Portland, OR: Amadeus Press, 1995).

Pedroncini, Guy. "La Justice militaire et l'affaire des quatre caporaux de Souain (mars 1915–mars 1934)," *Revue Historique de l'Armée*, no. 2 (1973): pp. 59–69.

Les Mutineries de 1917 (Paris: Presses Universitaires de France, 1967).

Pétain, général en chef, 1917–1918 (Paris: Presses Universitaires de France, 1974).

Perloff, Nancy. *Art and the Everyday: Popular Entertainment and the Circle of Erik Satie* (Oxford: Clarendon Press, 1991).

Pézard, André. *Nous autres à Vauquois* (Paris: La Renaissance du Livre, 1918).

Porch, Douglas. *The March to the Marne: The French Army, 1871–1914* (Cambridge University Press, 1981).

Prochasson, Christophe, and Anne Rasmussen. *Au Nom de la patrie: les intellectuels et la première guerre mondiale* (Paris: Éditions de la Découverte: 1996).

Prost, Antoine. *In the Wake of War: les anciens combattants and French Society*, trans. Helen McPhail (Providence: Berg, 1992 [originally published in French in 1977]).

Les anciens combattants et la société française, 3 vols. (Paris: Presses de la fondation des Sciences Politiques, 1977).

"Verdun," in Nora, Pierre, ed., *Les Lieux de Mémoire*, vol. II, *La Nation* (Paris: Éditions Gallimard, 1986), pp. 111–41.

Rebérioux, Madéline. *La République Radicale?: 1898–1914*, Nouvelle Histoire de la France Contemporaine, no.11 (Paris: Éditions du Seuil, 1975).

Renouvin, Pierre. *The Forms of War Government in France* (New Haven: Yale University Press, 1927 [originally published in French in 1925]).

L'Armistice de Rethondes (Paris: Gallimard, 1968).

Ricoeur, Paul. *La mémoire, l'histoire, l'oubli* (Paris: Seuil, 2000).

Ries, Frank W. D. *The Dance Theater of Jean Cocteau* (Ann Arbor: UMI Research Press, 1986).

Romain, Jules. *Men of Good Will* trans. W. B. Wells and Gerard Hopkins, 14 volumes (1961 [originally published in French in 1932–46]).

Rousso, Henri. *La Hantise du passé* (Paris: Les éditions Textuel, 1998).

Seigel, Jerrold. *Bohemian Paris: Culture, Politics, and the Boundaries of Bourgeois Life, 1830–1930* (New York: Viking, 1986).

Sherman, Daniel J., *The Construction of Memory in Interwar France* (University of Chicago Press, 1999).

Silver, Kenneth E. *Esprit de Corps: The Art of the Parisian Avant-Garde in the First World War, 1914–1925* (Princeton University Press, 1989).

Smith, Leonard V. "The Disciplinary Dilemma of French Military Justice: September 1914–April 1917: The Case of the 5e Division d'Infanterie," *The Journal of Military History*, vol. 55 (January 1991): pp. 47–68.

Between Mutiny and Obedience: The Case of the French Fifth Infantry Division during World War I (Princeton University Press, 1994).

"The French High Command and the Mutinies of the Spring of 1917," in Peter Liddle and Hugh Cecil, eds., *Facing Armageddon, 1914–1918: The War Experienced* (London: Leo Cooper/Pen and Sword, 1996), pp. 79–92.

"Remobilizing the Citizen-soldier through the French Army Mutinies of 1917," in John Horne, ed., *State, Society, and Mobilization during the First World War* (Cambridge University Press, 1997), pp. 144–59.

"Mémoire et mythification des mutineries de 1917," in Sylvie Caucanas and Rémy Cazals, eds., *Traces de 14–18: Actes du colloque de Carcassonne* (Carcassonne: Éditions "Les Audois," 1997), pp. 47–54.

"Le Corps et la survie d'une identité dans les écrits de guerre français," in "Dossier: Le Corps dans la première guerre mondiale," *Annales: Histoire, Sciences Sociales*, 55e Année. no.1 (January–February 2000), pp. 111–33.

"Narrative and Identity at the Front: Theory and the Poor Bloody Infantry," in *The Great War and the Twentieth Century*, ed. Jay Winter, Geoffrey Parker, and Mary Habeck (New Haven: Yale University Press, 2000), pp. 132–65.

"Jean Norton Cru, lecteur des livres de guerre," *Annales du Midi*, no. 232 (2000): pp. 517–28. Also published in English as "Jean Norton Cru and combatants' literature of the First World War," *Modern and Contemporary France*, vol. 9, no. 2 (2001): pp. 161–9.

Soutou, Georges-Henri. *L'Or et le sang: les buts de guerre économiques de la première guerre mondiale* (Paris: Fayard, 1989).

Spears, Brigadier-General E. L., *Prelude to Victory* (London: Jonathan Cape, 1939), p. 338.

Stevenson, David. *The Outbreak of the First World War: 1914 in Perspective* (New York: St. Martin's Press, 1997).

Stovall, Tyler. "Colour-blind France?: Colonial Workers during the First World War," *Race and Class*, vol. 35, no. 2 (1993): pp. 33–55.

Sweeney, Regina M., *Singing Our Way to Victory: French Cultural Politics and Music during the Great War* (Middletown, CT: Wesleyan University Press, 2001).

Tanenbaum, Jan Karl. *General Maurice Sarrail, 1856–1929: The French Army and Left-Wing Politics* (Chapel Hill: University of North Carolina Press, 1974).

Taranow, Gerda. *Sarah Bernhardt: The Art Within the Legend* (Princeton University Press, 1972).

Taylor, A. J. P. *The First World War: An Illustrated History* (London: Hamish Hamilton, 1963).

Terraine, John. *To Win a War* (London: Sidgwick & Jackson, 1978).

Veray, Laurent. *Les Films d'actualité français de la grande guerre* (Paris: AFRHC/SIRPA, 1995).

Vercel, Roger. *Capitaine Conan* (Paris: Albin Michel, 1934).

Watson, David Robin. *Georges Clemenceau: A Political Biography* (London: Eyre Methuen, 1974).

Whiting, Steven Moore. *Satie the Bohemian: From Cabaret to Concert Hall* (Oxford University Press, 1999).

Winter, Jay. *Sites of Memory, Sites of Mourning: The Great War in European Cultural History* (Oxford University Press, 1995).

Winter, Jay, and Jean-Louis Robert. *Capital Cities at War, London, Paris, Berlin, 1914–1919* (Cambridge University Press, 1997).

Index

NEW APPROACHES TO EUROPEAN HISTORY